NO SOUVENIRS

MIRCEA ELIADE

No Souvenirs

JOURNAL, 1957–1969

Translated from the French by Fred H. Johnson, Jr.

1817

HARPER & ROW, PUBLISHERS, San Francisco
Cambridge, Hagerstown, New York, Philadelphia
London, Mexico City, São Paulo, Sydney

This book (pp. 1–327) was originally published in France by Éditions Gallimard, rue Sébastien-Bottin, Paris, as pp. 229–571 of *Fragments d'un journal.* © Éditions Gallimard, 1973. The Preface and Index are published here for the first time.

FIRST HARPER & ROW PAPERBACK EDITION PUBLISHED IN 1982.

Library of Congress Cataloging in Publication Data

Eliade, Mircea, 1907–
  No souvenirs.

  Includes index.
  1. Eliade, Mircea, 1907–   2. Religion
historians—United States—Biography.   I. Title.
BL43.E4A34   1977   291'.092'4   [B]   76-9969
ISBN 0–06–062143–5

82 83 84 85 86 10 9 8 7 6 5 4 3 2 1

Contents

Preface

In 1973 the French publisher Éditions Gallimard brought out, under the title *Fragments d'un journal,* certain selections from a diary which I kept—with a few interruptions—between 1945 and 1969.* Even given its 570 pages, this book still represented something less than one-third of the original manuscript. Now, according to Leonard Woolf (in his preface to Virginia Woolf, *A Writer's Diary,* 1953, p. vii), "It is nearly always a mistake to publish extracts from diaries or letters. . . . At the best and even unexpurgated, diaries give a distorted or onesided portrait of the writer. . . ." A number of authors, however, do publish their journals in a more or less fragmentary form, and I suspect that they risk the perils of this enterprise for different reasons. For my part, the risk of "a distorted or onesided portrait" seems to be worth taking. Even in fragmentary form, a journal offered me the possibility of conveying certain stray observations, ideas, and queries for which the time and opportunity had never arisen before.

Different authors will always assign a different role and significance to their journals or diaries. It suffices to compare, for instance, Amiel's long, diffuse and repetitious self-analysis, Léautaud's indiscreet verbosity, Gide's obsession with the meaning and message of his *oeuvre,* and Jünger's *Strahlungen,* which is at once the notebook and the

*The present volume contains only those extracts written during my time in America, and omits those from the period 1945–1955.

secret agenda of an entomologist, a reader of strange, half-forgotten authors, and an incurable traveler. A diary can be anything, from a calendar to a diatribe, to a table of contents for the next *Summa Theologica*.

During my school days in Bucharest, I always kept a journal. I used to write down my current "discoveries" (authors, facts, theories) in thin copybooks, as well as conversations with friends, recriminations directed against some of my teachers, reflections relating to term papers and, later, to my master's thesis. From the pile of these notebooks, I extracted the material for the first articles which I published while still in the lycée, and after 1925 as a student at the University of Bucharest. During my first trips abroad (Italy, Austria, Switzerland), the journal traveled with me and became my confidant. It was also, in a certain way, the model for a kind of writing that I have never been able to achieve. In those years I was, of course, aware of the specific function of a personal diary, namely the possibility of "saving and preserving time"; that is, of capturing the ineffable quality of a particular moment—the last rays of sun on an old abandoned house, the bench in that park where I suddenly discovered that I was—or was not—in love, and many others. The few words that were scribbled hurriedly would be enough, years later, to bring back the *presence* of a certain afternoon or a certain town, or even the rapture of some fresh discovery. Of course I realized that I alone would relive—and recognize—the miraculous experience of those fragments of my personal past. This, for me, was the main justification for keeping a diary: the exhilarating experience of reading it much later and thus reliving a whole series of long-forgotten impressions. But in those years I also hoped to discover a dimension of the diary that was not strictly personal. In brief, I was hoping to be able to compose a work some day that would draw upon the specific experiences that had been preserved in my diary.

In the autumn of 1928, a few weeks after having taken my Licence ès Lettres, I left Bucharest for India, and returned in January 1932, with a suitcase overflowing with notebooks and folders. I called it my storehouse, for everything was there: descriptions of temples, monuments, and slums; narratives of Himalayan adventures and discoveries; my first, awkward translations from Sanskrit, as well as detailed reports of intimate experiences, discussions with my professor and guru, Surendranath Dasgupta, with Tagore, and with any number of yogis and sadhus from Benares, Hardwar, and Rishikesh. I also called those notebooks and folders my *chantier,* for they contained numerous works in progress: drafts of my doctoral dissertation on yoga, a monograph on Asiatic alchemy, projects, essays, sketches of literary works, and so on. For years, my Indian notebooks and folders supplied not only the materials for two volumes consecrated to India, but they were also used in the preparation of many articles and essays, and even some of my literary works.

Born in Rumania near the turn of the century, I belong to a cultural tradition that does not accept the idea of any incompatibility between scientific investigation and artistic, especially literary, activity. As a matter of fact, some of the most original Rumanian scholars have also been successful writers (Demetrius Cantemir, Hasdeu, Iorga), and the greatest of Rumanian poets—Mihail Eminescu—was equally a philosopher and one of the most learned men of his time. Long before the new fashion, which was initiated in France by such artist-philosophers as Gabriel Marcel, Jean Paul Sartre, and Simone de Beauvoir, it was not uncommon for a Rumanian scholar to be acclaimed as a poet, a novelist, or a playwright.

For me, a historian of religions and an Orientalist, the writing of fiction became a fascinating experience in method. Indeed, in the same way as the writer of fiction, the historian of religions is confronted with different structures of sacred and mythical space, different qualities of time, and more specifically by a considerable number of strange, unfamiliar, and enigmatic worlds of meaning. At that time I was unaware of any structural analogy between the scientific and the literary imagination. One can thus appreciate the enthusiasm with which I read, many years later, statements by renowned scientists, such as the following: "The step by which a new axiom is adduced cannot itself be mechanized. It is a free play of the mind, an invention outside the logical processes. This is the central act of imagination in science and it is in all respects like any similar act in literature" (J. Bronowski, in *The American Scholar,* Spring 1966).

I began teaching at the University of Bucharest in the autumn of 1933, and in the seven following years I brought out a number of books, fiction as well as nonfiction, and I founded *Zalmoxis,* an international periodical for the study of history of religions. Then, in April 1940, I was appointed cultural attaché at the Royal Rumanian Legation in London. I was convinced that in two or three years I would again find my way back to my rooms and my library, the manuscripts of unfinished works, and, of course, the innumerable folders and notebooks. But, in fact, I returned only once, for a few days in August of 1942. Being now a cultural counselor in Lisbon, I thought that longer and more frequent visits home might be expected. But when I left Portugal in September 1945, I went directly to Paris. I wanted to redress the time that had been lost far from any great Orientalist library. In this light, my first visit to the Société Asiatique had almost the ritual character of a pilgrimage. In Paris I also realized my dream of meeting some of the great French Orientalists, especially those who had appreciated my book *Yoga: Essai sur les origines de la mystique indienne* (1936), and who had contributed to *Zalmoxis:* Jules Bloch, Louis Renou, Georges Dumézil, Jean Filliozat, Paul Masson-Oursel, and others. Shortly afterward, I was invited to serve as a visiting professor at the École des Hautes Études of the Sorbonne, and in November I gave my first lecture.

I decided to remain in Paris, at least for the time being. Only here could I complete a number of monographs that I had begun to prepare while I was in London and Lisbon. First of all, I wanted to conclude *Traité d'Histoire des Religions (Patterns in Comparative Religion),* to write *Le Chamanisme (Shamanism: Archaic Techniques of Ecstasy),* and to revise and enlarge my book on yoga. I knew that such ambitious projects could not be accomplished in Bucharest, owing to the lack of rich and specialized libraries. Moreover, the discipline of history of religions could not be included in the curriculum of a Marxist university.

It was, of course, a trying experience to start a new career in another, great country at the age of thirty-eight and to begin writing in a foreign language. In 1946–1947, I published my first articles in *Critique* and *Revue de l'Histoire des Religions,* and in 1948 *Techniques du Yoga* appeared, followed in 1949 by *Traité d'Histoire des Religions* and *The Myth of the Eternal Return.* From 1950 on, I had the opportunity to lecture in many European universities, perhaps the most important for me being the University of Rome, where I was invited by the great Orientalist Giuseppe Tucci and the famous historian of religions, Raffaele Pettazzoni. I had already known Professor Tucci during my student days in Calcutta, but I made the acquaintance of Pettazzoni rather late, in Paris in 1948, although I had been corresponding with him for some twenty years.

This intense scholarly activity rendered literary work almost impossible. The first years of my Parisian journal are interspersed with the yearning to write fiction, but I defended myself as best I could against any such temptation. Although by 1948 I could write a reasonably correct French, I continued to write literary pieces only in Rumanian, for I considered myself to be a Rumanian author, belonging within the organic whole of Rumanian literature. The first translations of my fiction were published in Germany in 1948, and in France two years later. But I was so involved in other, scholarly projects that I did not pay much attention to my debut on the European literary scene. From time to time, however, to satisfy at least in part my nostalgias, I interrupted my work and wrote a short story or novella.

In the summer of 1949, though, I succumbed to temptation and began working on a long novel. Devoting only a month or two each year to this project, it took me five years to finish it. Allain Guillermou translated the eleven hundred typed pages, and the novel was published in 1955 by Gallimard under the title *Forêt interdite (Forbidden Forest).* For various reasons, the book did not have the success that had been expected by the author, the publisher, and the critics (cf. pp. 12–16). This incident did not change my opinion of the value of my novel, however, nor did it block my "literary creativity." I continue to write stories and novellas to this day. (Some of them, translated into German, have had unexpected success with both the public and the critics.) Rather, from that moment on I became almost indifferent to the destiny of my literary *oeuvre*. I still believe that one day *Forbidden Forest* and other books will be "discovered," but I cannot do anything to accelerate that discovery.

The truth is that I became more and more convinced of the significance and indeed the urgency of such disciplines as history of religions, Orientalism, and ethnology for a full understanding of contemporary history. The correct analyses of myths and of mythical thought, of symbols and primordial images, especially the religious creations that emerge from Oriental and "primitive" cultures, are, in my opinion, the only way to open the Western mind and to introduce a new, planetary humanism. These spiritual documents—myths, symbols, divine figures, contemplative techniques, and so on—had previously been studied, if at all, with the detachment and indifference with which nineteenth-century naturalists studied insects. But it has now begun to be realized that these documents express existential situations, and that consequently they form part of the history of the human spirit. Thus, the proper procedure for grasping their meaning is not the naturalist's "objectivity," but the intelligent sympathy of the hermeneut. *It was the procedure itself that had to be changed.* For even the strangest or the most aberrant form of behavior must be regarded as a human phenomenon; it cannot be interpreted as a zoological phenomenon or an instance of teratology. This conviction guided my research on the meaning and function of myths, the structure of religious symbols, and in general, of the dialectics of the sacred and the profane.

I was therefore happy when, in 1950, Olga Froebe-Kapteyn invited me to lecture at the Eranos conference in Ascona, Switzerland, the famous symposia that she had inaugurated fifteen years earlier. The ten or twelve days of meetings each year provided a unique opportunity to meet and talk with such brilliant and original scholars as the Islamicists Louis Massignon and Henry Corbin, the great specialist in Kabbala and Jewish mysticism, Gershom Scholem, the classical scholars Walter Otto and Karl Kerényi, the biologist Adolf Portmann, the learned theologians Hugo Rahner and Jean Daniélou, and many others. C. G. Jung also assisted at some of the Eranos lectures. Although my knowledge of depth psychology was rather precarious, these conversations with Jung impressed me in the highest degree. (The only comparable experience for me was the series of joint seminars I taught with Paul Tillich at the University of Chicago in the sixties.) Jung was the *spiritus rector* of Eranos, but one cannot say that the lecturers constituted a Jungian group. Most of them were only superficially acquainted with the problems of modern psychology. But from the group there emerged what can be called "the spirit of Eranos," one of the most creative cultural experiences of the modern Western world. Nowhere else is to be found a comparable sustained effort of scholars to integrate, in one all-embracing perspective, the progress made in all the various fields of study.

At the International Congress of History of Religions held in Rome in the spring of 1955, Joachim Wach told me that he had proposed to the Theological Faculty of the University of Chicago to invite me to be visiting professor of history of religions at that institution. Unfortunately, Wach died a few months later. And when I arrived in Chicago in the fall of 1956, it was Wach's disciple, Professor Joseph M. Kitagawa, who introduced me to the intricacies of an American university's curriculum. I delivered the Haskell Lectures (published by Harper & Row under the title *Birth and Rebirth*), and I taught several small classes on morphology of religions, on yoga, and on shamanism. In spite of a most friendly reception, my wife and I could not believe that we would be able to stay more than a year or two; everything was so different from our previous experiences. But, as is usually said, Chicago (like any great American city) "grows on you." When Jerald Brauer, the dean of the theological faculty, invited me to become a regular professor, I agreed in principle for a period of four years. However, as I came to know the merits and advantages of American universities, the academic freedom and the absence of any spirit of intolerance in our faculty, the interdisciplinary and creative teaching system employed within the Committee on Social Thought, founded and directed by John Nef, we decided to prolong indefinitely our sojourn in Chicago. A few years later I realized that the decision had been the right one. I witnessed with great satisfaction the growing interest of the American universities and the American public in history of religions. Today I do not doubt that this discipline is better taught in the United States than in any other part of the world. Such a fact is, in itself, highly significant; but this is not the place to go into details.

The following extracts from my journal reflect, although only fragmentarily, the stages and aspects of my American experiences and discoveries. But, as the reader will no doubt observe, some of these discoveries revealed their full meaning only during our summer vacations in Europe, which, after all, was to be expected.

MIRCEA ELIADE

Chicago
April 1976

Translator's Note

The translator's art is a meticulous task, yet without the translator an author's work might remain locked from a good portion of its potential readers. The task, in this instance, was lightened by the valuable assistance of my colleague Philippe Maucotel, by the efforts of John Shopp and others at Harper & Row, and of course by the author himself.

It has not always been possible to locate the original English text or the standard English translation of passages quoted, and in these cases I have given my own translation from the French.

NO SOUVENIRS

Summer Notebook

ASCONA, *July 1957*

Every time I go back to this room at Casa Gabriella, I see once again the cover of the first novel that I read of Alfredo Panzini: *Il padrone sono mì!* From my worktable I can see the terrace, the lake, and the mountain before me. Exactly as I used to see them on that fabulous cover from my adolescence.

I open the suitcase stuffed with books and manuscripts. I look for the folder of notes made for the Eranos lectures. So often I have knelt before this suitcase to look for books and notebooks, or to take out folders one after the other, sometimes tortured at the thought that in one or another of the places I've stayed the last few years, I could have forgotten precisely the notes I needed: in Jacqueline Desjardin's basement or in her upstairs library, in the Val d'Or or perhaps in Chicago. I still see myself a few weeks ago, in Lisette's apartment in New York, and, two weeks ago, in a little cabin on the *Liberté,* then, again, at the Collège Sainte-Thérèse, kneeling before this same suitcase that I was to prepare for the summer's work. And suddenly I realize that I've become a nomad, a "wandering scholar." I no longer have an apartment or room of my own anywhere. I live at the mercy of circumstances with those who invite me—parents, friends—or at the homes of hospitable people. I remember the melancholy and indignation of

Camil Petrescu when he confided to me, around 1937, I think: "At the age of forty, I don't even have a room somewhere." He seemed to me, then, to be the very picture of the exemplary martyr.

... What saddens me especially is that for a long time I'll be unable to write and read as I wish. I sometimes dream of a long, endless summer, waking up every morning overjoyed that the new day will be mine, all mine, and that, if I feel like it, I will be able to squander it, to use it up, writing a book.

I'm reading Jules Verne's *Journey to the Center of the Earth,* and I'm fascinated by the boldness of the symbols, the precision and richness of the images. The adventure is, properly speaking, an initiation, and, as in every adventure of this sort, one can find the wanderings through the labyrinth, the descent to the underworld, the crossing of the waters, trial by fire, meetings with monsters, trial by absolute solitude and by darkness, and finally the triumphant ascension, which is nothing other than the apotheosis of the initiate. How right these images of the underworlds are—the other worlds—how admirably precise and coherent, too, the mythology, which is hardly camouflaged by Verne's scientific jargon. How can psychologists and literary critics have so long ignored this exceptional document, this inexhaustible treasure of images and archetypes?

Some day someone will certainly write the history of the modern imagination. The chapter on the worlds below will have to take account of *Journey to the Center of the Earth,* of *She* by H. Rider Haggard, of *Om* and *There Was a Door* by Talbot Mundy. Probably none of these three authors understood much about mythologies or initiatory rites. Nonetheless, the images, the disposition of scenes evoking the underworlds that abound in their books, reveal their secret meanings only if they are reintegrated into the mystery from which they have been taken, the mystery inherent in every initiation.

C. G. Jung recently had a dream in which he was all alone in a huge theater. The curtain slowly rose, and Mme. Jung appeared on the stage—not as she was in the last years of her life (she died last year at seventy-five), but as Jung had first known her fifty years earlier. She didn't say a word. They looked at each other for a long time. Apparently Jung admitted that after this dream he no longer had any doubt as to the immortality of the soul.

How I admire E. M. Cioran for his incomparable mastery of the art of letter writing. I think I have penetrated his secret: Cioran never writes a letter out of obligation, or because he has nothing better to do, but only when he feels the need to communicate with someone, whether friend or stranger. And his letter reflects his mood at the moment, a nontemporal mood in a way—in any case, beyond the historical moment.

How well I understand that! . . . Today, suddenly, I felt the need to communicate with someone the first impressions that I had of Chicago eight or nine months ago. I felt them again, vividly and clearly, as I will probably never feel them again. I would have loved to have been able to sit at this table all afternoon and imagine the trees of Woodlawn Avenue or the carillon of the mysterious Rockefeller Chapel, which resembles an Aztec imitation of a Gothic cathedral.

Last night's storm. The lightning struck the lake several feet from the terrace, shook the house to its foundations, and blew all the fuses. We lit candles and finished dining to the accompaniment of thunder rolls. After that, in Corbin's room, around a potbellied flask of Chianti, by the light of a candle, we had a long discussion on Gnosticism and the apocryphal Gospels.

The storm continued just as furious until dawn. In the morning, the lake was nearly overflowing its shores.

I remembered what had happened to Haig Acterian, in 1927. While he was spending a night with friends in the little monastery of Ialomicioara, they were awakened by the noise of thunder. A candle was lit, and Marietta, his wife, began to read the Gospel of Saint John out loud. When she finished her reading, the moon was rising over Piatra Craiului.

The blackbirds' singing has awakened my memory of a summer spent at Sacele, one of the "Seven Villages" situated near Brasov. It must have been in 1922. I was fifteen years old, and I was fascinated by entomology among a thousand other things. I would leave at the break of day, go along the river, and scrutinize the tufts of wicker in search of butterfly larvae. Or I would climb the hill, settle down in the hay, or lose myself in reading until hunger gnawed at me. I read everything that my hand touched. In the house that we had rented I found a collection of old editions of *Revista Romana*. I remember a study by H. Sanielevici: "Why Do Birds Sing?" It was one of his first articles, published around 1910. I was so captivated by it that I read it two or three times. If my memory serves me correctly, the explanation was rather simple: if birds sing it is quite plainly so they will not die of asphyxia.

I've brought the last notebook of the journal with me, but I haven't yet opened it. I'm writing these pages in one of the notebooks that Olga put on my worktable. In recent years I've abandoned the journal, so to speak. That was a mistake. I had no illusions as to its importance, for I would hastily jot down all sorts of trifles, and if I was writing a book, I would hardly open it anymore. Nevertheless, I regret having interrupted it. With all those odds and ends, I would have been able to reconstruct an event, an itinerary, an encounter from memory.

I stopped writing in it during the summer of 1953, but even since the spring, I had already begun opening it only rarely. Nevertheless, I knew why I was feeling more and more detached from this journal, begun in 1928 and kept up continuously, with the exception of the year spent in England. One night, during the winter of 1955, I was awakened by a corpselike odor. The wart that I had had under the right arm—for a number of years—had become infected and was running. I was operated on the next day, but I had to wait for the results of the analysis for one week, a long one, to find out whether the tumor was malignant or not. I put all that down in the journal. But I did not write down this long, fantastic "waking dream" that I had after finding out the results of the analysis.

It was afternoon; I was stretched out on a couch. And all of a sudden I saw myself dead, laid out in a coffin and carried to the Rumanian church on rue Jean-de-Beauvais. On the coffin were some flowers and two little flags, one Rumanian, the other French. At one point in the ceremony the coffin began to rise into the air; it left quietly by the door, without any of the flowers falling, came to a stop for a few minutes about ten meters above the street pavement, then gained some altitude and headed toward the Institut Pasteur, where I had just been operated on. It circled above the Institute several times, climbed to fifty or sixty meters above the ground, and headed toward the south.

I would need several pages to describe the feeling brought on by this "miracle," the crowds which, in the streets of Paris, were watching the coffin as it sailed over the houses; the cars, the film and radio trucks, the helicopters which accompanied it as it went farther away from the capital. The evening papers indicated the places over which it was flying, and the various editions followed one after the other with the latest photos. The coffin was approaching the Alps. By now it was flying at a high altitude. Despite the gusts of wind, neither the flowers nor the flags moved in the slightest. No one could guess where it was heading. After several days, the coffin arrived here at Casa Gabriella and came to a stop some meters above the terrace as if it were to wait for Olga to come. When Olga came forward, a rose in her hand, the coffin slanted down so she could place the rose beside the other flowers. Next it regained altitude, flew over the lake, and, still without hurrying, headed toward Italy, crossed the Adriatic, Yugoslavia, entered Bulgaria, and stopped on the right bank of the Danube, across from the city of Oltnitza. It remained there several days, waiting. My friends had formed a committee which, through the mediation of the Red Cross, had asked the Rumanian government for assurance that the coffin would not be destroyed. Once this guarantee was obtained, the coffin once again calmly took up its slow progress toward Bucharest. Up to here I had followed it without any difficulty over mountains, seas, and cities. But this time I had to give up. Remaining on the Bulgarian side of the Danube, I watched it go farther away until it had completely disappeared.

This fanciful vision lasted about half an hour. Several times I tried to shake it off by immersing myself in a book, but a few moments later I would find myself once again behind the flower-covered coffin, which was sailing through the air somewhere between the Alps and the Danube. That summer I naturally told some of my psychologist friends about this waking dream, but I learned nothing from them that I hadn't already guessed for myself; it was connected with a death experience and an initiatory resurrection. Some unknown part of me, of my past life, was to die so that I could survive. From that moment on, it became more and more difficult for me to return to the journal. And that summer I abandoned it for good. In a certain sense, perhaps I had to let go of my recent past—the last fifteen years—just as circumstances had forced me to let go of everything I had loved, dreamed of, and worked for in my youth.

About a month after my arrival in Chicago, at a lunch of the Southeast Asia Club, Milton Singer, the anthropology professor, wanted to know what had most impressed me in the United States. "The squirrels," I answered. I tried to explain to him why, but I didn't manage to make myself understood. M. S. was smiling, reflective and happy, with an understanding air: he had certainly discovered in this a secret, ironic illusion to who knows what American "situation." At bottom, I wonder if it's so easy to understand. A few weeks ago in Paris, I was speaking about all this to Father Bruno. But over there, in the Carmelite Study Center, where one is not obsessed with the passage of time, I think I succeeded in expressing what I really felt when the first squirrel had approached my outstretched hand to take an almond. Every time distrust, enmity, the struggle for life, everything that characterizes the relations between man and beast seems to me to be abolished—even if it's only for an instant—a powerful and obscure emotion takes over inside me. As if the actual condition of man and of the world were canceled and the paradisiac epoch glorified by the primitive myths were reestablished. Then, *in illo tempore,* before the "Fall," before "sin," men lived in peace with the wild beasts; they understood their language and spoke to them as friends. Friendship with the wild animals and the understanding of their language are both paradisiac and eschatological syndromes. The day the suckling child plays with the viper and the young kid gambols beside the leopard, history will be nearing its end and the Messianic age will be at hand. Hermits and the saints recover—but only for themselves—that friendship with the beasts.

I have spoken of all this at length, in studies and articles which I don't intend to summarize here. What is encouraging is that a man of today can be so deeply moved by the friendship of an untamed animal. At the beginning of July, on the *Liberté,* I listened for a whole evening to various stories about the bears of the Canadian forests: how they approach cars to beg for sugar, and, if it is refused them, how they lie down across the road, certain that no one will have the heart to drive over them. It's a story of the same sort told me by V. Christian around 1934, a story of lizards and butterflies which supposedly took place in a forest not far from Bucharest. Perhaps he was simply evoking his poet's longings.

I was saying today to H. C. that the word "dilettante" has always had an impressive gravity for me. Without telling him why. It's connected in my memory with the gloomiest vacations of my adolescence. I was staying at our villa in Tekirghiol, and I had read all the books. Moreover, there weren't very many. The vacationers came to take mud baths, not to read. And there it was that I finally discovered the complete Works of Basil Conta, in the edition of O. Minar. A volume of about a thousand pages, with a portrait of the philosopher on the cover. I believe it was one of my aunts who had brought it and had forgotten it in a cabinet. First I read "The Theory of Universal Undulation," but without understanding very much. I was about twelve or thirteen, and philosophy had no appeal for me. Even without understanding anything, or very little, I persisted in reading every day, out of boredom, out of curiosity, and with the hope, perhaps, that I would understand in the end. I had gone through about half of it when, one morning, a student from the neighborhood, who had entered through the garden, came upon me by surprise as I was reading. He took the volume, leafed through it, and, with a disdainful smile, told me with a reproachful tone of voice, "Young man, what an idea to read Basil Conta! He wasn't a philosopher. Nothing but a *dilettante....*"

VENICE, *August*

I stop before this monumental Jesus, beardless and as luminous as an archangel, and I feel that a memory coming from very far away is trying to reach me as I am today. I wait, fascinated by this fragment of my forgotten life, a fragment which is trying so hard to come to recognition. And suddenly, I have it. It was in the spring of 1926. We had arrived late the night before, and, as it ought to be, our first visit in the morning had been to San Marco. I had left the others clustered around the guide, their heads tilted back, listening to his explanations of the scenes from the Old Testament, and I had gone into the basilica. I was convinced that I should go see for myself, without the guide's comments, that it was the only way for me to be able to discover. Discover what? I didn't know, I didn't even wonder. I only had a feeling that something would be "revealed" to me.

And it was at that very instant that I was greeted by that Christ in mosaic, a Christ that I couldn't even recognize as such for an instant, it resembled an archangel so much. *Christos Angelos.* One of the first mysteries that I couldn't be aware of, much less understand, at that time. I had an idea, nevertheless, that in the beardless youth and incomparable beauty of the Christ was hidden also the mystery of the androgyne. Suddenly I find myself again as I was in 1926. I rediscover the same obscure attraction, the same amazement, the same gestures, as if time had been stopped. I shove my glasses energetically against the bridge of my nose to see better, and I realize that this gesture is the continuation of a mannerism from my adolescence, when my vision was worsening at too rapid a rate for me to be able to change the corrective lenses in time. And then, another gesture which had been lost for a long time: I cross my arms behind my back. A habit acquired by a whole group of students, our last years at the lycée, after Nanu, our teacher of Rumanian, had assured us that it was the gesture of Titu Maiorescu when he spoke.

Vita di Giovanni Papini, by Ridolfi, is more than a biography; it is also a word of warning for every writer of Papini's spiritual family. For half a century, this disparate *enfant terrible,* too talented and capable, wanted to write only one single book: *Adamo,* or, as he was to call it later, *Appunti sull'uomo* or *Giudizio Universale.* The first page, of which Ridolfi gives a reproduction of the handwritten manuscript, is from 1903. From that time on, and until just before his attack of paralysis, he abandoned this magnum opus and took it up again a thousand times. *Giudizio universale* was almost finished in its final form in 1953. When I saw Papini in the spring of that year, he was hoping to finish it very quickly. And he could have if, some six months later, he hadn't lost the use of his right hand. He still could have finished it by dictation if he hadn't let himself be tempted by *Il Diavolo.* It's another one of his lyric-theological fantasies designed to delight, dismay, or exasperate his public, as he enjoyed doing in his younger days. Having made up his mind to finish *Il Diavolo* by dictation, Papini lost the last chance granted by Providence to finish the masterpiece of his life. He survived a little more than a year, working doggedly, in conditions that were almost miraculous, at dictating those *Schegge* published two times a month by the *Corriere della Sera.* But this long, unbelievable agony which transfigured his biography added nothing to the famous manuscript of *The Last Judgment.* This last work will also appear one day, but it will no longer be as he had wanted it, nor what he had hoped to offer to the world. Since the conception of the work Papini wrote about fifty others. Not all were within his realm, far from it. A good number of them could have been written by others, and better than he himself had done. The work for which he came into the world, with the exception of *A Finished Man* and some others, was *Guidizio universale.* But he let himself be tempted too often by works which did not take root within him organically. And when he tried to steel himself in one last effort to finish *Guidizio universale,* he collapsed in a chair, mute, almost blind, and paralyzed. A terrible example. Nevertheless, since 1912, Papini had understood it all. He wrote in *Diventar genio,* "Anyone, on the condition that he know clearly what he wants to become and that he not lose a single second of his life, can attain the level of those who dictate laws to things and create worthy lives."

If I still go to Venice, it's partly to see Evel Gasparini. I met him in 1950. Although he is a Slavic scholar, for many years his great passion has been ethnology. It all began with a plan for a book on Dostoevsky which he hasn't yet written. In order to better understand Dostoevsky, he first studied popular Russian culture. But as a result of comparing it with other popular cultures, he acquired the conviction that the Russian world is strange and exotic. He then took up ethnology, and he arrived at the conclusion that there is an abyss between the Slavs and other European peoples, simply because at the beginning of the century the Slavs still belonged to a culture of the matriarchal type. Since 1948, Evel Gasparini has been devoting his course in Russian language and literature to the Slavic matriarchal system.

MUNICH, *2 September*

The Congress of Orientalists. Evening, in a beer garden, with Edward Conze. A discussion on Buddhism, Prajnaparamitra, and on astrology. He believes in reincarnation. He remembers "two and a half existences" (the half is probably his present life). Extraordinarily likable. We hit it off well, and very quickly. He explained to me that it is because we are both Pisces. Christinel is Taurus. She is very down to earth; she probably won't like his book on Buddhism.

Moreover, he says that while reading the epic of Gesar, he rejoiced at the idea that, one day, "the Mongol horses will crush Europe and trample it underfoot." A great passion for the Mongols and the Tibetans. Limitless admiration for Padmasambhava that, according to Conze, only the certitude of having been one of his disciples can explain.

I was with Stig Wikander looking in the bookshop display windows. Stig saw a book of Swami Shivananda and asked me if I knew him. "Yes," I answered, "for close to six months he was my guru, at

Svargashram, Rishikesh. My hut was about a hundred meters from his. We would go down over the rocks at dawn to bathe in the Ganges." "Has he written anything else?" Stig asked me again. "It's quite a story," I told him. In the spring of 1931, the Swami had finished his first book and had left to find a publisher, in Allahabad or Benares. I haven't seen him since. When I left Svargashram, he hadn't come back yet. But I read his book a few months later. What happened afterward? I don't know, for in November I went back to Rumania.

A good many years later, I learned that he had published a whole library. Around 1950, in Paris, I received one of his numerous periodical publications, written entirely by him. On that occasion, I learned that he had written some four hundred volumes or brochures, as well as a considerable number of articles. All this in less than twenty years. He has become very popular in India, where he is considered to be a saint, the spiritual master of the century. In Europe, too, he is beginning to be translated and known. To judge from the photos, he hasn't changed much. He appears ever so slightly heavier than the day I saw him leave for Allahabad, in 1931, his first manuscript under his arm. A photograph shows him writing in his study. Shelves filled with manuscripts all around him and up to the ceiling. These are the manuscripts of books already published. Indefatigable, he continues to write, and always on the same subject: the illusory nature of the world (maya), the unity of the spirit (atman = brahman), the means by which man can gain freedom (Yoga and Vedanta). This extensive, but sketchy and monotonous, writing depresses me; as I am also saddened by the photos of the Rishikesh of today, with its post office, its hospital, its printing presses, its libraries, its meditation and rest houses, its Himalayan pharmaceutical industry, its elementary and secondary schools and colleges, all these constructions built thanks to the work and prestige of Swami Shivananda. I realize very well their importance and the need for them. The Swami is addressing a world which, from the traditional viewpoint of India, is nothing but corruption and stupidity, since we live in Kali Yuga. In an age dominated by the syndicated press, the *Reader's Digest,* and radio and television, the Swami puts himself on the same level as today's reader, and repeats the same simple, empty things to the point of exasperation; just as millions of tons of newsprint today really published more or less the same news and the same slogans. If I understand him correctly, he is trying to awaken his contemporaries to the spiritual life by adopting the publicity techniques of the modern world. He's a guru for our modern age of rotary printing presses and blurred print.

There is, nevertheless, a detail that I don't understand: his reverence for what *he* has written or said. One of his articles that repeats the same well-known themes ("The World is illusion. Read and meditate on the Holy Scriptures. You are free. You are atman. You are brahman, etc., etc.") ends this way: "Copernicus, great astronomer, born on . . . died on. . . ." As if, finding his inspiration suddenly cut off with a space of one or two lines still to fill, he had opened a biographical dictionary at random. In a magazine published by the Swami at Rishikesh, one of his young associates told this story: some radio reporters, who had come to record a speech of the Swami's, asked him to speak a few words for the equipment's volume adjustment. The voice test was quite satisfactory, so the radio men began to erase the tape, but the Swami objected:

"Why erase them?" he said. "Once uttered, these words have the right to remain."

For someone who believes that the Universe is merely illusion, this desire to *remain* seems to me to be very heavy laden with innuendoes.

Yesterday, during the intermission of *Parsifal,* I spied Father de Menasce. Today he said to me, "How beautiful it was! How beautiful it was!" We had met in front of Harrassowitz's stand. He noticed the German translation of my book *Shamanism,* picked up the volume, leafed through it, and exclaimed, "What an extraordinary book!" Then, turning toward me, he apologized—he seemed a trifle embarrassed to me—for not yet having read *Forêt interdite,* which I had sent him a year ago. I apologized in turn, more embarrassed than he was, perhaps: I wouldn't have taken it upon myself to give him this overly thick novel, done in such small print, if I hadn't known that he had been the original, and excellent, translator of T. S. Eliot, etc.

Alone, I remembered what Kurt Wolf used to say to me in Ascona: the print is too small, it is illegible. Or D.: Forgive me, I can't read it. It's too long. I haven't the time. . . . Dr. René Laforgue read only the beginning and the final pages. He didn't have the courage to resume reading it. "As a psychoanalyst," he told me, "I have come to understand that a personal destiny that ends in suicide cannot be humanly interesting." "But it's not a suicide," I objected. René burst out laughing. And Delia exclaimed, "He *thinks* that it *isn't* a suicide." And giving me her amused, incredulous look, she went further, "It's obvious that it's a suicide." René admitted how he regretted that I had lost so much time in writing this novel. His opinion was this: were I an excellent novelist, it would still be a great pity to spend my time writing novels. There have been, are, or will be at least a thousand great novelists in the world, whereas, at the present time, I am the only person capable of writing *Shamanism* and the others. . . .

The fact is that *Forêt interdite* hasn't been successful, as they say. Too few reviews and—except for the article by René Lalou in *Les Nouvelles littéraires*—published too late, when the book had disappeared from the bookstore windows. A host of reasons could be found to explain this failure: the book came out at a bad time, when people hadn't yet returned from vacation; I myself made no effort to "launch" it, etc.; it was a "traditional novel," that is, written to be read, whereas the critics and the literary elite are most interested in a shattered, disjointed epic, written as much as possible on the outer limit of semantic intelligibility.

It was a great stroke of luck for me to know "success" at the age of twenty-six, both with the critics and with the public, for, since then, I have become almost indifferent to the fate of my books. I am very glad, just as anyone would be, if a book of mine pleases, or if it succeeds, but I can't say that I suffer if it doesn't. The only thing that really occupies my mind is the book I'm writing or the one I'm thinking about. It is possible that one day people will "discover" *Forêt interdite,* just as it is equally possible that it will sink into total oblivion. I can do nothing to save it. Only one of my future books could do something in that direction.

But the issue doesn't lie there, or, more precisely, that is not the only issue, i.e., whether or not a book commands respect and whether or not it lasts. In a certain sense, a book exists in itself, independently of the author's will or the critics' opinions. That existence does not have to do with time, or, more precisely, it is neither sustained nor canceled by time. It partakes of that mode of existence which suffices unto itself. It's of no consequence to the book if its "duration" be an hour, a season, or a century. Books exist within an epiphanic structure: they *are* because they have appeared, have been manifested, shown. They can disappear in the next instant. Their destiny has been accomplished; their destiny was simply to *be*. No one knows a book's deficiencies, its defects, its excesses, better than the author. Personally, I realize all too well what has missed the mark, what is grating, false, or cheap in *Forêt interdite*. But, for all that, the admiration that I have for this book, the best one I have written, is in no way diminished. I even listen at times with a suppressed smile to the praises bestowed on my other books by men whom I admire and like. I say to myself: Despite your perceptiveness, your intelligence, your culture, *you have not seen*.

This reflection, privately made, is all the more innocuous, since there is no way to make them see what they don't succeed in seeing for themselves.

I have reread the preceding pages, not without a certain disillusionment. A writer has so much to say about his works that, despite his effort to say everything, certain aspects will always remain obscure. I would like to add a few brief remarks on *Forêt interdite*. The unhoped-for repercussions that my previous works on the history of religions and the philosophy of culture have had ought to have warned me that a mitigated acceptance would be offered to the novel. Everything, or almost everything, that I have published up to now, even technical works such as *Shamanism* and *Yoga*, caught the interest of the literary critics to a degree that could not have been anticipated. And this has been true not only in France. It is not difficult to discover the reason: the myths, the symbols, and the behavior of the archaic world and the Oriental world are fascinating because of their primitive and exotic character, but perhaps even more because they could furnish a point of departure for a new vision of the world which would replace the images and values, outmoded today, to which the preceding generations were attached. I could write an entire book on this phenomenon of regression toward the amorphous and the chaotic which is discernible in the history of all the arts in modern times. Its significance is clear, it seems to me: we are rejecting the world and the meaning of existence as known and accepted by our forebears. We are expressing this rejection by abolishing the worlds of the past, by shattering the forms and leveling the rough places, by dismantling all forms of expression. Our ideal would be to demolish everything down to ruins and fragments in order to be able to return to full, unlimited formlessness, in short, to the unity of the primeval chaos. It is yet another way to protest against the world as it is today and to manifest a nostalgia for another world, dawnlike, fresh, untouched. It's very clear: a coherent, poetic language no longer has any interest for those who are put off by any form that would simply be a reminder, however vague, of the spiritual universe in which they no longer believe. That would be to move back into an organized, meaningful world, that is, precisely a world that they claim is not possible today. A traditional novel such as *Forêt interdite* seems to them to be an anachronism. What suits them—even if they don't enjoy them as much as they say they do—are novels such as *Finnegans Wake, The Sound and the Fury,* or *Molloy.* These difficult, esoteric texts also have the advantage of flattering the perceptiveness of commentators who take it upon themselves to penetrate their mysteries.

I shall speak of all this at greater length some other time. One more word, however: the regression toward chaos is only one moment in a much more complex process. Today, still more than the destruction of languages, we are witnessing the desire to return to the primordial age, to the original plenitude. Rare are those who think of this precosmogonic moment, too rare those who have a presentiment of the new worlds which promise to appear, namely, the all-new languages which will articulate new value systems. What is curious is that literary critics, so taken with archaic and exotic myths, don't understand the meaning of their fascination with them; they don't understand that myth is, before everything else, a tale, that it has no other function than to reveal how *something came into being*. Modern man's attraction to myths betrays his latent desire to be told stories, to learn how worlds are born and what happened afterward. In the jargon of literary criticism, that is called a "traditional novel."

FLORENCE, *September*

Every time I return to Italy, I rediscover the old passion of my adolescence and early youth: the Renaissance. I defend myself against it as best I can: I don't go into bookstores, I avoid buying the latest novelties, but finally I yield. I begin by gathering together my memories: seventeen years afterward, I can still see the library I left behind in Rumania and I'm able, as in a dream, to go up to the bookshelves where I had put the texts and books on the Italian Renaissance. I can open them, thumb through them, find the bookmarks where I stopped reading, and the pencil underlinings, as if they were still in front of me. In the last drawer there used to be the filing cards and the manuscript I wrote on Campanella in 1928 for my graduate degree. But why feed my melancholy by letting my thoughts go through these records drowned in a time and a space that are prisoners of a magical circle? As is the case with any prolific author, I carry within me several books that will never be written. Notably, a history of the Italian Renaissance of which I dreamed at the age of twenty. It was to be monumental, as is necessary at that age—I don't know how many volumes—for I wanted to tell all, and I was sure that I would say things that no one had ever dreamed of. One volume, for example, was devoted to the relation between the mystical and occult currents of the Middle Ages—Joachim of Fiore, the Kabbala, alchemy, Hermeticism—and the humanism of Ficino and Pico della Mirandola. I still remember; I had worked on that volume for the whole autumn of 1928, until the eve of my departure for India. And with what seriousness, on the night of November 19, the last that I was spending in my garret on the Strada Melodiei, I had put all these documents —notes and texts together—on the last shelf of my library, not without wondering whether one day—but when?—I would see them again. I did see them again four years later, but at that time I was coming back laden with other documents and other manuscripts, and since then, I have given no further thought, other than by chance and in passing, to that gigantic project of my youth.

Nevertheless, afterward, how many secret, underground threads I was to discover between my passion for the Italian Renaissance and my vocation as an Orientalist. It was in the spring of 1928, in the library where Tucci held his seminar in Rome, that I found the book by Dasgupta, to whom I then wrote that I wanted to work with him in Calcutta. Those who had first introduced me to Indian studies had been the Italians: Carlo Puini, C. Formichi, Tucci. But that isn't the essential point. More significant is the very fact of my having chosen India as the principal field for my research at the same time that I was studying the Italian Renaissance in Italy. In a certain sense, I could even say that for the young man that I was, Orientalism was only a new version of the Renaissance, the discovery of new sources and the return to *forgotten, abandoned sources.* Perhaps, without knowing it, I was in search of a new, wider humanism, bolder than the humanism of the Renaissance, which was too dependent on the models of Mediterranean classicism. Perhaps, too, without realizing it clearly, I had understood the true lesson of the Renaissance: the broadening of the cultural horizon and the reconsideration of man's situation in a wider perspective. What, at first glance, is further from the Florence of Marsilio Ficino than Calcutta, Benares, or Rishikesh? Nevertheless, I found myself there because, as was the case with the humanists of the Renaissance, a provincial image of man didn't satisfy me, and because, ultimately, I dreamed of rediscovering the model of a "universal man."

It took me ten years to understand that the Indian experience alone could not reveal to me the universal man I had been looking for since my adolescence. Thus it is that, since that time, I have been oriented more and more toward the two universes which seem to me today to have an inexhaustible wealth of human situations: the world of the "primitives" and the universe of folklore. But even today, despite my passion for the myths of the primitives and for archaic and popular beliefs, I feel I haven't forgotten the lesson of the Renaissance.

In rereading the lines from yesterday in which I recalled my garret on the Strada Melodiei, I suddenly remembered that at the age of thirty-three I left the country with empty hands. I didn't even take my books and my published articles with me, to say nothing of the manuscripts and files of notes. I later found some of my books abroad, in the homes of friends. I had others sent to Lisbon during the war. But I was unable to reassemble all of them. As for the files of notes which I built up for works in preparation, I gave up on them long ago. I have never understood why, during my brief trip to Rumania in the summer of 1942, I didn't think of bringing to Lisbon at least the unpublished manuscripts. I felt that the war was lost for my country and I decided it was useless, if not downright immoral, to try to save something of my past work. Perhaps that was only a rationalist interpretation of a much deeper process. In reality, I felt that everything that I had achieved or even begun back there, and which I kept, was linked to a Rumania that was in mortal danger; if that Rumania was to disappear, my past no longer had any meaning. To be more precise, that past could recover its meaning and could be redeemed only if I renounced it, only if I sacrificed it. In one way or another, I felt that the only thing that I still had the right to do was to begin everything over: working in poverty in a hotel room in the Latin Quarter, trying to write in another language, and making my debut again, at the age of forty, before a public of a different sort.

Sometimes, in my room in the Hôtel de Suède, I longed to recover the manuscripts left behind in Rumania. At such times, I would stay with my eyes half closed for hours and hours, trying to remember them. Reconstructed in this way from memory or with the help of the imagination, some of these texts seemed better to me than everything I had written since. I would say to myself: The best things I ever did are buried. Once I even decided to compile an "Exhaustive, Annotated Catalog of All Manuscripts Left Behind." I never began it because my memory never succeeded in penetrating to the primary layers: the manuscripts from my early years in the lyceé. From my early youth I had a habit of collecting things: I kept everything, even the postcards my friends sent me from spas. I would have liked to begin the analytical catalogs with a detailed description, supposedly scientific, of those notebooks written in 1920 in which I recorded my observations on plants and insects. But I remembered nothing, or almost nothing. The fact is that I never looked through them. It was enough for me to know that they were there, in a little chest, along with the manuscripts of studies and novels begun in the lycée.

During these memory exercises at the Hôtel de Suède, I would make discoveries that brightened my day. Once, I remembered an article written in 1927 for *Cuvântul,* the only one that Nae Ionesco ever refused to publish: I can still hear his voice saying, "This is unbearable self-centeredness."

I had entitled it "Apologia pro causa sua" and had put down these verses of La Fontaine as an epigraph: "This animal is very mean-tempered—when it is attacked, it defends itself." It was right in the middle of the polemics about the young generation, and I shut up the "old fellows" once and for all.

Another time I remembered that I had kept the draft of an article entitled "The Magic Deed," written in December of 1928 on the ship *Hakone Maru,* between Port Said and Colombo. I had sent it from Colombo to Mircea Vulcanescu, for the magazine *Esprit et Lettre* that he intended to publish with Sandu Tudor and Paul Sterian.

It was odd, but the autobiographical novels written when I was a student—the last years at the lycée and later at the university—did not evoke memories, nor did *The Near-Sighted Teenager,* or *Gaudeamus,* or even *Peter and Paul* or *Stephania* (this last novel should have become the first novel of the series "New Life," sequel to *The Hooligans*). What attracted me most especially were the manuscripts from my adolescence, which I had never had the curiosity to look through as long as I was still in Rumania. I remember a *History of the Deciphering of Hieroglyphics,* written when I was in my next to last year at the lycée. A thin notebook with a blue cover. On the first page was a long fragment of *Oedipus Aegyptiacus* as an epigraph.

I would like to go through my very first literary attempts written before the short narratives and the articles published from 1920 onward in the *Journal of Popular Sciences*. I remember the subjects of these "novellas" because I got them from my father: things that took place during the war, or the retreat of the Rumanian troops in Moldavia. I would like to know what I did with them, how I told them. My memory has kept only bits and pieces of sentences, without any apparent connection. One of these little novellas began: "I met God at the end of a path. He had pulled a branch off a hazel tree and was trying to make a switch out of it. 'You wouldn't have a penknife, by any chance?' he asked me."

What I wouldn't give to know the rest.

We began the evening at the diplomat Pietro Gerbore's home at Lungarno Vespucci. I listened to him recall our first meeting in Lisbon, just after my arrival from London in the spring of 1941. We ended late, reading aloud in turns from Matei Caragiale. This sort of communion, considered to be one of the components of the Rumanian soul, lays bare, I feel, the secret sense of my being uprooted.

This took place in the Café Giubbe Rosse, one evening in 1910. The military band had finished playing a medley and the audience was still applauding. They were already announcing the first results of a charity lottery. Ardengo Soffici was verifying the numbers of the tickets he had bought when a little man approached him and asked him if he was indeed Soffici. He had hardly had the time to answer when the man punched him with such violence that Soffici fell over backwards with his chair. The aggressor was none other than the painter Boccioni, ridiculed by Soffici in an article in *La Voce* devoted to the Futurist Exhibition in Milan. Boccioni was not alone; Marinetti and a few other futurists were with him. Soffici got up with a bound and rushed at the group with his cane. Thus began a fight that was to end a few hours later at the police station. Panic took hold of everyone there: the women and children were crying, the men were vying with one another to escape, in the middle of a fine tumult of upset tables and chairs and broken bottles, saltcellars, and glasses. Soffici tells in his memoirs that on the floor, after the café had been emptied, besides a considerable number of broken glasses, plates, and bottles, were to be found purses, wallets, men's and women's hats, scarves, handkerchiefs, shoes, lottery tickets, and many other articles. The next day, all these objects, exhibited on tables, were available for retrieval by their owners.

Such was the first of the skirmishes between the Milanese futurists and the Florentine group from *La Voce*. Skirmishes that ended, shortly thereafter, in a close association and a sincere friendship between the two groups.

This episode seems to me to exemplify everything that was being done or was about to be done in 1910. One would have said it was a Chaplin film: men with mustaches and armed with canes, military music, a lottery; an aggressive weakling, a melee, panic, the march to the police station. And just as in a Chaplin film, two worlds side by side: the one didn't know that it was dying and would be dead within ten years; the other was not yet aware of its own existence and was pathetically seeking to express itself, not without borrowing the mannerisms and prestige of the world it wanted to bury.

With Pietro Gerbore at Arigo Levasti's. Levasti's anthology was the first collection of mystical texts that I read at the lycée. Tall, lean, almost airy, the face of an ascetic or an angel. A hallway; in the salon into which he brings us, some canvases done by his wife: a circus in the suburbs, some streets in Florence, a theater auditorium. While he was coming with me to Levasti's, Gerbore told me that, under fascism, his friend had lived goodness knows how, sometimes reduced to starvation. Now he is head curator of the Academic Library. We spoke of Papini, among others. Levasti told me that after Papini wrote *Storia di Cristo,* he was unhappy because he had lost his audience and was no longer read except by priests and pious types. That was why he tried to regain the audience he had had in his youth: from this came *Dizionario dell'uomo selvatico, Gog,* and *Il Libro nero.*

In a café, at a nearby table, two Americans are talking about Milton. One—very tall, almost bald, with a little dog tangled in its leash—is setting forth a personal theory when, without any apparent reason, the dog begins to bark. With one hand, the young man tries to calm it; with the other he is holding his coffee cup, without stopping his talking. And then suddenly he interrupts himself to ask for a glass of water. He has upset his coffee on his clothes. Concentratedly, frowning, he rinses the spots with a wet handkerchief. In the end, says the other, we must discover Milton. That will be difficult, says the young man, still drying his jacket. We have already discovered him once and we didn't understand very much. The moral of the story, continues the other, is that we must discover him a second time.

Convento di San Marco. In the center, a majestic cedar stretches lazily out of a bed of blue flowers. Above the flowers flutter some butterflies that haven't caught up with summer.

The Crucifixion of Fra Angelico. Adam's skull at the foot of the cross. On the walls of the cell, in the frescoes painted by Angelico and his disciples, the motif returns several times. Here the symbolism is stressed even more: we see the trickles of blood flowing from the Savior's body onto Adam's skull. This motif is also found in certain Florentine primitives (the Academy's collections), but it disappears in the great paintings of the Renaissance. Moreover, it was to be expected. The myth of Adam buried in the "Center of the World," at the top of the Cosmic Mountain, in the very same place where he had been conceived, and where, later, Jesus was to be crucified, in such a way that the forebear too, touched by the Savior's blood, would find salvation—this archaic myth has survived, especially in religious folklore. But if there was one area of Christian experience which the great painters of the Renaissance did not know, it was none other than this archaic religious folklore, taken and canonized, nonetheless, some ten or twelve centuries earlier by liturgical poetry and iconography.

The Last Judgment by the Blessed Angelico. All the redeemed—monks, soldiers, women—resemble one another. They all have the same childlike faces. Looking at them closely one after the other, one nonetheless realizes that they are not like the angels—those famous angels of Fra Angelico—these are men, of all ages, who have kept the face of their childhood. One might say that, for Christianity, this is the translation of an obvious fact: the religious symbolism of the child flows directly from the parables and acts of Jesus. But is the import of this symbolism clear to all Christians? To be like a child means to be newborn, to be reborn to a new spiritual life; in short, to be an initiate. Unlike all other modes of being, the spiritual life has nothing to do with the law of becoming, for it does not develop within time. The "newborn" is not a suckling child who will grow up only to grow old one day. He is *puer aeternus.* He will remain a child *in aeternum:* he will partake of the atemporal beatitude of the Spirit, and not of the flux of history. The second life—the life of the initiate—does not repeat the first, human, historical life: its mode of being is qualitatively different.

Beato Angelico says all that infinitely better, with a blinding simplicity, in *The Last Judgment.*

The little donkey in the *Flight to Egypt* seems just as meditative as Joseph and the Virgin.

Of the frescoes that decorate the monks' cells I remember—for reasons other than artistic—*The Transfiguration* and the *Two Marys at the Tomb* (nos. 6 and 8). In these two compositions the Christ is shown to us in his glory, as though in an immense egg of dazzling whiteness. I feel a limitless admiration for the metaphysical and theological genius of Angelico. In this image of the Divine Glory, similar to the Cosmogonic Egg, he says more than could be said in a whole book. The intuition of Angelico is truly stupefying: the light of the transfiguration, which blinded the apostles on Mount Tabor, is the same glorious light of the cosmos on the eve of creation, when the world was still in its embryo state, not yet detached from God.

Viola, one of Papini's daughters, recounts this memory, among others: In 1917 in Bulciano, Ungaretti, just returned from the front, would remain stretched out on the grass for hours at a time looking at scattered clouds moving slowly across the sky. When she asked him one day what he saw, Ungaretti answered, "Nulla."

Seated on a chair in the Council Room of the National Museum, a young woman was keeping watch in a reflective mood, ten meters from Donatello's *Saint George*. I found her there, looking, her hands on her knees. A quarter of an hour later, she was still immersed in the same discreet bliss. At certain moments, she seemed to me to be closing her eyes. Just as I was about to leave the room, I turned around, and I caught her hiding a little notebook with her hands: she was furtively writing something in it as soon as she thought she was alone.

I found the sentence from Pico della Mirandola that I've been seeking for a long time: "Nec te coelestem, neque terrenum, neque mortalem, neque immortalem fecimus. . . ." (De hominis dignitate.)

That indefatigable cat, sick or mad, whose heart-rending, unending meowings can be stopped by nothing and no one—he begins to cry before sunset and doesn't stop until dawn—this invisible cat, hidden somewhere in the Piazza SS. Apostoli, gave me a lesson tonight in monastic humility. After all, why shouldn't I also accept from animals signs and spiritual direction? The entire history of religions—including the Christian traditions—bears witness to this. I endured the trial with great courage—or so I flattered myself in any case—but around two in the morning I had had enough. Exasperated, I began to toss and turn in my bed. And suddenly I remembered what I had known for a long time, what I had read in the great books and had learned from the masters and disciples of all the religions: self-fulfillment is obtained only by resisting the spontaneous impulses of "life" (blood, nerves, pride) and by a behavior contrasting exactly with the needs of life.

Love your enemy. Turn the other cheek. Who doesn't know these teachings? But how difficult it is to put them into practice, to live them! And, nevertheless, what a miraculous transformation if one succeeds in observing one of these old commandments.

When I succeeded not only in accustoming myself to this sinister, poisonous lamentation, but also in picturing and in loving the cat as it was—wicked, hateful, wild—I suddenly felt myself to be another man. It is impossible to describe this experience, although it wasn't the first of its type. I only understood—once again—that there was a path, a way out.

Last night's dream. Two old men who are dying, alone, each in his own way. Disappearing forever with them, without witnesses and without leaving a trace, was an admirable story (which *I* knew). Terrible sadness. Despair. I withdrew to a room on the side, and I prayed. I said to myself: If God does not exist, all is finished, all is absurd.

I awoke with the taste of ashes.

The Rocks of Matsushima

September 1958

On the way from Sendai by car, I was listening to Hori tell me how close heaven and earth were in the beginning. One day a stranger who walked bent over, almost doubled over, arrived in a certain village. When asked why he walked that way, he answered that in his country the sky was so low that if he had stood up, his head would have touched the vault of heaven. I was getting ready to add that what we had here was a case of the well-known paradise myth (in the beginning, heaven was so close to earth that men could, at any moment, meet the gods, etc.), when the car turned abruptly, the ocean suddenly appeared before us, and I saw the islands that were closer in.

How many were there? Maybe twenty, or even more. But as I realized a half-hour later, from the hotel terrace, there were a good many more. More than a hundred. Some no bigger than a rock on which one could scarcely stretch out. Others a few square meters or a few dozen square meters, and even bigger, with a little grass and a lot of trees. One after another, some very close, others farther away, they stretched out over several kilometers. Sometimes a bird with huge wings rose from a cinderlike, arid rock.

At the Park Hotel, built in a pseudo-Chinese style, one could say. Probably luxurious around 1930. Today it seems old-fashioned, fallen. Only a few customers.

Hori took me into the immense garden, which is in front of the hotel. There's also a wharf where the motorboats leave for cruises among the islands and rocks. This is certainly a case, I said to him, of a rather widespread mythical motif, especially in Southeast Asia. The sky was so close that, in one of the versions of the myth, a woman who was doing her laundry raised her head abruptly and struck it against the vault of heaven. In a certain sense, one could say that the separation of heaven and earth had not yet taken place. This cosmic separation was to occur later. And almost always it would be the result of a hasty act by the mythical ancestors: one of them would get angry with God, or else would begin to cut the tree or the vine which attached heaven to earth, and then the sky would rise dizzily to where we see it today.

Hori reminded me of certain similar ideas in Japanese mythology. For example, Ame no Mihashira, "the Pillar of Heaven," which held up the universe and, in addition, allowed the gods and god-men to go up to heaven. (As I expected, these ritual pillars have their ritual counterparts on earth: *hashira,* the pillar identified with the High God, and later with the emperor. One day I must examine to what extent the *axis mundi*–high god–emperor complex can be compared to the mythology implied in the Vedic *rajasuya,* the ceremony of royal consecration. As he was being anointed, the rajah would stand on the throne, his arms raised; thus he incarnated the cosmic axis, one end of which was fixed to "the Center of the Earth"—the throne—the other touching heaven.)

This morning at Sendai, in the castle park, he asked me all sorts of questions about our trip to Kobe, Hakata, and Nagasaki. I was able to tell about the night spent at Beppu with Joseph Campbell, who had all the trouble imaginable speaking Japanese with the geishas. The next day, Professor Furuno came to take us in his car to Fukuoka. We stopped to visit a wooded hill, near Beppu, that teemed with monkeys. And while we were slowly climbing, he asked me if I had read Luigi Salvatorelli's *Introduzione bibliografica alla Storia delle Religioni.* I couldn't believe my ears. None of my European colleagues had ever spoken of this admirable book, long since forgotten. . . .

The castle was demolished under the Meijis, because the baron opposed the emperor. The statue of the castle's founder still looks toward the city. Completely destroyed by bombs, Sendai was quickly and poorly reconstructed. Several paths and streets are still under construction.

The park is something of a forest with giant trees several centuries old. We climbed up and suddenly came out on a thin bridge, suspended over a chasm of unexpected depth. It is from this bridge, Hori told me, that the inhabitants traditionally commit suicide. But candidates come also from other regions, he added. A sign tries to save them *in extremis:* "Warning! Do not be tempted to rash actions." Under the bridge, and over us, swarms of dragonflies.

Afterward, we went down into the city, where Hori lives in one of these new houses built by the Americans, which they turned over to the university this year. I continued my tale. Fukuoka, Nagasaki, Unzen—and again Fukuoka, to the University of Kyushu. Furuno had insisted on organizing a symposium with Joseph Campbell, Wilhelm Koppers, and Joe Kitagawa. Obviously, he added with a smile, the theme of the symposium was "Current Methods in the Study of the History of Religions." Hori smiled also. The day after tomorrow, I am to treat the same subject at the University of Sendai.

The passion of the Japanese for "methodology." Just like my students at Chicago, they have an almost religious respect for "methods." I understand the American students: they are descendants of the pioneers. Formerly, when the Americans lived in the mystique of the frontier, things seemed simple: give us the tools we need and we will extend settlement and farming to the Pacific. My students seem to be saying: Give us a method and we will explain everything, we will understand everything. Exactly like the young Japanese scientist from the University of Kyushu who asked me: "What is your method in the study of the history of religions? Up to now, I've used the method

of X and that of Y, but to judge from the results, I have the impression
that yours is better. What is it?"

In the evening Hori went back to Sendai. I dined at the Park Hotel.
Only two tables were taken in this huge restaurant; nonetheless I was
given a choice among a large number of entrées. . . .

In the lobby, as in all Japanese hotels, there is a television set. I
stopped for a minute. It was a "variety show." The bar was deserted,
and the two waitresses were also watching. When the variety show
ended and a film started, they put their chairs in front of the set and
settled down.

I went up to my room. And, as in all hotels in Japan, there is also
a radio. I heard the radios from several rooms, some far off in the
other wing of the hotel. If I didn't know that there are only ten or
twelve customers tonight, I would think the hotel was full.

I tried to put my notes from Fukuoka in order. Toward evening,
we had gone to visit the ruins of the ancient capital. There were only
a few stones left and a ground plan reconstructed by the archaeologists. Afterward, Furuno took us to a Buddhist temple, in unusually miserable condition. It was closed; we weren't able to visit it. Next
to the temple, an ultramodern building was being constructed. I wondered what the temple would look like beside this monumental edifice.

We crossed a village and came to a Shinto sanctuary. There was a
little lake and some bridges with lanterns where groups of children
were playing. And, as usual, the impression of simple, authentic grandeur.

I heard someone knocking at the door. It was Karl Löwith, returning from Hokkaido after a series of lectures in several universities. He
was impressed by the interest shown in contemporary German philosophy; professors and students who know as much about Heidegger
and understand him as well (or as poorly) as in any German university. On the other hand, a gross ignorance of Eastern philosophical
traditions. The same people who know the latest important article
published in Germany on Heidegger or on Jaspers know nothing of
Buddhism.

I remember my conversation with X. You are becoming "provincial." You are trying to make yourself think as they think in Germany or France today. You have within your reach the boldest logic known to humanity until Hegel—the logic of Nagarjuna, of Vasubandhu, of Dignaga, of Dharmakirti—and you leave it to the historians and Orientalists. Your philosophers are ignorant of it, or, in any case, make no use of it. It probably seems to you that it isn't "contemporary." But that proves that you don't know it. The problem of Nagarjuna and of those who followed him was this: to demonstrate logically that samsara is identical with nirvana, that becoming (cosmic "unreality") and being are the same thing (i.e., ontological blessedness). On another level, striving to reach a different goal and using different means—the madhyamika philosophers were faced with the same mystery of *coincidentia oppositorum* as Nicholas of Cusa. Now we meet the principle of *coincidentia oppositorum* today in certain principles of nuclear physics (Oppenheimer's principle of complementarity, for example), but the same principle urgently comes up at our moment in history: How is liberty possible in a conditioned universe? How can one live in history without betraying it, without denying it, and still partake of a transhistorical reality? Ultimately, the real problem is this: How to recognize the real camouflaged in appearances? I'm waiting for a Buddhist philosopher to present us with a total vision of the real.

And since Löwith added that none of the Japanese philosophers that he has known has been able to speak intelligently of Shintoism, I reminded him of Hirai's response: Hirai is a Shinto priest who studied the history of religions at Chicago with Joachim Wach. One day he took us to see a famous temple at Ise. Someone in our group, an American philosopher, told him: I see the temples, I attend the ceremonials, the dances, I admire the costumes and the courtesy of the priests—but I don't see any theology implied by Shintoism. Hirai reflected a second and answered: We have no theology. We dance.

Hori took me today to see a shaman *(miko)* at Shiogama. Her name is Suzuki. She is fifty-six years old and is blind (as are most of the shamans of the *itako* class). She went blind at the age of ten and was initiated at the age of fourteen.

Hori told me that blind people have always been numerous in the northern regions of Japan. Since they were useless, at one time they were brought together and put to death at the age of five or ten. But once it happened that a high official called a blind woman to him, led her into a garden, and asked her to describe it for him. The blind woman had been well trained, for she was studying to become an *itako*. She described the garden and said, among other things, that over there was a tree, and under the tree a stone lantern. From that time on, people began to make use of blind people's clairvoyance and no longer killed them.

We went into the room set aside for the ceremonial and knelt down near the shaman. A small altar where there were some candlesticks with candles, some boxes, and a little white paper boat. The *miko* put two dolls on the altar and began to purify them with soft, round, little gestures. (They were undoubtedly the Oshiro Kami dolls whose story I know from Hori: a farmer had a daughter and a horse. The young girl fell in love with the horse and, finally, married it. When the father found out, he tied the horse to a mulberry tree and cut off its head. Unconsolable, the young girl mounted the horse's head and ascended to the sky. The young girl and the horse were metamorphosed into gods; they returned to earth and lived in mulberry trees in the form of silkworms. From that time they became Oshiro Kami, and their likenesses have been made in mulberry wood.)

The *miko* took a little metal drum and began a litany, telling a long string of beads *(iratako)* between her fingers. She lit candles and burned some aromatic substances. Then she put the *iratako* on the ground and laid hands on a bow. Then came another litany, probably incomprehensible, because Hori, taking advantage of a little pause, asked her to explain it to him. She took up the litany again, striking the bow gently with a rod. It seemed that she was getting ready for the "trance": she turned her attention from the bow and took up the two dolls again, bringing them to her face. Suddenly she began to chant, without changing her voice. The same monotonous melody, at the same rhythm, indefinitely repeated. What she was saying was addressed to me, and Hori quickly took some notes so as to be able to translate for me after the séance. The *miko* was asking me which members of my family I had just lost. I had spoken to her of my father and my brother. (The "message" that Hori was to translate for me later came from my brother. It hadn't been a case of possession, and my brother wasn't speaking through the mouth of the shaman, but the *miko* was giving me news of him.)

She didn't claim to have fallen into a trance because, for the whole time, she had held in one hand the rod with which she had struck the bow, and in the other the two dolls with which she devotedly touched her face. The chanted message lasted about a quarter of an hour. When she stopped and began again to strike the bow, I understood that the ceremonial was drawing to a close. Everything ended five minutes later with a final ritual.

A conversation with Hori. Undoubtedly, I said to him, that wasn't shamanism in its exact sense. The absence of ectasy is decisive. And one can't even speak of the "possession" characteristic of the other *mikos*. But there are also some curious elements which suggest a Siberian and, ultimately, a central Asian origin: the dolls, for example, the bow, and, with certain *mikos,* the rod with the horse's head.

But I would have liked to know a little more about another category of shaman, those called "spouses for a night" *(ichiya-tsuma),* whose partner is a divine guest *(marebito),* who, in the course of his infinite wanderings, stops for one night to visit them.

Note of March 1959

Ecstatic possession is attested from the beginnings of Shintoism and finds its justification in the famous myth of the Sun Goddess, Amaterasu. When Amaterasu hid herself in the Cave of Heaven and light disappeared from the world, the gods met at the entrance of the Cave and the goddess Ame No Uzume began to dance. But a spirit entered her and Ame No Uzume fell into ecstasy; while dancing she bared her breasts and her stomach. Thousands of gods broke out laughing, and their laughter shook the universe. Amaterasu stuck her head from the cave to see what was going on outside; then a god pulled her out of the cave and blocked the entrance with a cord in such a way that, henceforth, Amaterasu was not able to hide there—and from that moment on the sun has shone on the world.

The dance of the goddess Ame No Uzume was the first ecstasy and, as such, the exemplary model of all trances and ecstatic possessions. And who hasn't undergone ecstasy in Japan? Empresses (such as Himiko, the famous matriarch of the third century), or peasants (such as the famous Ohotataneko, in the first century B.C.; she had been born in a hamlet but claimed to be a daughter of the gods); princesses of the imperial family or simple *mikos* who, while officiating in the temples, accepted séances in private houses. This surprising popularity of ecstatic experiences is explained if one takes into account the fact that for the Japanese everything was, or could become, animated by a spirit or a god—everything, from stones, trees, animals, to manufactured objects and, of course, human beings: children, women, men. Religious life particularly revolved around this objective: to assure and maintain a concrete link with divine powers and persons. And what relationship could be more concrete than possession, the incarnation of the spirit or the god?

"Possession" had become so indispensable to religious life that when Shintoism tried to stem the triumph of Buddhism, one of the first official measures was to prohibit mediumistic practices outside the precincts of the sanctuary. Obviously, it was an attempt to consolidate, by those means, the prestige and authority of the Shinto temples. The first decree was published in 780 and the second in 807, but without result. In vain the decrees proclaimed that ecstasy was authentic only in a consecrated space, and that the pseudotrances which took place in private houses were illusory and dangerous. For more than a thousand years, the Japanese continued to consult all sorts of mediums, sorcerers, or ecstatics where they found them: in the temple or outside the temple. The last decree, published in 1873, prohibited ecstatic practices even within the precincts of the temples. Shintoism officially rejected an authentic two-thousand-year-old ecstatic tradition. (Was that the consequence of the first phase of Westernization?) Since that time, and until 1945, ecstatic techniques were conserved and transmitted on the sly.

Points to be remembered: the need to communicate with a divinity and to be taught by it, or by a spirit provisionally incarnated in a human being; the tendency to confront the divine or the sacred *in concreto,* such as they are made manifest especially in a living being; indifference toward the abstract and the transcendent; in a word, longing for the primordial bridge which used to connect heaven and earth (the floating bridge, Amano Ukihashi, by which, *in illo tempore,* Izanage and Izaname ascended to heaven). The Japanese soul yearns for a concrete epiphany of the divine. I don't think that a doctrine of the incarnation of the Christian type (that is, historical and once-and-for-all) could interest a Japanese; he is attracted by a theology of the provisional, lightninglike incarnation of the spirit: gods, god-men, spirits, souls of the dead, souls of animals, etc., etc. The gods are travelers *par excellence, visitors* (they are, in fact, *marebito*). Everything in the cosmos can be transfigured, no one is unworthy to receive the visit of a god: a flower, a stone, a pillar of wood. The universe is constantly being sanctified by an infinity of instant epiphanies. The gods do not settle down anywhere in the world. The spirit descends any time, anywhere, but it does not remain; it does not allow itself to be caught by temporal duration. Epiphany is especially lightninglike. Every divine presence is provisional.

Thus, I could perhaps understand the passion of the Japanese for the art of flower arranging, and for those universes in miniature, their gardens. The extraordinary value that any object, any moment, any act can acquire, if only for an instant. It is in this sense that I could understand Japanese painting, this passion for the concrete, the empirical, this penchant for erudition and extreme specialization, this collector's passion. I could even understand the vogue for spiritual techniques founded on discontinuity and paradox. For example, the doctrine of absolute discontinuity implied by Zen: a universe formed of billions of discontinuous fragments, apparently illusory and insignificant; but each one of them is capable of being transfigured, and then it is revealed as "All-One." The transfiguration is instantaneous and paradoxical. Nothing can pave the way for satori; one can have it after fifty years of meditation, but also in this very moment while playing with a pencil or drinking a glass of beer, and only after having known satori can you realize, *in a certain way,* that you had always known it. But, obviously, no one has succeeded in explaining what is meant by *in a certain way* to someone who hasn't experienced satori.

September 1958

Exactly as with the bouquet of flowers (when it is composed on the traditional model), the stage represents a cosmos in miniature. In the past, there was a pine tree on the stage, symbol of the cosmic tree. Today a painted pine tree replaces the real one. It has been said that the pine tree is of Chinese origin; but as with everything that has been borrowed by the Japanese, this borrowing too has been "Japanized." On the stage the pine tree is a *yorishiro,* a seat of divinity. In this case, the seat is the cosmic tree itself.

Ultimately, the stage—as formerly, the temple—constitutes a space provisionally marked out (thus "consecrated") for the celebration of a ceremony. In the beginning, no temples were built because it was believed that the gods visited only to preside at a rite and then went off elsewhere. The ceremonial consisted in inviting and welcoming with pomp, then respectfully sending off the divine guest, *marebito.* The temple, *yashiro,* means literally "place to construct a temporary edifice." But it is not claimed that *yashiro* is a divine residence—only a place of offering and repose during the time of the ceremonial. This conception survives in the custom of erecting a new sanctuary in the grand temple of Ise every twenty years; and every seven years at Suna, etc.

In order to be able to invite a *marebito* to the ceremony, it is necessary to have a "seat": a tree, rock, stone, rod, column, artificial hill, or other natural or manufactured objects, sometimes even children. These symbols are found in the majority of Shinto temples—but also on the stage. Because the stage represents merely a stopping place on a long divine voyage and the *marebito,* those supernatural travelers, are identified not only with wandering ascetics but also with itinerant actors.

The mythico-ritual complex of the *marebito* has fascinated me since my youth, when I learned of the existence of a doctoral thesis (unpublished) of Masao Oka. The *marebito* are gods, god-men, ancestral spirits, souls of the dead—or strangers who come from beyond the seas, from the land of the dead, from paradise, or from the mountains. Normally they arrive during the periods of cosmic crisis, preferably during the change of winter to spring, or around the New Year. They visit villages, recount myths, bless the harvests, and probably (at least in ancient times) initiate the young—and then return home. The *marebito* are represented especially by the "mountain folk" *(yamabito)* or by masked and costumed priests. When the priests aren't wearing theriomorphic masks, they hide their faces under huge bamboo hats. The hat and the mask constitute the symbols *par excellence* of the *marebito*.

Note of March 1959

These religious conceptions are not the appanage of Japan. As early as 1938, Alex Slawik showed that they bore a striking resemblance to certain old Germanic rites and beliefs. But this is a case of a much vaster mythico-ritual complex. In the traditions of many peoples, the dead return in a group at a certain period (normally toward the end of the year); they are welcomed, honored, and finally taken in ceremony to the edge of the village. Often, the souls of the dead are represented by groups of young masked men who visit the houses, bless the people, the livestock, and the fields, and solicit gifts. The custom has been conserved also in Europe; especially eastern Europe (the Koledari of the Balkans, for example, or the masked cortèges of central Europe).

Besides the collective visit of souls at the end of the year, certain cultures have another ritual, even more dramatic: the individual visit of the soul, forty days after its death. Thus, for example, with the Mordvin: the whole village goes to the cemetery and invites the deceased to return home to enjoy himself and feast. The soul of the deceased is carried in pomp on a cushion, the widow waits for him on her knees in the courtyard, and the master of the house welcomes him with bread and salt. The cushion is placed where the deceased usually sat. Next the relatives and friends arrive with gifts, and the banquet begins, followed by music and dancing. At midnight, the musicians stop as though by chance, and someone shouts from the threshold, "He has arrived." A man who resembles the deceased, and is dressed in his clothes, enters and sits on the cushion. The widow calls him "my husband," and everyone shakes his hand and envelopes him with respect. The man relates his experiences in the other world; he exhorts the family to live amicably together, to work, and to remember him. The people of the household ask him to protect them. At dawn, "the deceased" is accompanied by everyone as far as the edge of the village. With the Mordvin, it was also customary for an old man to symbolize the god Nishkipaz. He would climb onto the roof of a hut or into a tree, and when the people called upon him: "Nishkipaz, give us grain!" the old man would shout from above: "I will." In other regions, the old man, in brand-new clothes, would walk in the street and be invited into a house, where a meal was waiting for him. The people would beg him: "Nishkipaz, give us livestock, a good harvest," and the old man would reply: "I will!"

Traces of an analogous scenario are to be found in Byelorussian poetry; God (Bog) walks in the street and behind him the head of household who has invited him: "Come to my house, Bog, come to my home with much grain and livestock!"

But neither with the Mordvin nor in eastern Europe (the Koledari, etc.) has the mythico-ritual scenario of the visitor who incarnates the souls of the dead or even God given birth to a theater. These scenarios have never gone beyond creative folklore; they have not been transformed into a spectacle detached from its ritual source, they have not given rise to the literary genre of the drama, as in Japan and perhaps in Greece, if we are to believe William Ridgeway. But if Ridgeway thinks that drama and theater everywhere derive from the cult of the dead, he attaches no importance to the cult of visitors. He believes that the first Greek actors were mediums. Thespis used white spectral masks to represent the heroes whose phantoms were to rise from the tombs, as, later, the phantom of Darius would appear in *The Persians*. But Thespis was a bold innovator: he piled his company into carts, traveled through Greece, and gave plays where he found a public; not for religious ends but, as he admitted himself, "to pass the time and earn money." Whence Solon's brutal reaction against this innovation, which he considered a sacrilege. The dramatic ceremonial, in Solon's estimation, was to be celebrated solely around a hero's tomb and not in just any profane space as Thespis did.

As usual, the mystery of the transformation of a *ritual* into a *work of art* remains impenetrable. Numerous folk cultures—from central and eastern Europe to Japan—have had the mythico-ritual motif of the visitors and have even sometimes elaborated dramatic scenarios around this ceremonial. But it is only in Japan that the *marebito* ended by being identified with the itinerant actors, and that the ritual complex of the divine visit gave birth to the drama and to spectacle.

September 1958

In Japan, the passage of ritual to theater can best be observed in the transformations which the stage underwent through time. In the beginning, the "stage" was located at the corner of a rice field, on a platform, or at a crossroads. Later, it was a space marked out by four bamboo sticks tied one to another with straw rope between them. At the four corners, branches of willow or pine were hung. *No* tried to synthesize all the earlier traditions. A *No* play implies a proper stage (that is, a podium), a bridge, and a dressing room. (In the beginning *No* was performed in the open; the stone enclosure appeared only in the seventeenth century.) The bridge that connected the dressing room with the stage symbolized the route by which *marebito* came (it was one of the actors, generally the head of the troupe).

But the cosmic symbolism of the stage has been preserved down to recent times. Under the podium were huge clay vases—replicas of the empty barrel on which Ame No Uzume danced before the cave of the goddess Amaterasu, but at the same time they symbolized the subterranean regions (the earthen vases are supposedly filled with sake; in other words, it signifies the subterranean waters). In sum, the vases represent the underworld, the audience belongs to the Earth, and the actors incarnate the divine beings *(marebito)*. On the stage and in the theater, the three cosmic regions—Hell, Earth, and Heaven—communicate with one another.

Wandering Scholar

I saw Jung, at Küsnacht. I believe I hadn't seen him since 1953 or 1954. Almost unchanged; his hair hardly any whiter; he has lost two teeth and walks with the help of a cane. We spent an hour and a half in the garden, in the shade. I asked him not to come that evening to the lecture I was giving at the Psychology Club on "The World Tree and the Tree of Life." I summed it up for him in a few words. Afterward, it was he who took over the conversation. He remembered, and quite well, everything I wrote in *Shamanism* on the symbolism of the tree. We spoke of several other things: of Dostoevsky's dream (while still young, Dostoevsky had dreamed of a very brilliant full moon. It had cracked in three pieces, and on each one of the pieces Dostoevsky had written: "Me too, me too, me too")—a dream that Jung interpreted thus: The moon, that is the feminine principle, revealed to Dostoevsky that trinity is not an exclusive mode of the "masculine" Spirit, as Christianity interprets it. We passed on to the *tao* (Paul Mus had come to see him a few days before and had spoken to him of the origin and history of the Chinese character which expresses the term *tao*). Jung finds E. Neumann too rationalist (Jung gives this interpretation of a dream of Neumann that has a little girl in it: Neumann hasn't integrated the "feminine creativity" of which he has spoken so much in his writings).

Then he explained the meanings of numbers for the primitives. He called to mind his African experiences. He repeated some Swahili words, each time with a different intonation, meaning, "five," "numerous," "very numerous."

When I told Jung that in *Mysticism: Sacred and Profane,* Robert C. Zaehner comments on and applies his theories on the collective unconscious, and their connections with mystical experience, he was delighted and took down the title of the work. For him doctors and psychologists are "too stupid and too uncultivated" to understand these things. When I confessed that *Psychology of the Transference* is one of my favorite books, he smiled and appeared surprised: "Here, no one has understood anything," he said.

Very cordial, very friendly, exactly as in 1950. Aniella Jaffé and everyone around him confided to me, however, that he tired very quickly and that he could no longer receive a lot of people all on the same day. Other changes ascribable to age: he is no longer interested in therapy or in case studies. He no longer reads contemporary theologians (E. Brunner, Karl Barth), but patristics still fascinates him.

While we were in the garden, the elderly English lady who lives with him came to tell him that a group of Germans was waiting in front of the entrance to photograph him. They conferred together on the best way to escape them: he would not take me back as far as the entrance to the garden and would go back into the house by a back door. Jung was furious: "They are no longer well behaved. They regard you as an object or a toothpaste that has just been put on the market! . . ."

7 June

I had lunch with Ernst Jünger and Philipp Wolff-Windegg (the editorial secretary of *Antaios*) at Halbinsel Au, on a hill which dominates the lake of Zurich. Wolf has come from Basel and E. Jünger from Germany so we could decide on the synopsis of the second installment of *Antaios*. Jünger asked me what my working hours are and was surprised that I work so much in the afternoon. He offered me *Jahre der Okkupation,* the last volume of his journal. Next we discussed numerous eventual collaborators in the review—Zubiri, Julian Marias, Narr, Jettmar, etc.—and since I knew so many things about them and about their works, I felt obliged to justify myself: the history of religions is an impossible discipline; one must know everything, consult at least a dozen auxiliary disciplines (from prehistory to folklore), always chase after genuine sources and forever be consulting specialists of all types.

PARIS, *9 June*

I'm back in the little apartment on the rue de l'Yvette that I had rented for two months. When I went there for the first time, the morning of the thirteenth of May, Cioran and I carrying my suitcases on our shoulders up to the fourth floor, the apartment had seemed low-ceilinged and crowded. Now I'm beginning to like it here. From the balcony I saw some houses facing me across the gardens. In the background, the Eiffel Tower. From the Jasmin metro station the street climbs up just as in an Italian town. In the tiny room in the back, I've set up a wobbly little table where I try to write. I'm writing down all these insignificant details in order to get used to the journal again.

13 June

Summer days such as I have never known in Paris. The sky is a mediterranean blue, unusually clear. An air resembling a sea breeze has been blowing all day. I am constantly tempted to write the short story "With· the Gypsy Girls," but I hesitate to begin. I have so many other things to finish.

20 June

Last night at Suzanne Tezenas's. I saw Henri Michaux again, after three years. Thinner, aged. I've been told he was taking mescaline five times a week. But he is still just as interesting; he still has things to say that one doesn't expect. This, among other things: when he sacrificed music and gave up composing (especially "research with the drum") so as to be able to devote himself exclusively to painting, he noticed that his painting took on a "musical rhythm." He felt the "rhythm" in his arm as he painted. An art that one gives up is not entirely lost. Its essence, its mystery, passes over into the art that one has resolved to cultivate by working on it undividedly.

21 June

René and Délia Laforgue invited us to have dinner on the Bateau-Mouche. For ten years Christinel and I have been wanting to take that excursion. We're glad of the chance.

Délia spoke to me about *La Forêt interdite,* which she has read twice. She asked me why I felt a need for a "double." Not knowing what to tell her, I answered somewhat peripherally, calling to mind that this business of the double had tortured me, and that I hadn't been able to breathe, finally, until I had killed off Partenie; at that point René intervened: the double is the superego. Consequently I had killed the superego, etc.

An odd meeting that should bring us to discuss that novel on Saint John's Night, making the boat excursion that I had been dreaming of for ten years, and ten years, or very nearly, after I had decided to write the book.

23 June

In Zurich, one of Jung's daughters, Mme. Baumann, whose speciality is astrology (and more particularly the possible connections between astrology and depth psychology) told me this story: A Dutchman who had fought in Indochina came to see her. While in Indochina he had contracted some tropical disease or other; once cured, he noticed that he was seeing people's skeletons, or more precisely, that he saw of people only their skeletons. He felt that he was going mad. He couldn't look at his wife anymore because he saw only her skeleton. In the street he saw the skeletons of men long dead. It got to the point that he wasn't able to distinguish the living from the dead. Desperate, he retired into a Buddhist convent, where a bonze taught him how to endure this condition, as well as a number of other things: the art of divining the future, of counseling people, etc.

The Dutchman had come to Mme. Baumann to see whether, according to Jung, he would have to endure this condition all his life. When he had arrived, he had told Mme. Baumann that there were two other women in the house. According to his description, one of these two women could be none other than Mme. Jung (deceased in 1955). But Mme. Baumann couldn't believe in her real presence, because, she said, "if my mother's soul is somewhere, it is surely very far from the house she lived in."

11 July

Last winter Alan Watts talked to me about Christianity. He had renounced Christianity, he said, when he had realized that God was accessible to the Western world only through the Father Image. It would have taken him ten or fifteen years to destroy this image in one, single individual and to open him to the absolute. He had estimated a work such as that much too long and too intense in comparison with the results looked for. That is when he chose Zen.

On another occasion, he told me that in two centuries half the United States will be Roman Catholic and the other half will practice "a sort of Zen."

12 July

We're leaving tomorrow morning by car with Sibylle and Jacqueline for Ascona. The same group as four years ago. But we'll take a different route.

I've spent nearly six weeks in this apartment. I've written "With the Gypsy Girls" but have done nothing, or almost nothing, for the Eranos lectures. It has only been these last few days that I've had the time to spend a few hours at the Musée de l'Homme and the Musée Guimet.

13 July

Provins. A few old houses at the foot of the keep, among the linden trees and sycamores. On the square, the Four Gables restaurant; we had an excellent lunch in the garden, but had to chase away the flies as though we were in a market town in Bessarabia.

At the end of the afternoon, we visited "the source of the Seine," near the village of Saint-Germain. The source belongs to the city of Paris.

There is the artificial grotto and the nymph, both set up in 1867 under Napoleon III. In the pool, a large number of coins. They were probably already being thrown in back in Gallo-Roman times.

Giant trees that reminded me of the sanctuaries in Japan. Above the Seine, which flowed, almost invisible, through a field of clover, some dragonflies.

Dijon. We passed a number of parks and gardens before arriving at the Hôtel Central, where we found two rooms for the night. In the bar, the inevitable television set; all the chairs were occupied. A group of English tourists, who had arrived by bus, was preparing to see Paris lit up by night.

The church of Notre Dame, superbly illuminated with its four rows of gargoyles. We passed by the Firemen's Palace; in the courtyard, an orchestra, some tight groups, a few couples dancing, and, from everywhere, firecrackers were exploding at our feet, at our backs, at our shoulders.

14 July

Dijon: the Carthusian monastery of Champmol, today a hospital. The superb Jeremiah; and Moses with his huge beard and the two horns. The angels which seem scarcely awakened from sleep.

The park with its old trees made me suddenly recall one of the forests of my adolescence. But which one? Overcome with sadness at not being able to place it precisely.

In France it is enough to walk and look around with just a bit of attention in order to understand that this country would be a museum today if it weren't for the vandalism of 1789. Churches and cathedrals in ruin greet you just about everywhere.

Evening in Fribourg. We stopped first at Froideville, in front of the Anthropos Institut. I rang and rang, and after five minutes, a monk appeared (the reverend librarian, I believe). But neither R. P. Rahmann nor D. Schröder was there. I hope to find them at the beginning of August when I return here to work.

At the Hôtel de l'Aigle Noir, on the terrace, we waited for the monuments on which the city prides itself to be lit up: the city hall, the churches on the hill.

On the evening of 9 July I had dinner with Father de Menasce at our restaurant of two years ago: the one on the corner of the boulevard Saint-Germain and the rue des Saints-Pères. I was telling him, among other things, how much I admired—and envied—the mathematicians and physicists of today: their intellectual courage, their daring. They have no fear of contradicting themselves, nor of formulating contradictory judgments on the structures of the real. How far behind we "humanists" are—philologists, historians of religion, ethnologists, etc. We are fearful, prudent, or myopic to the point of idiocy. And no change is in sight in the near future. Nonscientists are being recruited from among the mediocre and the timid, or from among young people who are afraid of life and who are looking for security in a profession without risks: teaching, scientific research, etc. The adventurous and the bold, creative minds are no longer coming to philology, to Orientalism, or to the history of religions as they were in 1870–1880; they are oriented rather toward the physical sciences and mathematics. An Oppenheimer, an Edmund Sinnott, a Jacob Bronowski, is inconceivable among us Orientalists, ethnologists, or historians of religion. We attract only paltry types who haven't a virile enough soul to face a world in a state of crisis or to risk their career for a daring idea.

15 July

We left Fribourg in a fine rain. We made a stop at Thun—which we were not yet familiar with—and had breakfast in one of the most picturesque streets in Switzerland. We had lunch at Interlaken, then climbed up toward Furka Pass. Rain and thick fog. Up above, in the gorge, the gloom was so complete that we went at a speed of ten or twelve kilometers per hour. But we had a half-hour of light at the Rhône Glacier. Extraordinary impression in the ice caves. On the return, the closer we came to the exit, the ice became more and more transparent, to the point that we expected to find the blinding sun of a summer noon outside. Whereas there was only the pale light of a cloudy afternoon. Paradisiac images.

We spent the night at the Gasthaus Saint-Gotthard in Hospenthal. The cold is such that we don't even dare take a walk after dinner. In front of us at a neighboring table, her gaze fixed insistently on us, was an extraordinary old woman whose mummified face resembled Beethoven's mask to the point of being mistakable for it.

16 July

After Saint-Gotthard Pass, we came back to the blue sky and warm breezes of Ticino. At Lucarno, the rose laurels are still in bloom.

Nevertheless, for the first time in ten years, catching sight of the Lago Maggiore through the trees and villas, I no longer felt that indefinable bliss that used to make me think that this countryside was, for me, sacred, a bearer of happiness. Is it only because this morning on the telephone Christinel had been struck by the hint of weakness and fatigue in Olga's voice?

Sure enough, when Olga greeted us on the threshold of the Casa Gabriella, we had trouble hiding our surprise. She has lost thirty pounds; her hands shake. For six months she had been bedridden by jaundice, and just after she had had to suffer the tenacious aftereffects of the Asiatic flu for the last two years.

We were saddened that, for the first time since 1952, we didn't find the flowers in our room that Olga was in the habit of placing there a few hours before the train's arrival.

This very evening I took out the notebooks and two or three books from my satchel. In one of my notebooks from two or three years ago, I found these lines copied from *Journey to the Center of the Earth:*

" 'We shall descend, descend, and everlastingly descend. Do you know, my dear boy, that to reach the interior of the earth we have only five thousand miles to travel!'

'Bah!' I cried, carried away by a burst of enthusiasm, 'the distance is scarcely worth speaking about. The thing is to make a start.' "

Last week I was speaking to Guy Dumur about the extraordinary

Journey to the Center of the Earth. What a fascinating doctoral thesis one could make, I was saying to him, on the imaginary universe of Jules Verne. Dumur encouraged me to undertake this study myself and tried to convince me that only a historian of religions, experienced in symbolism, could penetrate and describe the dream worlds of Jules Verne. He was undoubtedly right. But where would I find the time to write that book? I have already sacrificed so many potential books, aware as I was that I did not have the necessary leisure to develop them, let alone complete them. Among others, the study on Balzac, begun in 1948 and which was to include as well an analysis of all his work up to the *Les Chouans*. The manuscript—a fine, close handwriting—must be in the basement on the rue Duhesme, along with other cartons and dossiers.

17 July

This morning it seemed to me that I was beginning to understand Jung's interest in what he calls "synchronicity." If matter and spirit are the two sides of a single reality, there exists a correspondence between psychic events and cosmic processes. But then the "primitives" weren't as stupid as is sometimes believed when they took as a model of all creative activity the creation *par excellence:* the cosmogony. The ritual imitation of the cosmogony at the New Year, or at coronation festivals of the sovereign, or at the curing of the sick, etc., undoubtedly have spiritual consequences that we moderns can no longer appreciate.

All this throws an unsuspected light on the results I obtained on the function of cosmogonic myth in traditional societies.

21 July

This morning again I heard the sound of a flute coming from one of the neighboring villas. It's a very short tune, a naïve, childlike allegretto of great simplicity—a tune that the flutist repeats continually. From time to time there's a short pause, as though he were stopping to listen. And abruptly he begins again, keeping the same tempo, as though, patiently and without haste, he were repeating an appeal addressed to a being that he alone knows. I've been hearing this melody for several years. A feeling of reconciliation with the world, of inexplicable bliss.

22 July

Two years ago, having arrived in Siena by bus, we left our baggage at the hotel and immediately headed toward the old city. On the square, right near our hotel, we sat down on a terrace to have a drink. Leaden sky, lively square. We could hear a radio turned up uncommonly loud, amplified to a din. Modern American music, jazz, Negro spirituals, love songs. Suddenly, we both started: we seemed to recognize the melody. It was exactly like one we had heard in January 1957 at the Church of Deliverance, the church of a black sect in Chicago. Cornelius Bolle had taken us. A room as huge as a concert hall. On the platform, four pianos and a choir of several hundred men and women, all dressed in green and white. The pianos accentuated the jazzlike quality yet without managing to lessen the heart-rending melancholy, the nameless despair which breathed from that haunting melody. The refrain stood out: "Jesus, Jesus!" At one point one of the female choristers fainted. We had noticed her when her arms began to move like two broken wings. Afterward, they carried her outside.

I shall always remember the two black women seated behind us, extraordinarily beautiful, distinguished, soberly and yet so elegantly dressed.

24 July

I was awakened this morning by the noisy motor of a passenger boat going very slowly across the lake in the direction of Brissago. For a long time I was lost in my memories. I recognized the sound of the tugboat which used to cross the lake of Tekirghiol. I think I heard it for the last time in 1922 or 1923.

And this is happening just at the very moment I'm writing the end of the short story. Perhaps to make me understand better that Movila, Tuzla, Constantsa, evoked in "He Who Reads the Stones," belong to a mythical landscape and resemble little or not at all what these places were in 1939. More and more I feel the need to free my writing from the geographical and historical concrete. The Bucharest of my novella *Mântuleasa Street,* although legendary, is truer than the city I went through for the last time in August 1942.

26 July

Two years ago, Laurens Van der Post spent a few weeks here at Casa Gabriella. He left one morning, and in the evening of the same day, Olga received an express letter sent from Bellinzona. Van der Post wrote that he had forgotten his denture on the table in his room and gave the address of a hotel in Zurich where she was to send it. After having looked just about everywhere in vain, Olga telephoned him in Zurich: "Look for it in your mouth," she said. "Maybe it's there." Sure enough, that's where it was.

28 July

I've been reading *Seconda Nascita* of Giovanni Papini, with the same interest and the same curiosity as in 1925. But, actually, I'm disappointed, saddened. Written in 1923, it was to be the sequel to *A Finished Man,* but Papini didn't publish it: he contented himself with using certain chapters or fragments of it. Except for his meeting the family of his future wife, the book is even devoid of any biographical interest. Two polemical chapters call to mind, not without a certain nostalgia, the Papini of the *Stroncature.* The rest is only banal prose, broken here and there by brief poetic flashes. I understand very well why Papini never made up his mind to publish the *Seconda Nascita.* But if his other unpublished works are of the same quality! . . . I noticed *Giudizio universale* in a bookstore window in Lucarno, but I hesitated to buy it.

29 July

In a dream last night, I saw my class in Swift Hall, where I gave a course on the structure of myth. One of the students had just read a work on the origin of death in African myths. And in my dream I was trying to explain to the students the meaning of the apparent stupidity of the cause of the first death. God sent an animal to inform men that they were immortal, and the animal, inadvertently or by error, told them just the opposite. All this actually took place last year: I was explaining to my students that the "absurdity" of the cause that introduced death into the human condition is only the mythical expression of the incomprehensibility of the fact of death. I even set up a comparison between the literary expressions used by French existentialism (cf. *La Nausée*) to suggest the absurdity of existence, and the ridiculous explanation the myth offers us to take account of the fact that man is mortal. Actually, I was only summarizing a chapter—not yet written—from my book *Mythologies of Death*.

I relived all that, but in explaining the same theory, how much clearer, sharper, more inspired it seemed in the dream. I saw myself, I heard myself talking, and I was saying to myself: *That* is exactly it. How is it that I didn't understand it earlier?

The meaning of all these causes—apparently so idiotic, so ridiculous—seemed to me not only transparent, but immensely noble.

2 August

We're moving into the Villa Shanti for three days, next door to the Villa Gabriella, invited by Marie-Louise and Christian Dehollain.

Yesterday I bought *Giudizio universale*. I read with emotion the fragments of Papini's journal inserted at the beginning of the book. I remember our conversation of 1953. It is impossible that Papini hadn't guessed, and even rather quickly, the risks of an undertaking so out of proportion; to begin with, the inevitable monotony of the autobiographical speech that each character gives before the angel. A monotony accentuated by Papini's literary method: he allows the same number of pages (two or three) to each character. Although each one's drama is unique to him, the structure of the confession is always the same: all the characters speak as Papini's characters in *Gog* or *Il Libro Nero*. The clear, didactic prose with the well-known accumulation of epithets falls frequently into cliché. Nevertheless, there are some admirable pages, inspired portraits where the poet of the *Cento*

Pagine or of *Pane e vino* is found once again. The choirs are of an especially stunning beauty. Certain confessions—those of Hazal, Huller, etc.—excellent. I am persuaded that an anthology of a few hundred pages would bring Papini's genius to light better than these thirteen hundred pages of an unfinished work. What seems to me both terrible and tragic in this *Guidizio universale* is that the work such as Papini had conceived it could never be finished. Why three hundred or five hundred characters—real or invented—and not a thousand or five thousand? The infinite variety of the human condition cannot be exhausted by individual destinies, but by "existence-types" (shepherds, kings, criminals, etc.). That must be what Papini understood when he replaced the brief individual confessions by choirs.

5 August

Each time I go through Saint-Gotthard Pass by train, I remember the dreams of the Swiss officers that Dr. Franz Riklin told me. During maneuvers they sleep in the fortified tunnels set up in the mountain. Some of them came to consult him about their nightmares. They had the bizarre sensation of being swallowed up in the stomach of a colossal monster, but against all expectation, they weren't digested, but were flattened, crushed, dried, petrified.

A terrible sensation, that of an existence which is being petrified even while keeping the qualities of its corporeal life. One feels crushed, solidified, but nevertheless a three-dimensional volume of flesh and blood persists; a body somehow continuing to move which has become immobile, hardened.

FRIBOURG, 6 August

In the afternoon I took the bus to go to Posieux, to the Anthropos Institut. Dominik Schröder announced his departure in September for Japan. He will remain there for several years as professor of ethnology at the Catholic University of Nagoya. After five hours of work in the library, I filled my satchel with books and returned to Fribourg with a Spanish priest who is a candidate for the chair in history of religions at the University of Madrid. From what I could understand, the area which fascinates him is the problem of the Flood. He believes in the historical reality of the Flood which, about twelve thousand years ago, destroyed just about the entire population of the globe. Supposedly, it lasted only a few seconds, a few minutes at the most: the level of the ocean rose abruptly about one hundred meters. Atlantis.

7 August

In the bus taking us to Posieux, a young priest cited the name of Saint Sylvester. I didn't catch in what connection. The only thing I know about this saint is the definition he gave of God. Mircea Vulcanescu first told me of it. God, said Saint Sylvester, is like the onion—because he is good and makes you cry.

Last winter, when I was telling my students about Meister Eckhart and negative theology, I commented at great length on Saint Sylvester's definition. It is perhaps the best illustration of negative theology: of God, nothing can be said. The more adequate a definition seems (God is good, powerful, the Creator, etc.), the more false it is. And especially dangerous: because, in that case, man imagines that he has understood God, that he knows something specific about him. Saint Sylvester found the right formula to show that, since God is indefinable, anything whatever can be said about him. Saying that he is like the onion is no less correct than affirming that he is the *summum bonum*.

9 August

A terrible storm yesterday afternoon. At three o'clock the sky was black. At the electric power station, they cut the current. Between the rumblings of thunder, gusts of wind could be heard like a strange, endless, metallic breathing.

I worked without stopping. I had taken out some works from the Anthropos Institut on the Melanesian "cargo cults." I will take a certain number of examples from them in my first Eranos lecture. I would like to find the time to develop the following theme: the religious origins of the political movements and of the dramatic phenomena of history. The socioeconomic explanations of historical phenomena sometimes seem to me exasperatingly simplistic. It's because of these platitudes that original, creative minds are no longer interested in history. Reducing historical phenomena to lower "conditioning" is to empty them of all exemplary meaning: thus, everything that is still valid and significant in human history disappears. The terrible banalization of history has been the fatal consequence of the systematic banalization of the world, accomplished especially in the nineteenth century. But, at that time, banalization of the world at least had a historical justification: modern, Western man was emptying the world of all extranatural meaning in order to give himself the means of "knowing it objectively" and mastering it. Today, even this historical justification can no longer be invoked.

ASCONA, *15 August*

This afternoon I dozed off for half an hour and had this dream: Far off, through my spyglass, I saw the chalk cliffs of a mountain. I made out crevices and caves; then I noticed the entrance to a cavern. I got rid of the spyglass and headed toward the cave. I began my visit and was alarmed, surprised at everything I discovered as I went farther in. Then, without any apparent reason, I woke up abruptly— nevertheless I managed to go back to sleep for a few moments, and I found the cave without difficulty. But I could no longer penetrate into it. I remained outside, in the light, and I said to myself—I remember very well—I'm going to wake up soon, but if I engrave well in my mind the spot where the cave is located, I can explore it in future dreams.

When I was awake for good, I retained the certainty that I could return to the cave as often as I liked.

21 August

Dr. Riklin told me that W. Pauli, the physicist, couldn't take a taxi for several years because, each time he took one, something happened (accident, motor trouble, etc.) that prevented him from reaching his destination. This series of coincidences was so well known in Zurich that they spoke at the university of the "Pauli effect."

23 August

Last night, I finished writing my second lecture. The only thing left for me to do was write the conclusion, a few pages. I hoped to do it this morning before leaving for the Casa Eranos. I wasn't able. The lecture was interesting, amusing (because I spoke about the "cargo cults"), but without conclusions. I'll have to write them in Chicago when I revise the whole manuscript.

FLORENCE, *27 August*

We're traveling toward Florence in Alain Daniélou's car. Anne Hunwald is also with us. We're having lunch in Parma, a city which we won't see, so to speak. Only speed seems to fascinate Daniélou, who has but one idea: to hurtle along at 120 kilometers an hour on the superhighway to gain time. Without us, he would have left Ascona earlier and would have arrived in Rome in the evening. Because of us, he has to stop tonight in Florence. Since there were no more rooms in Berchielli, we're spending the night in the new Hôtel Continental, opposite the Ponte Vecchio. From our window we can see the outlines of the landscape and the ruins, also the tower where, at this very moment, at sunset, little bats slender as larks are taking flight.

28 August

For a long time I had been wanting to read the *Vita di Girolamo Savonarola* by Roberto Ridolfi. I bought it this morning, and I'm cutting the pages in a café on the Lungarno Acciaioli. It was while listening to an Augustinian monk preach in Faenza that Savonarola was converted, and he wasn't moved by the monk's fervor, but by this sentence from Genesis: *Egredere de terra tua!*—"Leave thy country, leave thy father's house and family."

I'm thinking again of the "mystery" of my departure from my native Rumania, in 1940, a few weeks after the death of Nae Ionesco. Naturally, I thought I was leaving for a year, two at the most. But this departure saved my life to begin with, then my freedom, and finally allowed me to become what I am: a writer who can write and publish what he thinks. That would have been impossible had I stayed.

The legend, according to which Savonarola supposedly refused Lorenzo de Medici *assoluzione sacramentale:* Savonarola imposed three conditions—to have faith (Lorenzo replied that he had it), to restore everything he had taken (which Lorenzo also accepted), finally, to restore liberty to Florence. At that Lorenzo turned his back. That is supposedly when Savonarola left without absolving him.

I learned while reading Ridolfi (pp. 75–79) that this legend, accredited by Silvestro Maruffi and commented on enthusiastically by Villari, supposedly flourished in the time of the neo-Guelph, romantic Risorgimento. This archetypal image—Savonarola the prophet of civil liberties, Lorenzo the absolute tyrant—was too "true," too suggestive to be invalidated by documents or specific testimony. Even a critic as learned as Villari believed in its historical authenticity. Ridolfi cites the letters of Poliziano and of Carlo del Benino which attest that Savonarola, called to give communion to Lorenzo, went without hesitation. Even better: Carlo del Benino affirms that the monk's visit was a great consolation for Lorenzo.

And, nonetheless, the last encounter between the tyrant and the founder of the People's State was "truer" in legend than in history. In history, Savonarola conducted himself as any Christian monk, absolving the repentant sinner. In legend, he *had* to demand liberty for Florence, and Lorenzo *had* to remain silent, turning his back.

29 August

Pietro Gerbore took me to the Countess Seristelli's, at her palace on the street where Joseph Bonaparte died. The countess is eighty-eight years old. Following a recent accident, she is in a wheelchair. In front of her is a little table on which she eats, writes, and reads. She points out that the little table was sent to her by Berenson when he learned of the accident. Vivacious, very intelligent, her memory intact. She is Spanish, spent her childhood in Paris; her husband is a descendant of Machiavelli. She has known all her famous contemporaries, from D'Annunzio and Papini to Anatole France and Paul Bourget. Her memories of D'Annunzio are amusing. They were friends and frequented the museums together. I don't know, she adds, if everything he told me about Etruscan art was true, but it was very beautiful. Until D'Annunzio began to court her too. "D'Annunzio, why me rather than another, since, for you, all women are alike?" D'Annunzio replied: "True enough, for me woman is a spool onto which I wind the golden thread of my imagination." And the countess: "*I* do not want to be a spool. . . ."

Watching her speak, I can imagine how beautiful she must have been thirty or forty years ago. I don't know why she reminds me of the heroine in Papini's short story "An Unreturned Letter." I asked her about Papini. Her remarks were very much to the point. This one among others: Papini was always afraid of passing for a polite, likable, well-bred man. He prized highly his reputation for being a barbarian, an *omo selvatico.*

She also knew Tucci, and quite well. In Rome the countess received her friends in the morning, in her boudoir. One day when Tucci came to see her, she asked him what the "Mongolian blemish" was, and whether people other than the Mongols could have it. Obviously, replied Tucci. Me, for example. It's a brown spot on the back. "Show it to me," said the countess, and Tucci began to get undressed.

A few seconds later, realizing that she was in bed and Tucci about to take off his shirt, she cried: "Tucci, friends will be arriving; who will believe that you got undressed to let me see the 'Mongolian blemish'!"

30 August

The Florentines accepted all the reforms proposed by Savonarola—even the principle of universal peace—but they never accepted that their wives should wear simple, modest dresses, nor that they themselves should give up their coiffures and their ornaments (Ridolfi, pp. 253–254).

2 September

I'm rereading certain pages of Giordano Bruno. Stunned by the boldness of his thought. He recognizes the religious authenticity of paganism. He was already urging the mystery of God's abandonment of the world, the transformation of God into a *deus otiosus*. God, *come assoluto, non ha che far con noi* (*Spaccio,* Gentile edition, II, 192). God's withdrawal or eclipse, which obsesses the theological thought of today, is a much more ancient spiritual phenomenon. Moreover, it begins with "civilization." *Deus otiosus* characterizes all cultures which have gone beyond the hunting and gathering stage and have taken up gardening and the cultivation of grain.

3 September

This evening, two young reporters from *La Nazione* came to interview me. Along with a photographer, Caragatza also joined us, making the inadequacy of my Italian even more obvious. We talked about Papini, Yoga, alchemy, etc. While we chatted tranquilly, seated in a bar drinking coffee, the photographer, stationed behind some chairs, kept on the lookout for a happy expression on my face. It was raining. The young men seemed intelligent, cultured. But the article, which appeared today, is commonplace, dull, and teems with inaccuracies (I studied Yoga in Tibet, etc.). Only the title is attractive, and true: "Imparò l'italiano per leggere Papini."

4 September

We're taking the Ciat bus for Assisi. These last few days the sky has been dark. It drizzled. Today, a brilliant sky.

The Sieve bridge and the river of the same name.

Arezzo. At last we saw the frescoes of Piero della Francesca. It was the end of Mass. Stunning. Cortone on the hill. The country of Signorelli and of Saint Catherine. Must return there some day.

Next, Perugia. The walls, the cathedral, the palaces, the great fountain. Will these words mean anything to me later on?

We approached Assisi; it was three o'clock in the afternoon. In the distance we saw the Convento di San Francesco, and the whole town, yellow-white-gray, crowding up the side of the mountain.

I came here for the first time in the spring of 1927. I no longer remembered anything except the two churches, the one superimposed on the other. I was fascinated in those days by the thought of Ernesto Buonaiuti. I was attracted by the relationship he was discovering between Joachim of Fiore and Saint Francis, on the one hand, and the Franciscan movement, the Renaissance, and Savonarola, on the other. But it is only now that I have even begun to understand the inter-dependence of all these movements of *renovatio*. They imply in a more or less clear fashion the reconciliation of man with the cosmos, the acceptance of the idea that the world and life are good. The "pagan" Renaissance took shape from the moment the Church refused to accept the message of Gioachino (i.e., the third age is imminent, which will be dominated by the Holy Spirit), and did not assimilate Saint Francis's love for life and nature.

We spent two hours in the lower basilica and the upper basilica trying to read the frescoes with the help of an illustrated guidebook. Giotto seems to me to be less inspired here than in Padua, but how spontaneous, fluent, human, he is.

A long walk across the city. The first medieval Italian town to my knowledge where the modern buildings blend perfectly into the whole; they seem to be camouflaged. The same yellow-gray stone, the same style.

We rented a room for tonight at the Hotel Subasio. It is deserted, or almost. From our windows we can see all the Umbrian countryside, dotted with olive trees.

In the evening, we went back up to the Convento delle Suore Svedesi. Almost nobody in the street. A cold wind was blowing down from the mountain.

ASSISI, *5 September*

The weather has changed again. Drizzle. We saw the convent again; then, in the rain, we went up to the Cathedral San Rufino. No slightly above-average bookstores where one could buy Franciscan works or works on Assisi. Everywhere, in all the windows, the same little books, the same picture cards.

We are leaving for Rome by bus around three thirty in the afternoon.

ROME, *6 September*

At the River Hotel, Via Flaminia 39. A brand-new hotel, opened a few days ago. And since the Via Flaminia is still blocked with construction, no one has yet heard tell of this hotel. We are the first and, for the moment, the only customers. N. B. reserved us a room on the seventh floor. The owner sent a bouquet of carnations to Christinel: she is the first "signora" to be a guest. From the terrace, we can see all of Rome, from Saint Peter's to the Villa Borghese, which is directly out our windows.

In the article "Antaios—Held oder Widersacher?" that Hainz Demisch published in the *Frankfurter Allgemeine Zeitung* of 22 July (he accuses us of wanting to encourage the telluric forces to the detriment of the Olympian forces), I find a long quote from Stalin. Bolshevism reminded Stalin of Antaeus because, like Antaeus, Bolshevism is strong only if it keeps close relationships with its mother, the masses.

7 September

At N. B.'s I found the copy of Papini's *Mostra personale* that I had offered her ten years ago in Capri. I had read the book at the Villa Monacone during those burning hot afternoons when, for two hours every day, I would stop writing *La Forêt interdite*. I still remember with what emotion I read the preface letter in which Papini explains to his "friend Felice" the reasons he is forgotten, unknown, criticized, or misunderstood in Italy. The rest of the book is trite. For me, I realize, Papini represents something else as well: my adolescence, the youthful years spent in Italy, my life in my own country, work, the library I left behind. Every contact with Papini's work stirs up the subterranean waters in which my whole past is bathed.

I'm wasting hours writing and copying the six pages on "The Sacred in the Asian Religions." A text which has no importance for me, nor for others, for it adds nothing new to my previous work, nothing which has not already been said. Thus, I'm squandering my time writing trifles, fragments, things that don't interest me. And, one fine day, I will wake up and it will be time to depart, without having had the time to write at least one book in my more mature period.

9 September

I'm trying to write the preface V. Buescu asked me for the Portuguese edition of *La Forêt interdite,* translated by his wife from the French edition. When I agreed to write this preface a year or two ago, I thought I would be able to take the opportunity to comment on the novel, maybe even write that "Theory of the Novel" of which I've been dreaming for so long. But I won't be able to. This afternoon is particularly beautiful. My dental neuralgia that I felt in Florence is beginning again. In two hours I'm to see a dentist. I wonder what I will still be able to say in the preface.

In *Convivio,* IV, v, 8, Dante has this extraordinary idea: Christ didn't come down upon the earth until the world, under the empire of Augustus, had known peace.

12 September

Visited Pettazzoni. I knew that he had been seriously ill, almost in agony. We found him, as he said himself, "in convalescence": pale, thin, affable. He admitted to us that he had been highly impressed by Japan. It's because you went to India, he added, that you are an excellent historian of religion: you got to know the land and men of Asia.

Leaving him, we were a little melancholy. Will we see him again next September in Marburg? Pettazzoni is seventy-five years old. Serious difficulties with his kidneys. I read his first book in 1923–1924. We have been in correspondence ever since. I had sent him five pounds sterling from Calcutta so he would be able to get me the whole collection *Studi e Materiali di Storia delle Religioni.* He remembered twenty years later when we met in Paris. He had just learned that the Bibliothèque Nationale didn't have a copy of *Studi e Materiali.*

13 September

Yesterday I met the painter Omiccioli. In the evening, in his studio, to see his canvases. He was Communist until the Hungarian insurrection. Very good, rather taciturn, reserved, likable. I was haunted for several hours by some of his portraits: the fishermen, the brickmason, the man with the bicycle. Self-educated, he nonetheless talked with me about Quevedo. He invited us to Romolo in Trastevere. He became quite verbose on the subject of Ustica, where he spent five or six months, and from which he returned ten years older.

Original sin, according to Dante:

Into that breast, you think, from which was carved
the rib that went to form the lovely cheek
for whose bad palate all mankind was starved.
—*Paradiso*, XIII, 37–39

14 September

"Roma non perit, si Romani non pereant" (Augustine, *Serm.* 81).

15 September

We left Rome at two in the afternoon, in a fine autumn rain. The River Hotel was once again deserted. On the Via Flaminia the construction work continues.

Omiccioli gave us a little painting—and, to me, the learned work of Bragaglia, *Pulcinella*.

After Civitavecchia, the sky cleared. I suddenly realize that I risk losing myself in this perpetual vagabondage. I no longer have a refuge; I mean that I no longer have any place that I can call home, a universe of my own, in direct possession, but private, with the memories that constitute "my history."

I perceive this risk, and I am afraid of succumbing to it. Moreover, I feel as though I am a precursor; I am aware of being somewhere in the avant-garde of the humanity of tomorrow or after. Lunik has landed on the moon. I don't know whether interplanetary travel will be interesting or not, but it is inevitable. Personally, it holds no attraction for me; but I feel as one with all those who will no longer live, definitively, anywhere on earth.

PARIS, *16 September*

A fine, cold, persistent rain that I'm watching through our window on the rue de l'Yvette. First rain for I don't know how many weeks, they tell me.

21 September

Dreams: Eugene Ionesco related this to me: His old friend Jenny Acterian (dead of cancer a few months ago in the old country) appeared to him, young and beautiful. Eugene knew in the dream that she was dead. Jenny took him in her arms, crying: Betrothal, betrothal! A short time afterward, a second Jenny, like the first in every detail, came into the room. Eugene looked at both of them and woke up. Rodica Ionesco told us about the dream of a scientist from Leipzig, Dr. Block, whom she knew in Cerisy. In Venice, the scientist meets a young woman, exceptionally beautiful, who invites him to her home. A palace. Once they reach the bedroom, she undresses and gets into bed. The doctor, intimidated, wants to put out the light. "Don't bother," she tells him, "I'll put it out myself." And her arm suddenly grows several meters and reaches the switch. That is when the doctor woke up.

NEW YORK, *29 September*

Will we ever be content with what we have done, persuaded that what we have done saves—or at least justifies—our existence? I find it hard to believe. I was wondering in the plane: If an accident. . . . What upset me was not death, but the fact that *I hadn't finished anything.* I must have written some thirty-five books. I never judged them so harshly as at that moment. I felt that I had to write at least two or three excellent books, since destiny made a writer of me. And only the books that I hadn't written, or hadn't yet finished, seemed any good to me. I had with me the manuscript of *Mântuleasa Street* and two notebooks of my journal. I don't know why I considered those pages so precious then, but I know that I considered *Mântuleasa Street* (once finished) as my only free literary work, purely and simply because writing it had been a delight.

Chicago

We're moving into Coach House, 1214 Fifty-seventh Street. The only furnishings we possess are a bed, some dressers, a couch, a kitchen table, and the minimal necessary items.

In my seminar—which I have entitled "The Psychology and History of Religions"—I'm beginning to discuss Freud's theory on the origin and function of religion. An obviously elementary theory, rather polemical. One point amazes me, nevertheless: for Freud, religion is the result of a crisis of the unconscious. Which is true. Religion is indeed the result of "the fall," "the forgetting," the loss of the state of primordial perfection. In paradise, Adam knew nothing of religious experience, nor of theology, that is, the doctrine of God. Before "sin," *there was no religion.*

15 October

Fascinating article by Paul Ricoeur, "Le Symbole donne à penser" (*Esprit,* July–August, 1959). Ricoeur asks how one can base thought on religious symbols. He chooses his examples from my *Patterns in Comparative Religion.* His first exegesis of them is the one I tried myself. Ricoeur, being a philosopher, uses a hermeneutic that

I didn't dare use in *Patterns*. First I had to convince the "scholars" —Orientalists, sociologists, philosophers—that I was right to base my argument on documents and not on "speculations." Next, I tried to systematize my ideas on symbols in a few articles (the latest will appear this month in the volume prepared with Kitagawa in memory of Wach). But I haven't yet had the time to write down, at my ease, all my thought on this problem, which is, at the same time, the key by which modern man can still penetrate into the religious phenomenon. It is also the path by which we can restate the problems for contemporary philosophy.

16 October

For the last few days I've been trying to write a preface for the American translation of *Mythes, rêves et mystères* [*Myths, Dreams, and Mysteries*]. Benjamin Nelson, whose idea it was to ask me for this book, told me in New York three weeks ago: "You are unfair with your books. The prefaces don't give any indication of their value. No one reading the preface of *Mythes, rêves et mystères* could suspect the novelty and richness of the book. You speak in your preface solely of the difference in mode of being between myths and dreams, but the book touches on several other problems. Next, you introduce your book as a collection of articles, whereas it has a unity, a structure. . . ." He told me several other things as well, in Melvin Arnold's office at Harper's. He was right. I had to write the preface to *Mythes, rêves et mystères* in a great hurry, during the first few days of June 1956, just after having put the finishing touches on the manuscript of *The Sacred and the Profane* and before preparing my Haskell lectures that I had to do in October. Haste wasn't the only reason; it was rather my inability to be of service to my books, the inhibition that paralyzes me each time I am to bring out the meaning or message of my books. Often, the very idea of rendering them accessible is repugnant to me. I will willingly write articles or simple essays, devoid of all learned documentation—but I find it wearisome to summarize the content of a book in an article or preface (to emphasize, first of all, the "originality," the original way in which the problem has been posed).

17 October

Reading Charles Andler's *Nietzsche: His Life and Thought* (Volume IV) and different fragments of Nietzsche, I sometimes wonder whether I shouldn't be sorry for my literary luck, when, at such a young age, in my native country, I was accepted and covered with praise. This premature success killed any personal ambition in me, any desire for "glory." I knew what glory was and felt what it meant to be recognized, praised, adulated. Not only did I no longer thirst for glory, but having had it so early made me modest and indifferent about success. Indirectly, this fact had a negative influence on me: I never considered myself an unrecognized "genius," something which would have aroused in me a certain megalomania and would have given rise to the need to show off, continually and ponderously, my merits, the novelty of my work, etc.

I wonder what would have happened if Nietzsche had known the taste of success from the very beginning. I wonder if he would have continued speaking of his own genius with the same ostentation. In any case, it seems tragically sad to me that he became enthusiastic over the three little notes that Taine had sent him, that he spoke of them in I don't know how many letters, that he became angry at Rohde, who had been imprudent enough not to seem convinced of Taine's genius (in whom Nietzsche saw one of "those who immortalize their age," etc.; cf. Andler, IV, 476). And in Turin, in the cafés, he read only the *Journal des Débats* "because Taine had recommended to a young editor of this newspaper, M. Jean Bourdeau, that he write an article on *Beyond Good and Evil.*"

22 October

I've finally finished the preface for the English translation of *Mythes, rêves et mystères.* I see the history of religions as a total discipline. I understand now that the encounters, facilitated by depth psychology, with the stranger within, with that which is foreign, exotic, archaic in ourselves, on the one hand—and, on the other, the appearance of Asia and of exotic or "primitive" groups in history—

are cultural moments which find their ultimate meaning only from the perspective of the history of religions. The hermeneutic necessary for the revelation of the meanings and the messages hidden in myths, rites, symbols, will also help us to understand both depth psychology and the historical age into which we are entering and in which we will be not only surrounded but also dominated by the "foreigners," the non-Occidentals. It will be possible to decipher the "Unconscious," as well as the "Non-Western World," through the hermeneutic of the history of religions.

28 October

Today the frame of my working glasses broke abruptly, without any apparent reason. There they were, on the table in front of me, when I suddenly noticed that the frame was broken. Since I don't have another pair of glasses, nor the time to go into town, I asked at the drugstore next door for something to glue the frame. They gave me some Duco Household Cement, and now I'm waiting for the results.

I've been using these glasses for nearly twenty years. Since March 1940, to be exact, when I went to the Bucharest military hospital for my discharge examination. They are round glasses with a very thin frame which make me look miserable, tired, and a little sappy! For years I've been planning to buy another pair to have in reserve in case of accident, such as today, but I've never done it. On my way from Rome last September, a young Englishman who was looking at me quite pointedly couldn't control his curiosity; he asked me how long I'd had these glasses, for he had never seen any like them. I told him, and that gave us a chance to begin a conversation.

I've broken my glasses several times during the last twenty years, but never the ones I use for reading. The lenses are a little worn, and gray around the edges, and yet I cannot bring myself to give them up. And now, all of a sudden, I understand why. These glasses are the last object that I still have from *my own country*. I don't have anything else, not even a "souvenir," not even a photo of my family or of myself. Of course, I have a few of the books that I published back there, but I don't have them beside me, I don't carry them with me.

That's what I came to understand while looking at my glasses pressed between two thick books in front of me, waiting for the twenty minutes to go by in order to be sure, according to the Duco Cement instructions, that the gluing operation would work.

3 November

At the annual colloquium organized by the Roger Williams Fellowship I spoke of "The Sacred and Reality." I repeated what I've said over and over again so many times in so many books: that *homo religiosus* thirsts for the real, that he wants to *be,* fully and at any cost. I showed how nature, for him, was full of signs and hierophanies. During the discussion I came to understand that modern science would not have been possible without the Judeo-Christian tradition, which emptied the cosmos of the sacred, and thus neutralized and banalized it. Science would not have been possible without a nature that was desacralized and emptied of gods. That is in fact what Christianity did, emphasizing personal religious experience. But it didn't have to desacralize nature, because, for Christianity, the cosmos remains no less the creation of God. However, from the moment that historical time and irreversible duration triumphed, the religious charm of the cosmos was dissipated. There was also something else: nature had been inhabited by pagan gods that Christianity had converted into demons. Nature, as such, could no longer interest Christians existentially. Only the peasants of eastern Europe kept the cosmic dimension of Christianity.

4 November

On 27 January 1824, Goethe said to Eckermann: "Basically it has been nothing but toil and work, and I may well say that I have not had four weeks of real enjoyment in all of my seventy-five years. . . . There were too many demands on my activities from outside as well as from within me. My real good fortune has lain in my poetic reflections and creations. Only how greatly these have been disturbed, limited, and hindered by my external situation! If I had been able to hold myself back from public and business endeavors and activities and been able to live more in solitude, I would have been happier and would have accomplished far more as a poet."

As always, I see Goethe's destiny as my own. But obviously on a different level. I'm thinking of these three years of teaching at Chicago. How much wasted time! How much I could have accomplished if I hadn't had to teach six hours of class a week, and for six months. (Let alone the time for preparing them, or for trips.) The most fertile years of my life are the years of poverty I spent on the rue Vaneau. I woke up every morning without a schedule. Now, during the academic year, I have only two days a week to call my own: Friday and Saturday. The other days, I prepare for my classes, I write tedious articles, I receive students preparing a doctorate on some subject in the history of religions. Certainly, this work fascinates me. Guiding a young person, helping him to see things as I see them now, after thirty years of research, is equivalent to a cultural creation. Sometimes, after a successful class, when I think I've been understood, I have the feeling of having written a book. I suppose my best books will be written by someone else.

5 November

Immersing myself again in the Eranos manuscript, I'm taking up the problems that tormented me last summer. And, first off, the cultic dimensions of eating. The extraordinary importance of the "first-fruits": to taste a fresh, new cosmos, as it was in the beginning, when it had barely come from the hands of the creator.

Eating signifies assimilating a part of the cosmos, or, more precisely, the mystical essence of the cosmos. Thence for a long time—up to the time of Plato and even afterward—the importance of eating for the moral and spiritual development of man. The author of *The Republic* forbade game and pastry; he allowed grilled meat only for young soldiers. One of the things which has both astonished me and drawn me to Nietzsche is the seriousness with which he speaks of eating, especially in *Ecce homo*. I see in this a whole prehistoric mystique which he has rediscovered, as is often the case with Nietzsche, in one of his admirative bursts of enthusiasm for "science."

6 November

Last week, to the "Fireside" students who were questioning me about the atomic bomb, I replied: A Christian shouldn't fear the bomb too much. For him, the end of the world would have a meaning. That would be the Last Judgment. Nor should a Hindu be concerned about it: Kali Yuga will end by a regression into chaos, after which a new world will appear. Only the Marxists are right in being terrified by the eventuality of an atomic end, since, for them, paradise is in the future. Paradise has never existed on earth. What corresponds to it, approximately, is the classless society of tomorrow. A Marxist accepts —and takes upon himself—innumerable slaughters solely because the future will be like paradise. All history and all the sufferings of humanity would have no meaning whatsoever if the world were to disappear before having known the Communist eschaton.

7 November

As soon as I finally finished revising the Eranos manuscript, I went to the library to verify a text in Burckhardt's *Weltgeschichtliche Betrachtungen*. I could find only the English translation, done by my colleague J. H. Nichols, but also a volume of *Letters* and *Judgments on History (Historische Fragmente)*. I brought all of it to my office, where I spent some delightful hours. I relocated Burckhardt's prophetic pages on the catastrophic tension between France and Germany (following the Prussian aggression and the defeat of 1870), on the politization and "acculturalization" of Europe, on the fatal consequences of democracy (Caesarism, dictatorship), etc. One gets the impression that Burckhardt foresaw the entire tragedy of the nineteenth century down to the smallest details.

It is his success in the USA that astonishes me. Ultimately, the Americans ought to have the same opinion of Burckhardt as Croce had: a dilettante of genius who sins by excess of pessimism. The fact that Burckhardt believed neither in democracy, nor in progress, nor in liberalism ought to have made him disagreeable to Americans. And it's the exact opposite which took place. One is forced to believe that, in the USA, there subsists a minority for whom the pessimistic vision of history is the only one acceptable.

8 November

Today when I was leafing through my *Patterns in Comparative Religion,* I lingered especially over the long chapter on the sky gods; I wonder if the secret message of the book has been understood, the "theology" implied in the history of religions as I decipher and interpret it. And yet the meaning emerges rather clearly: myths and religions, in all their variety, are the result of the vacuum left in the world by the retreat of God, his transformation into *deus otiosus,* and his disappearance from the religious scene. God—or, more precisely, the Supreme Being—no longer played an active role in the religious experience of primitive humanity. He was supplanted by other divine forms—divinities which were active, fertile, dramatic, etc. I returned to the subject of this process in other studies. But has it been understood that "true" religion begins only after God has withdrawn from the world? That his transcendence merges and coincides with his eclipse? The movement of religious man toward the transcendent sometimes makes me think of the desperate gesture of the orphan, left alone in the world.

10 November

These thirty years, and more, that I've spent among exotic, barbarian, indomitable gods and goddesses, nourished on myths, obsessed by symbols, nursed and bewitched by so many images which have come down to me from those submerged worlds, today seem to me to be the stages of a long initiation. Each one of these divine figures, each of these myths or symbols, is connected to a danger that was confronted and overcome. How many times I was almost lost, gone astray in this labyrinth where I risked being killed, sterilized, emasculated (by one of the terrifying mother-goddesses, for example). An infinite series of intellectual adventures—I use the word "adventure" in its primary meaning of existential risk. These were not only bits of knowledge acquired slowly and leisurely in books, but so many encounters, confrontations, and temptations. I realize perfectly well now all the dangers I skirted during this long quest, and, in the first place, the risk of forgetting that I had a goal, that I was heading toward something, that I wanted to reach a "center."

12 November

At John Nef's I met Sir Julian Huxley. Naturally, I spoke to him of Aldous. I would have liked to know since when and following what intellectual encounter Aldous had become a "mystic." "He always was," answered Sir Julian. "Even in his first books. Remember what he says about music and poetry."

I learned some interesting details. At the age of seventeen, as I already knew, Aldous went through a brief period of blindness. He learned the alphabet for the blind very rapidly. And he didn't seem depressed. It's a great advantage to be able to read that way, he used to say. When it's cold in your bedroom, you can do it under the covers.

13 November

Snow has begun to fall here and there. It was hard to believe. This morning's fine, cold rain changed imperceptibly, and suddenly I saw that it was snowing. In a few minutes the snow covered the streets. Toward evening, the city was white.

All of a sudden I was reminded of last winter's snows. We were living in the delightful apartment of Kitagawa at 5712 Woodlawn Avenue (he was in Japan). In December and January it had snowed without stopping. At that time I was working with a savage appetite on the history of the religions of Dacia. I especially remember that night I spent until four o'clock in the morning with Strabon, Altheim, R. Eisler, etc. I was writing *Les Daces et les Loups*. Christinel was in New York with Lisette. At dawn, when I went to bed, the trees were weighted with snow. In the light of the street lamps, they seemed artificial—as if someone had put them there surreptitiously. I only had to realize this "as if someone" to feel a terrified, ardent fervor which rushed up from the depths and took my breath away.

15 November

I received the copy of the *Cahiers du Sud* devoted to St.-John Perse. Reading Pierre Guerre's article "Encounters with St.-John Perse," I remembered my meeting with Perse, in January 1957, in Washington, at Brill's, who had invited both of us to lunch. Perse spoke about China. He said, among other things, that the Chinese are a people whó do not know religion. (Certainly, they do not know religion as *we* understand it.) Afterward, imperceptibly, we moved closer to each other. Your place is in Paris, in Europe, he told me. Don't settle down in the United States. Here there are no cultural centers. There are only institutions. I asked him why he had chosen to live in Washington (and not in New York, for example). This city doesn't exist, he answered. It is something unreal; it is an administrative creation. Living in Washington, I don't have the feeling of living in the United States. I'm living in an abstraction.

16 November

Gill Patrick, vice-president of the India section of the Rockefeller Foundation, whom I met in the spring of 1958 here in Chicago, tells me that there was recently a meeting in Paris of some Tibetanists (Tucci, Stein, Petech, etc.) organized by the Rockefeller Foundation. The subject was how to make use of the lamas and the Tibetan scholars who have taken refuge in India. It was proposed to attach them to different centers in Europe and the United States.

Something has happened that will not be without consequences for the culture of tomorrow: a considerable number of Tibetan scholars have taken refuge in India. And from there they will go farther. It's the first time in history that such a thing has happened. It can be compared to the flight of the Byzantine scholars after the fall of Constantinople.

19 November

In the *Carnets* of H. de Montherlant, 1937 (pp. 254–255, Gallimard edition), I encountered this confidentiality: "I think that few living French writers are less concerned than I about the development and propagation of their work. . . . I like to pass unnoticed in my literary life as much as in my private life."

I don't know what to think. I remember Mihaïl Sebastian's surprise when, in 1936, he received a copy of *Pitié pour les femmes* with a long, glowing dedication. What had happened? Only this: Sebastian had written an article on *Les Jeunes Filles* in *Vremea,* and the Hachette branch in Bucharest had sent it to Grasset. Flattered by the attention that a Rumanian critic had given him, especially in a weekly, Montherlant hastened to consolidate this admiration by sending his next book along with a dedication.

Why linger over these insignificant details? Most certainly because what Montherlant says about himself can be applied in my own case. I do nothing to propagate my work, but I don't consider this attitude a quality. I know why I don't move: out of shyness, laziness, or indifference. Not doing what bothers you does not constitute a virtue. Cioran told me about ten years ago that it was the custom in France to thank a critic for his article. Several hundred reviews of my books have been published in France, and I don't think I've written ten letters to thank their authors. I've never written to foreign critics. Ultimately, this indifference is a defect, just as my "modesty" is a sin against the mind. An author who is sure of the importance of his work owes it to himself to spread it and have it accepted. Proust's literary strategy, such as we know it today, forty years later, is depressing. Perhaps the necessity to hasten recognition for his work forced him to it. It's true, ultimately, that the only thing that counts is to gain recognition for the value of the work.

It is indeed possible that, one day, I will bitterly regret my laziness, my shyness, and my indifference. There is an opportune moment for gaining acceptance for a work. Once this moment has passed, the thing becomes almost impossible. And someone else's work, more or less like your own, will be accepted.

21 November

Edward Shils gave me a mimeographed study: "The Macrosociological Problem." He's letting me read it to see for myself how he has used my pages on "the center of the world" and the symbolism of the center (*The Myth of the Eternal Return,* etc.). This is Shils's thesis: "Society has a center. There is a center zone in the structure of society." Macrosociology studies this center—which is a phenomenon, says Shils, in the domain of values and beliefs. Better still, *"The central zone partakes of the nature of the sacred."*

That means that Shils understands society as a religious structure. But what is more interesting is that Shils finds in macrosociology the same decisive function of the center that I had discovered, on my part, in the history of religions, namely, that the world is organized (that is, is created ritually) around a center. Man, in traditional societies, cannot live in chaos: he must situate himself in a cosmos that always has a center, an absolute fixed point. Absolute because it is revealed through a hierophany, or constructed ritually, which implies a break at the ontological level.

22 November

While I was speaking to my students this morning about the origin of the concept of karma—an origin that I see in the theory of sacrifice—I suddenly remembered that, for Vico, *il vero è nel fatto,* consequently, only that which is *done* is *true.* More precisely, only he who acts, who does, knows the truth. (Referring, of course, to the "truth" that is relative to what he is doing.) From this gnoseological valorization of the "fact," we came later to the absolute valorization of history. If man can only know what he does, and not what God has done (nature, for example), it follows fatally that the sum of human acts, history, becomes the only real, significant knowledge.

I return to the origin of the concept of karma. Brahmanist India bestows a great value on action. The universe is what it is because, *in illo tempore,* Prajapati *made* it, and since then, sacrifice remakes it, *upholds* it continually. The universe, like man, *is not;* it is created. For a thing to exist, it must be made or done. Man today is what he alone has made himself to be in the course of a long series of previous existences. Man is the result of his own karma—that is, the result of his own history. And that is precisely what post-Vedic India no longer accepts. The yogis, the rishis of the Upanishads, and the Buddha revolted against the fatality of karma. What the West, through Hegel, Marx, and historicism, considers as the only solution possible (to recognize oneself as the work of history and to take this condition upon oneself) is seen in India as slavery, suffering, and ignorance. Absolute freedom can be conquered only by canceling karma, that is, by abolishing history.

I must take this idea up again and develop it in an article.

"I'm just the little worker-bee, gathering honey for the queens to eat" (*Gaudy Night,* by Dorothy L. Sayers). That is what philologists, scholars, and bibliographers should apply to themselves. But it is exactly the opposite of what happens. Normally, those who are most infatuated with and surest of the importance of their work are the specialists on detail. Their capacity for work and their devotion, it must be admitted, are impressive. But the piece worker cannot represent a scientific ideal. His importance is on a social level, and, in the best cases, on an ethical one.

23 November

It's strange that the first installment of *Antaios* begins with my article on "Le Vol magique" (published in 1955 in *Numen,* republished in *Myths, Dreams, and Mysteries*). Instead of showing the spiritual value of contact with the earth, I illustrate the importance of the symbolism of flight and of ascension to explain the deepest and most secret longings of man: his desire to break away from the earth, to transcend the human condition, to be free. When Joachim Wach heard my paper at the History of Religions Congress in Rome (April 1955), where I set forth this thesis for the first time, he became so enthusiastic that he spoke and wrote about it to all his acquaintances. You have succeeded, he told me, in establishing the psychological and existential origins of transcendence and freedom.

What seems significant to me is that this particular article was chosen to be translated and published in the first edition of *Antaios*. Without realizing it, I was taking a position against the myth of the Earth Mother.

25 November

This evening, while I was making the trip from the campus to town, I watched the headlights of the cars on the road through the train window. They formed a single, dazzling, slightly wavy line. All these people were going home, that is, twenty or a hundred kilometers from their offices in the center of Chicago. Wherever one goes in the United States, one can always see the same thing everywhere: people hurrying to go home or to go to work; thousands, or tens or hundreds of thousands of cars next to one another, one after the other.

What makes it serious is that there is nothing that can be done about it. Tomorrow, or the day after, it will be the same thing in Europe. (The sadness that overwhelms me at night in Paris every time I go home and look at those rows of cars parked on the two sides of the street.) For that is the very problem that is obsessing me: although I see man crushed, asphyxiated, diminished by industrial civilization, I can't believe that he will degenerate, decline morally, and finally perish, completely sterile. I have a limitless confidence in the creative power of the mind. It seems to me that man will succeed—if he wishes —in remaining free and creative, in any circumstance, cosmic or historical.

But how can the miracle be brought about? How can the sacramental dimension of existence be rediscovered? At this point, so much can be said: all the things that have existed we have not definitively lost; we find them again in our dreams and our longings. And the poets have kept them. This is to say nothing of the religious life, because the authenticity and depth of the religious life among my contemporaries seems to me a most mysterious problem.

There must be a way out. Aldous Huxley proposes mescaline, alcohol, drugs. There would be a great deal to say on that score.

27 November

The weariness that invades me sometimes in front of this mass of documents that *I must* interpret, comment on, systematize, before I dare to draw my major books from them. Perhaps this weariness is a warning signal. I should hurry, continue nonstop. In point of fact, why shouldn't I give up the exegetical work that I've begun in order to devote myself to my "personal" books? These books that I call personal reflect tomorrow's philosophy better and more directly than all the exegetical work.

2 December

I have so many things to do I don't know where to begin. Even if I worked without stopping, I know I couldn't do everything: my classes for tomorrow (in the morning, the synthesis of the five sessions on the Upanishads; in the afternoon, a discussion on Otto Rank—on this latter subject, I still have three books to review), the texts for *Religion in Geschichte und Gegenwart* (that I was to have sent off four or five days ago), revision of the typed text of the Eranos lectures, etc. So I'm letting everything drop and I'm starting to go through my drawers. I find manuscripts, notebooks, files full of notes, and I leaf through them. For a long time it has been my defense against fatigue and despair. In that way I tear myself away for a half-hour or an hour from being obsessed with things that must be done, or are half done, or already done or redone, etc., etc., etc.

At Cascaes, during the winter of 1945, I got into the habit of gathering up the sheets and pages that were lying around on my desk. I filed them in folders that I entitled (not knowing what other name to give them) "notes found on the desk." Later, at the Hôtel de Suède, I would do the same thing, until the day that I decided to put these folders on the floor, in order to clear off the desk. And I forget them there. Waste paper, the cleaning woman who took them away must have said to herself. When I noticed it, it was too late. Along with other notebooks and folders (I never knew exactly either the number or the contents) the "notes found on the desk" were burned.

Sometimes I would find a note forgotten in a book. I would reread it with emotion, almost with devotion. Not that I had hoped to discover I don't know what luminous truth in these hurriedly jotted-down lines, but quite simply that, in this way, I could recover forgotten times and facts—which had got lost somewhere between memories and sleep. The taste of dust, among others, of those afternoons in 1946, 1947, or the humidity of the last days of autumn that I had spent in the Jardin du Luxembourg, in 1945.

(I'm writing these lines with that obscure delight one feels when he wants to do something further in a room that he knows he must leave half an hour later.)

Here, in a notebook, is this little note (written at Val d'Or, in I don't know what spring, after reading some of the Upanishads): God (= The Spirit) is buried in us as in a cave; he isn't dead, but only hidden somewhere in there. Brahman, says Katha Upanishad (v. 6), is *guhyam,* "hidden." That means that the Spirit is like "the inhabitant of a cave." The heart—where the Upanishads locate the presence of the atman—is a "cave." Atman is tiny as a grain of sand, etc., it dwells in the middle of the body like a "dwarf." In the mythical universe of the North, dwarves work in the caverns of mountains; they are miners who dwell in the caverns. They guard treasures, or dig in the earth to reach treasure. The archaic image of the soul likened to a treasure hidden in the midst of the body (= Mountain).

Writing out this note, a whole series of parallels come to mind. *Tong,* the Chinese term for "cave," also means "mysterious, deep, transcendent." I've spoken of all that in *The Forge and the Crucible.* How many things there still are to say! The "heaven-cave" of the Taoist traditions which indicate a hidden paradise. How to reach the heaven-cave, through subterranean galleries hollowed out deep in the Mountain. According to Taoist traditions, all these mountains can be reached from one another by caves and galleries. The symbolism here is clear: the transcendent is *one.*

Some day, I must compare another series of images: the primordial revelation in the form of a book, hidden for a long time in a cave, and rediscovered by chance; God who hides himself, the pearl that is difficult to find, etc. And the "Mysteries" celebrated in real or artificial caves (cf. the Mithraic mysteries).

It is highly probable that all these symbols or images depend, directly or indirectly, on the sacredness of the caves, and on the secret cults celebrated there since the Paleolithic age.

5 December

A new *Phänomenologie des Geistes* must be written on the basis of the results of psychoanalysis and ethnology. The importance of the history of religions for understanding archaic behavior.

For several years, another thought has been haunting me as well: if it is true that Marx has analyzed and unmasked the social unconscious, and that Freud did likewise for the personal unconscious—if it is then true that psychonanalysis and Marxism teach us how to pierce through "superstructures" to arrive at the true causes and motives, then the history of religions, as I understand it, would have the same goal: *to identify the presence of the transcendent in human experience:* to isolate—in the enormous mass of the "unconscious"—that which is *transconscious.* It's for that reason that the study of symbolism appears to me so fascinating and decisive. A symbol can reveal what is happening in the depths (psychoanalysis) as well as in the heights. I would need a good many pages to clarify all that. I said a word or two on it in the chapter "Symbolisms of Ascension" in *Myths, Dreams, and Mysteries,* but nowhere have I explained the analytical function of the history of religions, the way in which it helps us to unmask the presence of the transcendent and the suprahistorical in everyday life.

15 December

Listening today to Symphony no. 41 *(Jupiter)* by Mozart, divinely interpreted by Ionel Perlea and the Orchestra of Bamberg, I remembered a curious encounter from my adolescence. I must have been fourteen or fifteen. Miron Grindea (who, ever since he was young, liked to meet people and have them meet one another) took me one day to see a "genius." It was a family of rich Jews who lived somewhere between Bulevardul Domnitei and Calea Mosilor. The boy was the same age as I but seemed older because he was tall, handsome, and had an extraordinary forehead, which both fascinated and intimidated at the same time. I have an even better recollection of his sister, who was precociously and darkly beautiful. Very brown, enormous eyes with rings under them, she watched her brother with a provocative admiration; the rest of us—all of us, such as we are scattered throughout the world—we hardly existed. (More precisely, we existed intermittently, we appeared thanks to a sort of incomprehensible curiosity, we survived a few seconds before her quickly wearied gaze, only to disappear then into nothingness.)

The boy, who was a musician, was telling me that he would soon be the greatest orchestra leader in the world. For him, universal culture had so far produced three geniuses: Hafiz, Goethe, and himself. And he added: "If one brought me convincing arguments, I would give up Hafiz, and perhaps even Goethe, but never myself, for no argument could convince me that I am not a 'genius.' "

It was enough to listen to him speak, to look at his forehead, to agree with him.

21 December

I'm rereading Marx's criticisms of Christianity ("the specific religion of capitalism"): it is not enough to draw attention to the inconsistencies or contradictions of Christians, or to prove that no one behaves like a true Christian, etc., for Christianity does not consist in its contradictions or incoherencies, just as it is not threatened with disappearing because of them. Christianity exists and subsists by the myths, the symbols, the longings that answer a deep need in Western man. It is futile to criticize Christianity by philosophical or historical arguments, just as it is equally futile for modern apologists to defend it (claiming, in the first place, that if Christianity hasn't saved the world, it is the fault of Christians, etc.). "True" Christianity has roots that are too deep for it to be shaken or abolished. (At least for several hundred more years.)

1 January 1960

Every exile is a Ulysses traveling toward Ithaca. Every real existence reproduces the *Odyssey*. The path toward Ithaca, toward the center. I had known all that for a long time. What I have just discovered is that the chance to become a new Ulysses is given to *any* exile *whatsoever* (precisely because he has been condemned by the gods, that is, by the "powers" which decide historical, earthly destinies). But to realize this, the exile must be capable of penetrating the hidden meaning of his wanderings, and of understanding them as a long series of initiation trials (willed by the gods) and as so many obstacles on the path which brings him back to the hearth (toward the center). That means: seeing signs, hidden meanings, symbols, in the sufferings, the depressions, the dry periods in everyday life. Seeing them and reading them even *if they aren't there;* if one sees them, one can build a structure and read a message in the formless flow of things and the monotonous flux of historical facts.

This problem to be taken up again in the lecture on myth (Harvard, April).

NEW YORK, *2 January*

I've just learned of the death of Raffaele Pettazzoni. . . . One afternoon in 1924 (it was my last year of the lycée) I discovered by chance this title in an Italian magazine: "I Misteri-Saggio di una teoria storico-religiosa," by R. Pettazzoni. It was the year I had just discovered Frazer. I immediately ordered R. P.'s book, and, confused but exalted, read it for several nights in my garret. Then I wrote him, at just about the same time as I had written to V. Macchioro (I had been taken with his studies on Orphism). Pettazzoni answered me and offered me, in addition to some extracts and brochures, his work on religion in Sardinia, and the first volume of his *Dio.* I was to meet him for the first time in Paris in the spring of 1949. But after then, I saw him almost every year, whether at Rome or at some conference. In September 1958, in Tokyo, he fell sick and had to stay a few days in the Italian hospital. I saw him in Kyoto, thinner, but full of enthusiasm for Japan. And yet, at the end of the conference, he didn't want to extend his stay in Japan—not even by three or four days as I had proposed (suggesting that he accompany us to Beppu). It's too hot, he told me, wanting to return to Italy as fast as possible to go for a rest, with Mme. Pettazzoni, somewhere in the mountains. Did he have a presentiment of something?

... I can still see myself in my garret on the Strada Melodiei, elbows on the table, immersed in *I Misteri* (for the first time I had the impression that I understood something about the mysteries of Eleusis). In the years that followed, I was so obsessed by the underground currents of Mediterranean spirituality that I had formulated the project of writing a work on *The Origin of European Thought,* in two volumes. I had even announced it in my articles on Orphism published in *Adevarul literar.*

CHICAGO, *6 January*

It could be that Marxism and the materialist interpretation of history were the last trial of man. Trial; that is, the risk of perishing. Exactly as he almost perished, so many times, in prehistory. Or as he risks disappearing today by thermonuclear arms.

To think like a materialist or Marxist means giving up the primordial vocation of man. Consequently, to disappear as man. But it is not in vain that this temptation and this risk exist. It is even good for man to live with the awareness of his imminent disappearance as man. Fear = initiatory suffering.

NB: I feel that, in initiatory doctrine and rituals, I have discovered the only possibility of defending myself against the terror of history and collective distress. I mean that if we succeed in experiencing, taking upon ourselves, or imposing a value on the terror, the despair, the depression, the apparent absence of meaning in history, as so many initiatory trials—then all these crises and tortures will take on a meaning, will acquire a value, and the despair of the universe-as-concentration-camp will be spared us. We will find a *way out.* In that way we will transcend history in the most authentic fashion (taking upon ourselves, therefore, all the obligations of the historical moment).

To be gone into and made more precise.

10 January

I'm in a corner of the room, standing, so I can better see a drawing by Omiccioli on the opposite wall—and suddenly I feel the

top of my head touching the ceiling. Exactly as it was under the slope
of my garret on Strada Melodiei.

Instantaneous transfer to the years 1922–1925. A curious, strong,
almost drunken feeling that the meaning of my life, *now,* these days,
this year, consists in joining these two garrets, reintegrating into a
single universe these two worlds: adolescence and maturity. But how?
How?

14 January

List der Vernunft: I rediscovered these lines in Karl Löwith,
Meaning in History (that I'm rereading for my seminar): "It is not by
chance but of the very essence of history that the ultimate outcome
of great historical actions is always something which was not intended
by men. Caesar and Napoleon did not and could not know what they
were doing when they consolidated their own positions."

I compare this *List der Vernunft* of Hegel with the Freudian (or
Jungian) *libido:* something is being created, is being done, that the
conscious mind does not know. It would be perhaps even more
proper if I brought together the Hegelian concept and my conception of the symbol and its function in psychical life. To wit: symbols bring into the reality of experience transpersonal values and
events that the individual was not capable of apprehending con-
sciously and voluntarily. Thanks to symbols, psychic life is neither
insipid, mediocre, nor sterile. Even those who cannot suspect the
metaphysics and theology buried in their imagination and their
longings nevertheless enjoy—"unconsciously"—a rich, meaningful
psychic life.

This is the observation on which I should base what I say when I
speak (symposium at Harvard) of the importance of myth (or of what
is left of it) for the modern world. I will begin by emphasizing that
his psychic life is infinitely more interesting than the individual's
conscious mind. Then the question: Shouldn't the function of symbols
be compared to the *List der Vernunft?*

18 January

I've extracted, somewhat haphazardly, from the vocabulary of Communist trials: Titoist, Trotskyite, assassin, agent of imperialism. These are categories, characters, archetypes which do not correspond to human, historical personalities. One has the impression that in Soviet trials it is not men, not individuals, who appear, but types, archetypes, characters. Exactly as in the ahistorical horizons of archaic societies (cf. *The Myth of the Eternal Return*). Whence comes this need of identifying (historical) individuals with a (mythical) archetypal character, of transforming the concrete man into an exemplary category? Is it a return to popular archaic thought? Or is political propaganda condemned to rediscovering and reusing the categories of the popular mentality?

23 January

Ecce Homo. Nietzsche's rage against Germany and German culture is probably only the expression of the rancor of an unrecognized author. Venom bursts forth from his jealousy and his envy. "I believe only in French culture," he writes. I understand, but I don't agree. And when he speaks of his contemporaries, his poor taste and his provincialism border on the grotesque. His hatred of Germany transforms him into a provincial intimidated by the finesse of the City of Light. Nietzsche, who boasted of his mind's having penetrated to where no one had reached before him, wrote about the Paris of the 1880s: "I don't remember, in all of history, any other century in which a handful of psychologists as penetrating as they are subtle were found together at the same time as in the Paris of today." And he cites Paul Bourget, Pierre Loti, Gyp, Meilhac, Anatole France, Jules Lemaître; he goes into ecstasy over Guy de Maupassant. "Everywhere that Germany extends its preponderance, it *ruins* culture," he adds.

He would probably have neither thought nor said anything of the sort if Germany had given him recognition, if he had been able to win there even a tenth of Wagner's glory.

26 January

After a long mythological period, and a short historical period, we are on the threshold of a biological (economic) period. Man will be reduced to the condition of a termite, an ant. It is impossible for me to believe that this phase will succeed. But for several generations, or, perhaps, several thousand years, men will live like ants.

28 January

Our seminar discussion had to do with this theme: "What is the meaning of historical man?" First this: we are the result of events that can no longer be undone. We are what we are because, before us, hundreds of thousands of years before us, this or that happened.

But the so-called ahistorical man (the "primitive," the man of traditional civilizations) also considers himself the result of certain decisive events, which took place well before him, *in illo tempore*. Such events constitute the mythical history of the clan. Nevertheless, these represent two different ways of being constituted. For the primitive, myths unveil to him those exemplary events that have made him what he is today. Exemplary events; namely: the creation of the world and of man, the founding (by superhuman beings) of civil and religious institutions, etc. One could say that the primitive views himself as the result of a *cultural* history. Myths reveal to him how institutions were founded. Cultural history—and as such, paradigmatic history.

To recognize oneself as the result of historical events, in the modern meaning of the term, is to consider oneself the product of all the liberties and extravagances of one's forebears and contemporaries. And more particularly: the product of the fantasies and follies of others. A Rumanian, I am what I am, I am where I am, not only because Trajan conquered Dacia, and the Westerners were not able to unite in order to resist Bayazid victoriously, but also because there were Genghis Khan, Stalin, Hitler. These personalities are far from being paradigmatic in the primitive sense of the function—but to what an extent were they creators of history by their demented and bloody liberties!

3 February

I think that after Eugene Ionesco, the theater will have to become Shakespearean once again, to use historical events as dramatic pretexts—and to recover, nevertheless, the poetical language of Shakespeare. To use historical events doesn't mean accepting them as a man of today, understanding and judging them through modern man's awareness (which, whether he wants it or not, is "historicist"). Some day, I would like to go to a play in which the historical characters were filled with "mana," such as their contemporaries saw them, such as they lived in the mythologies of those times, as we sometimes find them, for example, in legends and ballads. These existential modes are not completely outgrown by modern man. They reappear sporadically in dreams or in the life of the imagination. I would like to go to a play in which Stalin, or Churchill, Gary Cooper or Mistinguett, etc., behaved and spoke as they do in the dreams, the longings, the daydreamings of certain contemporaries whose lives have been totally modified by the existence of these historical personalities. I believe that such a dramatic presentation is truer than any "history" or "psychology." With the condition, of course, that it recovers the poetical language of which modern man is so ashamed.

5 February

In Swift Hall, hanging on the wall of the stairway that leads to the top floor, is a plaster reproduction of the famous Eleusinian bas-relief with Demeter, Kore, and Triptolemus. The other day, going up to my class, I saw a vigil light lit on a tripod and, beside it, four verses in Greek, taken from the Homeric hymn to Demeter. I was told that the classical language students had gotten into Swift Hall at night, had washed the bas-relief (I realized later that they had damaged it a little, without intending to), and had lit the lamp to give homage to the goddesses. If they thought they were committing a sacrilege in venerating a pagan goddess within the precincts of the theology faculty, they must have been disappointed. The lamp was left to burn until the oil ran out.

6 February

When Goethe discovered the principle of the metamorphosis of plants, that is, that their reproductive organs are only specialized leaves, he exclaimed: "If I could only communicate to someone my vision and my joy! But it is impossible. It is neither a dream nor a fantasy; it is the discovery of the essential form with which one could say Nature constantly plays, and in her play produces the widest possible variety of life."

On a more modest level, and without going into the ecstasy of Goethe confronting his discovery, I too had a similar experience when I came to understand that the "historico-religious forms" are only the infinitely varied expressions of some fundamental religious experiences. When he discovers the sacredness of heaven or of the earth, religious man expresses his discovery by forms (divine figures, symbols, myths, etc.) which never succeed in translating exactly or totally what is signified by the sacred, be it celestial or telluric. That is indeed why other expressions replace them, just as incomplete and approximate and, in a sense, different from those whose places they are taking.

If one analyzes all these expressions, one begins to see the *structures* of the religious universe: one finds out the archetypes, the models of these divine figures, which try to be entirely realized and communicated and manage, nevertheless, only a new "expression." For everything that is realized, that is concretely expressed, is inevitably conditioned by history. Every religious expression is therefore only a mutilation of plenary experience.

9 February

Tired, sick (this mysterious "virus" that is located now in a leg or an arm, now in the throat), I've taken up again with an incomparable joy the *Life of Goethe* by Bielchowsky. I note at random: Goethe's "transfiguration" after his long excursion in the Harz Mountains, in the winter. He returned to Weimar completely changed—and *he knew it.* He became more reserved, less involved in worldly activities. The fundamental experience of the ascent to the mountaintop, which others have felt also. (I remember having read in Switzerland, some years ago, a book lent me by Godel: mountain climbers' experiences, so close to the religious experiences of ascending toward a center of the world.)

15 February

Had a visit from a student from South India. I opened the door to him saying: "Svâgatam! Ayusmân bhava!" (Welcome! Long life!) without understanding why I spoke to him in Sanskrit. I never spoke that language fluently, and I haven't used it for nearly thirty years. (I had to use it in Rishikesh to make myself understood by the ascetics of South India.) I thought I had completely forgotten the little Sanskrit one uses in conversation—as I have forgotten 90 percent of my Portuguese, which I can still read without any trouble.

The student's swarthy face threw me suddenly thirty years into the past.

18 February

The meaning of my "learning": I grasp the true meaning only after having gone through all the material (enormous, inert, somber documentation); I would compare my immersion in the documents to a fusion with the material—to the limit of my physical resistance: when I feel that I'm suffocating, that I am being asphyxiated, I come back up to the surface. A descent to the center of dead matter, comparable to a *descensus ad inferos.* Indirectly, the experience of death. Drowned in the documents, what is personal, original, living, in me disappears, dies. When I find myself again, when I return to life —I see things differently, I *understand* them.

21 February

I'm reviewing, for my course, the material in the file containing the Dionysiac documents, from *Bacchae* to the latest archaeological information that I've been able to gather. Whence this attraction, this mystery: to eat raw flesh, the flesh of the pursued animal, trapped and torn apart with the nails? Isn't it probably a regression to a very archaic stage, perhaps even prehuman? The wild stage? This unfathomable fall into the world of animals of prey can constitute a spiritual and physical shock that is extremely creative. A feeling of *freedom;* you feel that you are no longer a man, no longer subject to laws, to prohibitions. There is even more: you *relive* a primordial stage, you rediscover a world that was thought to be lost, you are immersed in the time of purely zoological existence, a time thought to have been abolished. The Dionysiac ecstasies: to rediscover the time from before the world, when time was only presence without beginning or end (that is how I picture, more or less, the experience of time among animals).

25 February

Greek religion—more precisely, Mediterranean religion—has survived down to our time under a Christian veneer. In the Mediterranean basin, in the Balkans, in Southern Italy, etc., certain religious themes of Cretan or Aegean origin can still be found. To a certain extent, it's what I call "cosmic religion." Demeter survives in folklore, whereas Jupiter has long since disappeared.

But how did they disappear, Jupiter, all the Homeric gods, and everything that is connected with Olympian religiosity? They disappeared from *religious experience,* but thanks to Homer and to the Greek genius, they found their place once again in European *culture.* They make up part of the learned heritage of every European. One could say that Greece fertilized Europe on two levels: by popular religion (pre–Indo-European), which passed into folklore and peasant Christianity (cosmic religion); and the gods of Olympus assimilated by the literate world and Western book culture.

1 March

The Homeric conception of existence: to enjoy life and youth exclusively; to love the perfection of forms (and it is perhaps in the discovery of this perfection—seen especially in the divine "forms"—

that the specific religious experience of the Greeks resides; cf. Walter Otto). From the religious point of view, the Homeric conception is more childish, more simplistic, than Mediterranean religiosity (as it is manifested especially in the Mystery religions). The Aegeans had a bold conception of the soul and of existence beyond the grave; they had kept initiatic techniques. Nonetheless, the Homerics fascinate me: they accept historical life (more precisely, *biology*) as the only real dimension of human existence.

3 March

The pessimism of Ionian poets; one gets the impression that, for them, the gods withdrew from the world, that they became *dei otiosi,* and that they lost their interest in the fate of man, exactly as with the primitives who believe that God, after having created the cosmos and man, became detached from his own creation, withdrew into the highest heaven, and became *deus otiosus.*

But with the primitives, the place of the Supreme God was taken by other divine figures (fertility goddesses, demiurges, etc.)—expressions of the sacredness of the cosmos and of life. In forgetting the "true God," the primitives are consoled in venerating the divinities of wealth and fertility. With the Ionians, the process is much more radical: even the secondary divinities withdrew from man and became indifferent to his fate. In the place of cosmic theophanies, the Ionians exalt life, health, youth, love, that is, precisely what remains after the desacralization of these theophanies.

But then why are these Ionian poets so pessimistic, so tragic? On the contrary, the fullness of the joy of life, once discovered, should have brought them to a luminous conception of existence. Or else, man probably cannot rejoice over the gifts of existence if he does not take them as signs that have come from the beyond.

11 March

The resurrection of the body, the redemption of matter, the efforts of Christian theologians to bring spirit and matter together—in Christianity, all this prepares for and announces modern civilization, the modern interest (since the Renaissance) in substance, matter, the world. Just as—I've already said it elsewhere—by its antipagan polemics, Christianity desacralized the cosmos (old receptacle of hierophanies and theophanies) and made possible the objective, scientific study of "nature." A substance capable of being transformed imperceptibly into a hierophany could not be studied *quantitatively*.

17 March

What a paradox: The Greeks, who, as I just said, loved life, existence in the flesh, the perfect form, had, as an ideal of survival, the survival of the pure intellect (mind, *nous*). Christians, who are apparently ascetics and scorn the body, insist on the necessity of the resurrection of the body, and cannot conceive of paradisiac blessedness without the union of the soul and the body.

19 March

Freud discovered the importance of the unconscious. In the morphology of the conscious mind he deciphered the dynamics and the intentions of the unconscious: sex, death, etc. Yes, but the explanation Freud gives of the ultimate motives of the unconscious is rationalistic, that is, conscious. The ultimate goal, according to Freud, is life or the tensions between Eros and Thanatos. It seems to me that an error in method is revealed there: Freud thinks he is able to explain rationally the meaning and goal of the dynamics of the unconscious. In other words, he wants to explain rationally life and its teleology. But if that is precisely what escapes us, if there remains something irreducible in the unconscious—that means that the rationalist explanation is partial. It is true that sexuality dominates, it is true that the unconscious is dominated by the libido, and even, perhaps, for the *conscious mind,* the meaning of the complexes (Oedipal, etc.) is that which Freud gives. But the ultimate goal of the unconscious escapes us, it is mysterious. Perhaps this dynamic is necessary to make it possible to transcend the human condition, or perhaps for some other end. There is a mystery in this.

3 April

Surprised to find this sentence in Gide's *Journal* (Pléiade, p. 964): "I am inclined to consider . . . the Cosmos as a game of God." A purely Hindu conception: *Lîlâ,* the divine game which is manifested by the cosmic creations and destructions.

4 April

E. Heller, professor at Northwestern University, told me that one of his students claimed that 75 percent of his peers were undergoing psychoanalysis. They all suffer from "repressed chastity," the student supposedly said.

8 April

My arthritis already has a "history." I'm writing these lines on my lap, settled in an easy chair. Last winter I spent two nights here, a week apart, reading the *Life of Goethe,* by Bielchowsky. I was feeling such atrocious pains (in the left arm the first time, the right leg the second time) that the horizontal position in bed was intolerable. I could stand the pain only in an easy chair, with my arm (or my leg) immobile. Toward three or four in the morning I couldn't stand it anymore, I was so tired my eyes were closing, but I kept reading, terrified at the idea that a change in position might bring back the pain.

14 April

Stone, the mathematics professor, told us about his conversation in Bombay with an illustrious Soviet mathematician. When he asked him which he liked more, the Taj Mahal or the Himalayas, the Soviet replied: The Himalayas, because the Taj Mahal is the work of man, whereas the Himalayas are the work of God. And as Stone was kidding him (What! you speak of God? I thought that God didn't exist, or that if he exists, he is Russian), the Soviet scientist interrupted him: "You who are a man of science understand what I meant by that."

18 April

The sun woke me up. An unusually clear morning, even for the Midwest where I've seen the most limpid skies. It's the rhythm of Chicago; from one day to the next, sometimes even from one hour to the next, the season changes. There's also something else in this morning's dazzling sun: it's as if I were awaking from a long dream, and rediscovering the light after having wandered far astray for a long time among caves and labyrinths. The winter was long and difficult. I was constantly sick. For weeks I haven't known what it is *not to hurt anywhere*.

7 May

The imagination and freedom the scientists of other centuries had at their disposal! Thomas Young, physicist and doctor, discovered the law of light interference and established the basis of modern optics. He studied archaeology in Göttingen just as deeply and, in 1796, asserted the thesis that only an alphabet of forty-seven letters could exhaust the possibilities of the human voice. He became a great specialist of alphabets and calligraphy and tried to decipher the inscriptions of the Rosetta Stone. Whatever he did he liked to do it well. One day he got the idea of amusing himself by dancing on a tightwire. . . . He practiced zealously, and soon became capable of exhibitions on the shaky wire—to the great scandal of his Quaker community (E. Doblhofer, *Le Déchiffrement des Écritures,* 1959, p. 57).

15 May

It rarely happens that I speak with a cultured American without the name of Camus being uttered emphatically and admiringly. The extraordinary prestige of Camus in America. Along with Gandhi and Albert Schweitzer, he is considered one of the most representative men of his century. Why? Because during the German occupation he was in the Résistance, because he undertook "action," wasn't a contemplative, an artist; he didn't live in his ivory tower. Because he understood "the absurdity of existence" and, nevertheless, accepted it; "he didn't flee from the world." The admiration of Americans for Camus' humanism. To love, to respect man—even in an absurd universe and in a society terrorized by history (by the political police)—there, at least, is a worthy, virile, moral solution. The sensitivity of Americans before a philosophical position of which politics and ethics are the essential elements.

19 May

Peggy Feldman was talking to me last night about spiders (her great passion: she has several boxes in which spiders spin their webs; Peggy feeds them gnats and flies). She is revolted that one of the young American poets identified spiders (in poetic images, obviously) with vampires, striges, and other cruel, hideous, and aberrant animals. Especially revolted by this image of the poet's: mummified wasps caught in the spider's web—when we know, Peggy points out, that the spider never attacks a wasp (it wouldn't stand a chance, she adds). The poet describes the spider's web, cluttered with cadavers, as a sort of remote, aerial cemetery—when we know that spiders never keep carcasses. They cut the threads and the mummies fall. The web is almost always clean.

We passed from spiders to insects—I discussed Fabre's *Souvenirs Entomologiques.* And while talking with her, my memory took me back to my garret on the Strada Melodiei, with my collection of insects—it was around 1923, I believe—the lizards that I nourished on living flies, coleoptera. The articles that I used to write for the *Journal of Popular Science.*

We talked for a long time of these universes which are so mysterious and yet so close. (Like religious symbols, I thought to myself, impenetrable and yet within the grasp of anyone.)

20 May

I vaguely remember a hotel room in an Italian port. I was very young. Was it Ancona? Bari? I went to Ancona in the spring of 1927, and to Bari—I believe—the following year. I find it impossible to connect the picture of that hotel room to the memories (very approximative ones, moreover) of Bari or Ancona. I can still see myself in the bed, on a dark morning, looking through the open window. The sky was low, the sea was gray, and I believe I was also able to see a part of the port. I had awakened overwhelmed with an incomprehensible sadness. I stayed in bed and tried to find out what had happened.

21 May

Last night, at Crossroads, a Catholic center for international meetings, we talked, among other things, about the theories of Teilhard de Chardin. I remember what he told me, in January 1950, about the necessity to renovate dogma: "The Church," he said, "is like a crustacean; periodically, she must throw off her shell in order to grow." His great confidence in "the progress of science." (The electronic brain, all alone, in a few seconds, does the work of a dozen mathematicians working for a century. Scientific instruments help man to "swallow time" and "conquer space." Scientific progress also had a religious function for T. de Ch. The entire cosmos—that of the galaxies, not that of the Greco-Roman world—will have to come to know the Christological mystery.)

What impressed me the most in my conversations with Teilhard was his response to the question that I had asked him: What did the immortality of the soul mean for him? Difficult to summarize. Briefly: according to T. de Ch., everything that can be transmitted and communicated (love, culture, politics, etc.) "does not pass into the beyond" but disappears with the death of the individual. But there remains an irreducible, incommunicable foundation, or, more precisely, what is impossible to express or communicate—and it is this mysterious, incalculable foundation that "passes into the beyond" and survives the disappearance of the body. An interesting theory because it appears to imply that if we succeeded some day in communicating and transmitting *absolutely all* human experiences, immortality would become useless, and would then cease. What interested Father Teilhard was the principle of the conservation of human experiences. Nothing must be lost. All experience must be expressed (by language, by culture), and it is thus that it is recorded and kept in the noosphere.

31 May

In September 1916, a few days after Rumania's entry into the war, Uncle Mitache came back from a café very excited. He had met an inventor there. This man had discovered a substance from which coats of mail could be made that bullets did not go through. He had presented his invention to the Ministry of War. In a few months, by spring at the latest, Rumanian soldiers would become invulnerable to bullets and shrapnel.

When he was asked what this substance was and whether it could be found in great enough quantities, the inventor supposedly answered: "But you're walking on it, my good man, you're walking on it!"

1 June

On March 17, 1832, five days before his death, Goethe wrote his last letter to Karl Wilhelm von Humboldt, and wondered (troubled and depressed) what welcome posterity would give his *Faust*. "But the present age is so senseless and confused that I know I should only be poorly rewarded for my many years of sincere effort at erecting this strange building. It would be driven like a wrack on the shore and lie there, getting gradually covered by the sands of time. The world is ruled to-day by bewildering wrong counsel, urging bewildered wrong action. My most important task is to go on developing as much as possible whatever is and remains in me, distilling my own particular abilities again and again. You, my friend, are doing the same up there in your castle."

Alongside other texts of Goethe, alongside letters and texts of Burckhardt (only fifteen or twenty years later), this fragment impressed me by its prophetic character. Goethe felt that "Nature" was giving way to "History," and for him that meant "aculturization," chaos, sterility. (More bizarre to me is Burckhardt's reaction in the face of contemporary history, 1848 in this instance, the '48 ideologies, democracy; because all this was part of history, and Burckhardt believed in the cultural significance of history. Obviously, what he was seeing in 1848 was the disappearance of Europe and the decline of the European genius.)

Since Goethe, nature has been more and more desacralized and emptied of its cultural and, finally, philosophical significance. I think I can count myself among the rare Europeans who have succeeded in revaluing nature, by discovering the dialectic of hierophanies and the structure of cosmic religiosity. That seems to me all the more important since, by contrast with Nietzsche, for example, who tried to rediscover nature by cultural techniques and values (Dionysus is, above all, a subject of classical philology), I arrived at cosmic sacralities by reflecting on the daily experience of Rumanian or Bengali peasants. Thus, my base of departure was contemporary historical situations and *living* cultural values.

I believe that modern man has rediscovered—in my books—a dimension of cosmic sacredness which is neither a lyric creation nor a philosophical invention; because I have always made an effort to draw the *facts* and their interpretation from those who still participate in a pre-Christian religious universe.

ELLISON BAY, WISCONSIN, *14 June*

Subject for a novel. A few hundred years from now in eastern Europe. The peoples who live there today have been exterminated (wars, deportations, etc.). Of each people, there survive only a few thousand individuals who live in reservations (like the North American Indians of today). The narrative begins when a group of noble men from the occupying nation (the occupiers could only be Euro-Asiatics) try to obtain more humane conditions for the natives. There are lectures, books, articles, but also intercessions with the authorities. People sing the praises of the Poles, the Hungarians, the Rumanians, the Serbs, etc., in the same way that John Collier today speaks of the Choctaw or Creek tribes. It is pointed out that the survivors of these peoples have nothing to be ashamed of in their culture and their history, although this culture is anachronistic. I would want especially to emphasize the inferiority complex that the Euro-Asiatic occupier discovers in himself—as it happened to the North American intelligentsia of thirty or forty years ago.

The lake, in the morning. Some kingfishers; also a good many crows, which like to rest in groups on a dead tree.

Newport—a little abandoned town. Over there was the post office, and there, the school. . . . Only a few walls still stand. And enormous clusters of white and blue lilacs. I climbed up on a ruined wall to gather a few sprigs, and I discovered a bird's nest. A few meters from there, Christinel saw a green snake.

Two kilometers away, in the forest, an abandoned and, so they say, haunted house. Its history: a happy young couple. The husband drowned. His widow, very pretty, refused to remarry. She claimed that she had no feeling of loneliness, that she felt her husband still near her, saw him, etc. A short time after, she died in her turn. Since then, noises have been heard in the house. Harriet believes that some foxes had dug their hole under the floor. The house deteriorates and falls into ruin a little more each year. Someone with business sense has bought this ground and all the surrounding acreage. But he doesn't want to subdivide or sell it for ten or fifteen years, when there will not be the smallest speck of land for sale in the whole peninsula.

In the afternoon, we visited Jensen's park. The forest as it was fifty or sixty years ago. On the edges, the roots of the pine trees show among the rocks. How fragile the stone seems here confronted by the implacable vitality of the vegetable life which thrusts its roots among the stones, like so many serpents, to the point of breaking them.

The room "of rest and meditation" where Jensen took refuge. He was the Norwegian forester who saved Chicago and other midwestern cities by persuading the city councils to preserve the parks and forests that surrounded the cities. He had this room built when he was eighty or eighty-five years old. He died here at ninety-one. Viking House; before the door a birdbath where a nightingale drinks and bathes.

22 June

In an essay by Thomas Mann on Goethe, I found this passage from *Divan:*

> Du beschämst wie Morgenröte
> Jener Gipfel ernste Wand
> Und noch einmal fühlet Hatem
> Frühlingshauch und Sommerbrand.

Obviously, the rhyme in the third line should have been "Goethe." What a superb awareness of his own genius. "Splendid Narcissism!" cried Thomas Mann. Goethe's certitude that, in creating himself, he created at the same time one of the masterpieces of universal culture.

But it is necessary to compare the work Goethe put forth to fulfill himself (i.e., to realize his "personality") with the asceticism and contemplation practiced in India as a means of integrating one's own atman. The *separation* and *integration* of opposites—these two "methods" are as characteristic of India as of Goethe.

Encounters

PARIS, *20 July*

This morning I made the acquaintance of a young Rumanian refugee. He fled the country, hidden under a wagon. He told me terrible things about Communist prisons. The tuberculous have permission to carry a bottle attached to their neck to spit into. They empty it into the latrines, rinse it, then fill it with water to drink. The worst punishment: the inmates are forced to eat their fecal matter. If they're lucky. Most often, they are forced to consume the excrement of others, preferably the sick. They are also made to drink the contents of the bottles that the tuberculous carry around their necks. It is easy to understand why no one here in Paris wants to believe it when the refugee recites such ignominies. By the end of a year, he was so disheartened by the indifference and imbecility of the Westerners that he had made up his mind to return to our country. Happily for him, a functionary at the Paris Consulate recognized him and told him what awaited him in Rumania. That is how he was saved.

ASCONA, *21 July*

In Basel, a dark, handsome young man came into our compartment and asked us in French if this was indeed the train for Milan. At first I thought he was Italian. But he was reading *The Bostonians*

by Henry James, then some American magazines. As far as Bellinzona he almost never looked out the window. One felt, nevertheless,
that this was his first trip to Switzerland. In Lucerne, he asked us if
it was Bern. Once or twice an hour, he raised his eyes and looked out
the window. If he saw a lake, he would ask its name and go back to
his reading.

In Airolo we were welcomed by a washed-out blue sky which grew
lighter as we descended. I don't remember ever having seen such a sky
here in Ticino.

We found Olga much thinner. Her hands tremble. After the eye
operation that she underwent and for the week that she had to wear
the black bandage, she suffered a terrible anxiety. She couldn't live a
single instant without the nurse's hand. She was afraid of being shut
into a cage or a cellar. During that time, she had a whole series of
visions. Later, she dictated them to her secretary and sent them to
Jung, who wrote a commentary on them in three letters.

23 July

I've finished *My Family and Other Animals* by Gerald Durrell.
As I felt last winter, when I was reading Lawrence Durrell's *Bitter
Lemons,* I have the impression of spending an enchanted holiday:
once again I find the sun, the flowers, the insects, the calm serenity
of the Mediterranean. A meaningful existence, not yet detached from
the cosmos, a concrete life close to the earth, where trees, flowers, and
seasons hold a major role. As if there were so many doors opening
onto a better world, or—to employ a different metaphor—the "ci-
phers" of other transcendent realities. I am writing very quickly, and
a little confusedly, thoughts which deserve being meditated upon for
a long time and written at leisure. A Sartrean reader happening upon
these lines would say that my reveries are only meaningless escapes
into an unreal world, etc., etc. But this is a case of something else
entirely. A certain *joie de vivre* and a "wisdom of the body" and a
feeling of fellowship, brotherhood with the living beings and the
plants of this world. A heavy existence, concrete, filled with signs.

That does not necessarily mean an escape from history. It only means that history cannot, by itself, satisfy all the dimensions of existence. It also means that, from the opposition of History and Nature, the erroneous conclusion has been drawn that all feeling of solidarity with the cosmic rhythms is unworthy of an authentic man. Ultimately, the whole problem of the relationship between what is natural and what is historical in man should be examined with the same seriousness that theology puts into debating the relationship between Nature and Grace.

25 July

Olga had me read the first two visions, as she had dictated them to her secretary, and her own commentary sent to Jung. The first one, rather significant: a ruined cathedral, at night; Olga was on the scaffolding, up high, near the dome; at a certain point, she realized that she herself was the cathedral; then she knelt and waited to be run through with a lance in the back.

All during the time she spent at the clinic, she saw masons and painters in her room busy repairing and repainting the walls. Admirable symbol of renewal and regeneration. As Jung wrote in his answer to the letter, the operation that she had undergone also had a psychic homologue. Olga was threatened with cataracts, with blindness, that is, with foundering in the unconscious, with spiritual death. The operation was equivalent to a birth: the recovery of sight, the salvation of the conscious life.

Yesterday morning, I began to write my childhood remembrances. Three whole pages. I would have written more because I felt that I had found the right tone—but about five o'clock Veith and his wife arrived and we chatted in Olga's salon until dinner.

26 July

I'm continuing my "Remembrances." I'm writing a few pages on the two years spent at Cernavoda, when I was five and six. Am surprised myself at the preciseness of my memories of this aspect of my early childhood. I notice, however, that if I write without any plan, as I am doing, I forget to note certain essential details; the fact, for example, that of three brothers, I was the only one nursed by a Tzigane wet nurse. When I was in the lycée, I used to like to think that it was thanks to this happenstance—thanks to this exotic breast which nourished me—that I had become an Orientalist.

28 July

Bill McGuire, from the Bollingen Foundation, came to see us. He told Olga that the fourth volume of *Papers from the Eranos Yearbooks* will appear in a few days. On the subject of that volume he told us the following story. Among the collaborators of volume 4, there is a certain M. C. Cammerloer. He spoke only once at Eranos, and his lecture had appeared in *Jahrbuch II* in about 1934. When McGuire tried to write his bibliographical notice, he discovered that M. C. Cammerloer did not appear in any bibliography. He wrote to Olga, who knew nothing about him. Then to Jolande Jacobi, who had known him in Vienna (she is the one who had proposed him to Olga for Eranos). But J. Jacobi didn't know anything either. She hadn't seen him for twenty-five years and she didn't know if he was still living, or where. She finally remembered, however, that she had written, about ten years ago, to his daughter in a little town in Austria. M. C. Cammerloer had borrowed from her the notes from one of Jung's seminars, and Jacobi had written to his daughter to see if she couldn't get them back. There was no answer to the letter.

But McGuire did not become discouraged. He wrote the daughter, addressing his letter to the mayor of the town to be sure that it would reach its destination. A month later, he was answered with a few biographical pages. M. C. Cammerloer had studied medicine, then Orientalism, had become a psychologist, was especially knowledgeable about raising Siamese cats, from which he made his living. His Jewish wife died in a concentration camp. After the war, M. C. Cammerloer had grown old and had become poor. He was so poor that, at his death, a coffin couldn't be afforded; he was taken to the cemetery in a little wagon and buried in the common grave.

The daughter wrote to McGuire that a great number of manuscripts had been found.

13 August

Three days ago, toward evening, we were on the terrace on the Shanti house with the Dehollains. The lake was gloomy, almost sinister. Abruptly, ten meters in front of us, we saw a bizarre little "boat." What else can I call it? It didn't look like anything else I knew. After a few minutes, we thought we understood: it was a pedal craft, with a cabin no bigger than an umbrella and the tired motor of an old motorbike. It didn't move any faster than a novice swimmer. In front of the "cabin," standing, a strange personage. An old man, he seemed to us at first. But when he lit a cigarette, we saw that it was one of those women of indeterminate age, with very short hair, dressed like a man. She began to smoke, looking at us. We hardly dared to speak any further. In the evening mist, she seemed an apparition come from a yet unborn world.

ABANO, 25 August

I've bought *Papini vivo,* especially for the photos. The extraordinary transformation of his last four years. I'm learning some frightful details of his long agony. Little by little, Papini had found himself reduced to the condition of a living corpse. Everything had remained intact: intelligence, memory, his unlimited curiosity, his enthusiasm —but little by little, all means of expression had been taken from him: the ability to write, the spoken word, gestures. I think about his tragic solitude: almost blind, deaf, paralyzed, and I remember that terrible Tibetan initiatic trial of which Alexandra David-Neel has spoken: the yogi shuts himself up in a stone coffin and lies down on a decomposing corpse. A disciple then puts the stone cover back on, and the yogi remains in there, all alone. I don't know just how true this information is. If this is an actual rite, I imagine that its goal is the following: the yogi acquires such magical force that it would be easy for him to remove the stone cover. And if he fails, that means that he wasn't worthy of being counted among the *mahasiddah,* among "the great magicians."

When I read this story in David-Neel, I was frightened by the absolute, definitive solitude that the yogi confronts. At that time it never occurred to me that being walled in while alive could also be the result of a disease. In Papini's case, it even has a symbolic value: the most curious, the most universal, and the most extravagant man of the century is gradually reduced to the most rudimentary expression: sounds, signs. Gathered into himself, reintegrated, after a life of dissipation. This initiatic agony is perhaps the most beautiful, the most authentic, and the most exemplary part of Papini's life. All his work is ennobled, perhaps even saved, by the courage and the serenity with which he accepted the condemnation to a slow death.

26 August

At four in the morning, the first mud bath. For twenty minutes, bound up like a mummy. Memories: the mud baths of my childhood in Tekirghiol. But my thoughts go further: to the sick in India buried in a ditch or hole in the form of a uterus; the meaning: *regressus ad uterum,* the return to Mother Earth's womb. This warm mud, and the feeling of being enveloped in a shroud.

30 August

How far I feel, sometimes, from the spirit of Western Christianity. The conflict between Jansenists and Jesuits leaves me cold. The problem of grace—as it was discussed, and lived, in France in the seventeenth century—seems foreign to *my* Christianity. Speaking of *Phèdre,* Mauriac writes *(Mémoires Intérieurs):* "The Redeemer, of course, had not yet come, and no drop of blood had been spilled for Phèdre." This pharmaceutical conception of grace—"the drop of blood" that the Redeemer supposedly shed for so-and-so—seems to me intolerable. I know well that we have here an image, a cliché, which only means this: Jesus suffered and died on the Cross for *each one* of us, as a particular, historical individual, not for humanity in the abstract. Nonetheless, it is a pharmaceutical conception, a grating, profane image which not only dissipates the mystery of the redemption, but minimizes it. What an ideal target for materialists or anti-Christians of any stamp.

VENICE, *4 September*

Night, Piazzale Roma, waiting for the bus to Padua. In the neon-lit bar, the same, inevitable jukebox into which you put a coin and listen to your favorite record. As is the case every evening, a group of young people, from fifteen to eighteen. They are the same as in Ascona, or Paris, the same as in the café-bar-restaurant in that humble village in Door County, Wisconsin. I remember so well that June night when, having arrived in Bob and Harriet Platt's car, we dined in the restaurant on Ellison Bay. At the bar, perched on chairs, three or four boys and girls. One of them put in coins. And the box poured forth these melodies that I'm listening to now on the Piazzale Roma.

BASEL, *9 September*

The Holbein Exhibition at the Kunstmuseum. I saw once again *Descent from the Cross,* by Holbein the Younger. Like a corpse at the morgue. What an extraordinary courage; showing *only the man* in Jesus, 100 percent. And on this corpse, which will resurrect in three days, no sign of his divinity.

The Nativity and *The Magi Kings,* still Holbein the Younger. Strange landscape; abandoned palaces in ruins. In *The Nativity,* a romantic moon can be seen through the clouds. An impression of solitude and abandonment. What could its meaning be? That Jesus was born in a ruined, finished world? Or that his birth brought the old world to an end? One has the impression that the palaces have just been destroyed. Abandoned, but not decrepit.

MARBURG, *13 September*

Superb autumn days. The arthritis pains are returning each night. I don't manage to sleep more than two or three hours. Yesterday I gave up the idea of giving my announced lecture: "Mythology and Eschatology." I needed four or five hours to put the finishing touches on the text. I wasn't able to find them.

PARIS, *20 September*

Back at 62 *bis,* rue de la Tour. It's raining, and this unexpected cold. We're warming ourselves with electric heaters.

I feel as tired as at the beginning of the summer. The result of "vacation." I feel that life is slipping through my fingers. I run from city to city. I can neither rest nor work. On a recent night, I woke up with this imperious warning deeply engraved on my mind: You must climb back up the slope! . . .

22 September

Marvelous afternoon. I took a walk on the boulevard Saint-Germain, I looked in the store windows, I stopped at the Deux-Magots to have coffee. And, yet, I feel that all these things *are past,* that, for me, it's a walk among the ruins, that I am no longer *of this place,* that I am no longer a part of this band of Parisian intellectuals, eager to read every new author, to discuss him, to become enthusiastic, and to launch ideas, names, myths. I am not tired, but detached. None of these new books that I see in the windows interests me. If I had the possibility of choosing, I would end my days on a Mediterranean island, and I would write some personal, noncurrent books (an autobiography; the history of religious experiences, from the paleolithic age to the gnostic period; short stories, theater). I would especially like to be able to write some books to appear after my death, that is, which would not be connected with current events or with the scientific prestige (more or less ephemeral) which I enjoy at this moment.

25 September

Avenue de Saint-Ouen to look for some files in boxes brought here from Val d'Or, two years ago. Since X. Y. wants to sell his apartment, the few pieces of furniture that remained there are there no longer. Even the bookshelves where I had put some of my books have disappeared. Rubbish, old newspapers, dust, a dirty floor. A terrible melancholy when I move among the boxes of books and the stacks of periodicals. Where to look first? In which box? I began completely by chance with a cardboard box. I had the pleasant surprise of discovering two files containing the reviews and the articles written about my books, and that I thought lost. In an iron chest I found the typed and corrected manuscript of *Forêt interdite* lost among other files and envelopes.

All these boxes of books, the collections of scientific magazines, etc., will be put in the downstairs storage of S.'s new apartment. When will I see them again, in the light of day, put in order on bookshelves and in a room *of my own?* (In the downstairs storage of the rue Duhesme there are packages and manuscripts that I haven't opened since 1950!)

CHICAGO, *3 October*

A glorious American fall morning. I remember our first arrival in Chicago, the first of October, 1956. The same light that enchanted me from the very beginning. The afternoon of that day with the Kitagawas, going by car to Evanston; the evening at the Bamboo Inn, the Chinese restaurant in the Loop. We lived at the Quadrangle Club. I hadn't yet finished the Haskell lectures, and as soon as I had a free minute, I would go back to work.

That was my last book. Since then, I've written only articles or studies. I've started several books, but I haven't finished one.

7 October

Marxism doesn't reflect the objective, scientific spirit (not even the spirit of positivism)—but rather the tension and aggressivity of prophetic theologies. Marx and the Marxists write just as aggressively and polemically as the theologians of the Reformation and Counter-Reformation.

LAKE GENEVA, WISCONSIN, *17 October*

I came here two years ago. "Faculty Retreat." I gave my lecture on cosmogonic myths. That was also a marvelous autumn, but it never seemed as beautiful as today. The forests are golden. This incredible maple tree which not only does not lose its leaves, but whose every leaf is a perfect, transparent, uniform yellow.

The walk along the lake shore, alone. Houses, cabins, villas, in groups, or isolated in the forest a few meters from the shore. I've been told that one can go all around the lake, about twenty-five miles, by following the little path near the shore, under the trees. I realize, once more, that in the United States, beauty has withdrawn from the great cities or from the so-called urban and industrial centers—and that it is maintained solely in the residential areas, in the suburban villages and in the forests, in the parks, around lakes. I rarely find here a house or cabin that is really ugly.

20 October

Among the interesting letters of the past few weeks, I am singling out that of the Trappist Father C. E. from Our Lady of the Holy Ghost Abbey, Conyers, Georgia. He wrote to thank me for *Patterns in Comparative Religions,* which "enlarged and deepened [his] concept of religion and brought [him] a deeper understanding of Catholicism. I will refer to it to the end of my days," he adds.

The end of the letter brought up this detail: during the war, he was for a long time a prisoner in a camp near Brasov, and got to know the Rumanians quite well. "And it is only thanks to their goodness, there in the Sinaïa hospital, that I am still alive."

22 October

Dr. G. C. Amstutz, professor of geology at the University of Missouri, sent me two little works: *Syngenese und Epigenese in Petrographie und Lagerstättenkunde* (extract from *Schweiz. Min. Petr. Mitt.,* vol. 39, 1959) and "Lunar Craters, Ore Genesis, Evolution and Life" (typed copy of a lecture that will be published this year). According to the letter that accompanies these two texts, I understand that he has read *The Forge and the Crucible.*

"Lunar Craters" is fascinating. "The Human Factor," therefore "the relativity," introduced into studies and especially into geological theories, is sensational. The origin of craters, as well as of metal-bearing beds, had been explained for a hundred years almost exclusively by external factors: meteorites, late transformations of the crust, etc. Amstutz believes that these exo- and epigenetic theories are explained by an unconscious process, compensation of the religious and aesthetic function, neglected or scorned in the age of radical rationalism. It is particularly a case of the unconscious veneration of "unknown depths" and of "unknown outer space" (the meteorites)— a veneration that was translated by the geological hypotheses in fashion for nearly one hundred years. There are so many things to add. To be connected with Pauli's remarks on archetypal images which crystallize and organize scientific theories. What interests me above all in this sort of reflection by men of science on their own research is the courage to accept the relativity introduced by the human factor; to accept it as a constitutive element of knowledge. In comparison, I think of my poor colleagues who torture themselves to be "objective" and believe they attain this objectivity by scorning, reducing, minimizing, and banalizing the spiritual phenomena they study.

26 October

Professor Ishizo stayed for several days on campus. I met him in Tokyo. I would often see him during the Congress. Then, invited by him and by Hori, I went to give a lecture in Sendai on "The Methodology of the History of Religions." Ishizo tells me that my visit to Sendai has taken on the proportions of a legend. Here, as a matter of fact, is what happened. The train was leaving at three o'clock in the afternoon, and at two o'clock, Ishizo, Hori, and a group of students came to get me at the hotel. At the station, we were informed that because of the latest typhoon, the northern region was flooded and the train would be about an hour late. We all went to the restaurant upstairs, ordered coffee, and continued our discussion on methodology. Since the students didn't understand English very well, I would stop from time to time so that Hori or Ishizo could summarize in Japanese what I had just said. A student would go down from time to time to get information on the train's arrival. (We had been told that it might gain ten or fifteen minutes.) At one point, the conversation became very animated (I believe that I was speaking about the interpretation of myths). An hour and a half had gone by somehow. But I can still see the frightened face of the young student who was shouting from the restaurant door that the train was coming into the station. We went down in a second, just at the moment the train was leaving. I tried to catch it in motion, but I was on another platform and I wasn't able to catch up with it.

This incident became legendary because I had waited for the train for an hour and a half. Fortunately, around six o'clock, there was a plane for Tokyo. We headed for the airport in several cars. To avoid all risk, Ishizo and Hori planted me in front of the gate where the word *Tokyo* was written and hardly opened their mouths anymore. We were seated on a bench, our eyes fastened on the sign that carried the magic word: *Tokyo.*

3 November

Eric Voegelin visited me. I had just finished reading the first volume of *Order and History (= Israel and Revelation),* surprised by the affinity of our positions. He is still a young man (he appears to be barely fifty). He is working now, he tells me, on volume 4. He believes that our era is "gnostic." He is astonished that no one has yet written on the gnosticism of Hegel, for example, or of Heidegger. Bultmann seems to him just as influenced by gnosticism as Jung. And he can't get over the fact that no one has ever seen these things up to now.

10 November

The sun returns intermittently bringing the Indian summer light—the beginning of a glorious autumn. At these moments I don't know how or from what corner of our attic the ladybugs appear. Everywhere, at all the windows, on the windowpanes, on the drapes. *Coccinella tripuntata.* I remember the *Coccinella septempuntata* of my adolescence. When they made their appearance, I knew that I had to get my insectarium ready. I would leave every Sunday, very early in the morning, for the forests around Bucharest. I would return late at night, with a supply of butterflies, coleoptera, lizards, frogs, larvae.

29 November

. . . Around eleven at night, returning home, we were greeted by red signal lights right in front of our house. That superb old tree, that made me thrill with joy each time I opened my window onto the street, lay felled to earth. The wind had taken it down a quarter of an hour earlier. Moreover, it had been sick. And it used to lose its leaves as soon as July came.

The melancholy this morning when I saw it blocking the way with its dead branches. Then the "specialists" arrived in a truck and began to cut up the trunk and the branches with an electric saw. The heart of the wood was almost entirely rotten.

2 December

I was saying last summer, half joking, half serious: it is useless for the U.N. to send troops to the Congo if it doesn't at the same time send some historians of religion familiar with archaic myths and "primitive" millennialist ideologies.

I repeated the same thing every time I had the opportunity: no fruitful dialogue is possible as long as the white partner in the discussion does not understand the mythology (camouflaged or not) of the "native" that he wants to help today (after having oppressed and exploited him for centuries). The history of religions and religious ethnology are of a much more urgent usefulness in the politics of today than are economics or sociology.

4 December

The interpretations proposed by Freud are more and more successful because they are among the myths accessible to modern man. The myth of the murdered father, among others, reconstituted and interpreted in *Totem and Taboo*. It would be impossible to ferret out a single example of slaying the father in primitive religions or mythologies. This *myth* was created by Freud. And what is more interesting: the intellectual elite accept it (is it because they understand it? Or because it is "true" for modern man?).

7 December

It was the great merit of Christianity to revolt against astrological fatalism, so powerful in late antiquity—and thus to restore man's confidence in himself and in the possibilities of his freedom. Today Christianity—as well as all the spiritualities that are conditioned by it—opposes Marxist determinism. It opposes it in the name of the same belief in man's freedom, but much less successfully than in antiquity.

14 December

Because I had told him that I would be curious to reread Barbellion's *The Journal of a Disappointed Man*, Burton Feldman gave it to me today in a pocket edition. I've skipped through it with melancholy, but so far I'm only half conquered. It's strange that I remember certain pages so well, notably the last years (those terrible years 1915–1916). I read this journal for the first time in Calcutta, around 1930. I was extraordinarily impressed. I recognized myself in Barbellion, attracted at one and the same time by science (entomology! the "science" of my adolescence), by art, and by life. I was also attracted by his way of handling his journal; those delightful little things that alternate with serious confessions, the experiences of a beginning naturalist, impressions garnered in a museum, his ambitions, the despair of knowing he would die young, unknown, the hopes he pinned on the publication of the journal.

I would read it, in the room on Ripon Street, at night, after ten hours of Sanskrit and Indian philosophy. One of Mme. Perris's sons would be sleeping soundly in the bed next to mine, his breath puffing. In the other bed, the radio employee, almost naked, would be dreaming with a smile—in a cot similar to mine, his mosquito net poorly hung. Sometimes reading the *Journal* took me so far from my preoccupations (Sanskrit, Indian philosophy, yoga), obsessed me with so many questions, authors, problems, that I would close the book and go out for a walk. Even late, after midnight, the streets of Calcutta are alive, busy, noisy. Those extraordinary smells—eucalyptus, cinnamon flowers, melted butter, curry, laundry. . . .

15 December

I am more and more convinced of the literary value of the materials available to the historian of religion. If art—and, above all, literary art, poetry, the novel—knows a new Renaissance in our time, it will be called forth by the rediscovery of the function of myths, of religious symbols, and of archaic behavior. Ultimately, what I've been doing for more than fifteen years is not totally foreign to literature. It could be that someday my research will be considered an attempt to relocate the forgotten sources of literary inspiration.

16 December

About two weeks ago, my colleague Bobrinskoy, professor of Sanskrit, sent me a Nepalese amulet with a microscopic inscription, asking me to decipher it. It took me several days to make out the characters. And I managed only with an enormous magnifying glass lent me by Margaret Boell. But I wasn't able to decipher it. I doubt that it is in Nepalese. When I called him on the telephone to admit my failure, I learned through his secretary that, the preceding evening, B. had been attacked and beaten. It occurred about six thirty in the evening. A young man stopped him to ask him for a light and gave him a blow on the temple. B. is a robust man, but the blow sent him to the ground. The young man took his wallet, went through his pockets, and disappeared.

All that in the middle of the campus. At that hour, from five to seven, the young drug addicts absolutely need five dollars (as one of them said in a recent investigation) for a new dose of heroin. It's been recommended that we always have at least five dollars on us and ten at the most. If they don't find any money, or if they find too much, these youths lose their heads, and then anything is possible.

18 December

Forêt interdite. Why do so many readers stop, discouraged, after one hundred pages? Kay Atwater, my former student, for example. I had given her the novel two or three years ago. And she only read it this fall. She wrote me a long letter. She seemed moonstruck, unable to escape the bewitching charm of the forests through which I had made her walk. I am therefore sure that, once he has arrived at the heart of the novel, any intelligent reader would be captivated, obsessed, and would not then be able to put it down. The fate of this book hangs on the first hundred pages, where everything is camouflaged. The reader could have the impression of holding an ordinary novel in his hands, one a little confused, wordy, and awkward. In order to realize that it is a case of *something else entirely,* in order to remove the camouflage, he must get through the first hundred or two hundred pages to arrive at the heart of the work. But why should he force himself to do that? Yes, indeed, why? . . .

21 December

It's been snowing since last night. Snowdrifts in the morning, as in Bucharest in the winter. And abruptly one begins to *perceive the silence*—grave, mysterious, inimitable. As if all sounds had been smothered under a pavement as immense as the sky.

3 January 1961

Today, coming home from the university, in the vicinity of the Oriental Institute, I suddenly experienced my life's *duration.* Impossible to find just the right word. I suddenly felt, not older, but extraordinarily rich and full; expanded—bringing together in me, concomitantly, both the Indian, Portuguese, and Parisian "time" and the memories of my Bucharest childhood and youth. As if I had acquired a new dimension of depth. I was "larger," "rounder." An immense inner domain—where, not so long ago, I was penetrating only fragmentarily by trying to relive such-and-such an event—was revealed in its totality: I'm able to see it from end to end and, at the same time, in all its depth.

A vigorous, strong feeling. Historical human life suddenly takes on meaning and significance. Optimism.

10 January

This morning I'm leafing through Barbellion's *Journal.* His enthusiasm after reading (December 22, 1912) *Ancient Hunters* by

Sollas. The perspectives opened to him toward the Paleolithic consoled him in his miseries and his illness. Even better, it revealed to him the certainty of his *indestructibility*—as matter but also as "epiphany." He writes: "For nothing can alter the fact that I HAVE lived; I HAVE BEEN, if for even so short a time." It is indeed what I would call the indestructibility of human existence as epiphany. But B. adds: "And when I am dead, the matter which composes my body is indestructible—and eternal, so that come what may to my 'Soul,' my dust will always be going on. . . . When I am dead, you can kill me, burn me, drown me, scatter me—but you cannot destroy me. . . . Death can do no more than kill you." B. wrote that because he was a naturalist. But I have met similar experiences, expressed almost in the same terms, among numerous "mystics" (cf. especially the experience of "cosmic consciousness").

19 January

The principal objection made against me: I "idealize" the primitives, I exaggerate the importance of their myths, instead of "demystifying" them and emphasizing their dependence on historical events (colonialism, aculturalization, pagan-Christian syncretism, etc.). But I have never affirmed the insignificance of historical situations, their uselessness for understanding religious creations. If I haven't emphasized this problem, it is precisely because it has been emphasized too much and because what seems to me essential is thus neglected: the hermeneutic of religious creations. Ultimately, the insistence with which Western scholars repeat that the myths of "primitives" are *only* the result of their historical situation will end by irritating the future elites of these peoples. A Bautu or Indonesian critic will only be able to wonder: How were the Westerners able to write thousands of volumes on the "beauty" and the "eternal values" of *The Divine Comedy,* the work of a political exile, and see in *our* mythologies and *our* messianic symbols only a protest of oppressed peoples? Indeed, why am I suspected of "idealism" each time I try to analyze these primitive and archaic creations with the same care and the same sympathy that we bring to commenting on Dante or Meister Eckhart?

This truly paradoxical thing will come about: one day the so-called progressive ethnologists of today will be considered by the elites of the new states in Africa, Oceania, etc., as the defenders of the absolute supremacy of Western culture; because their work is limited, ultimately, to showing the origin and sociopolitical character of primitive mythologies and messianisms, and implies that "primitive" cultural creations, facing the political situation, never succeed in rising to the level of freedom, as opposed to the creations of Western cultures.

26 January

I believe that my interest in Hindu philosophy and asceticism can be explained as follows: India was obsessed by *freedom,* absolute autonomy. Not in a naïve manner, but taking account of man's innumerable conditionings, studying them objectively, experimentally (Yoga), and making a real effort to find the instrument that would permit them to be abolished or transcended. Even better than Christianity, Hindu spirituality has the merit of introducing freedom into the cosmos. A *jivanmukta*'s mode of being is not *given* in the cosmos; very much to the contrary, in a universe dominated by laws, absolute freedom is unthinkable. India has the merit of having added a new dimension to the universe: that of existing as a free being.

31 January

On the *ephemeral* character of "absolute reality" (obviously within the framework of human existence, not within the cosmos). Let's imagine a man dying of thirst in the desert: at that moment, *water* has the character of *absolute reality.* The rest is without interest. Water is the only truly *real* thing, the only one that can *save him.* Then imagine this man being *saved* at the last minute, either because he finds water or because someone brings it to him. In a few seconds, water loses its character of *absolute reality;* it becomes once again what it is for all of us, an important thing, but easily accessible and, as such, without interest.

Another example: You are on the point of being drowned; at the point, the only *real* thing would be a life belt. Someone throws it to you and you are saved. At that very instant, its character of *absolute and saving reality disappears.*

What can I name this sort of reality, absolute and ephemeral at the same time? Probably: epiphanic realities. In the sense that they are manifested as absolute reality only for a few moments, and for certain persons at certain times. But they are no less absolute for all that, because, if they had not been manifested, man would have disappeared as a living being.

1 February

At moments of great melancholy, when I feel the end of Western civilization near, I meditate on destiny and on the lesson that Hector gave us. Deep down, he knew that Troy was destined to perish. In that extraordinary scene in the sixth song of *The Iliad*—when he advises the old men to offer sacrifices to the gods and sees Andromache for the last time—one senses clearly that Hector had no illusions about Paris, and especially about the end of the war. He had a presentiment that he was going to die and that Troy would be destroyed. He suffered over the fact that all this had to happen because of a frivolous person like Paris: but he continued to do his duty and to struggle.

I fear lest that also be the fate of our Europe. (The "Asia" vanquished at Troy will have its revenge.) But I would want us to fall as Hector did. Doing our duty, at peace with our conscience, and, nevertheless, without illusions.

Sometimes I have the impression that all the "exemplary destinies" of the Europeans were anticipated by the Greeks.

2 February

Today, while looking for some extracts in the stacks of paper and magazines piled up these last few years, which I persist in saving on the lower shelves of my library, I fell on the mimeographed brochures with the title which is so touching: "Collected Haiku by Kosetsu Shoson Miyamoto." Japanese text, transliteration and translation by Bob Morrell, Jim Curtis, and Miyamoto. I can't help rereading them. Admirable Miyamoto. In 1958–1959, he had lived in the little apartment in Channing House that we had also occupied ourselves in 1956–1957. He was visiting professor in the History of Religions Department. He took his job very seriously. He wrote out his lessons in their entirety. I used to see him fairly often, but he almost never had time; he had to write out his lessons.

But, at the same time, M. wasn't forgetting that he was a poet. (He told me that his American experience had reawakened in him his poetic vigor.) In the spring, he began to distribute to us those mimeographed collections of haiku poems. He translated them himself, and his two collaborators helped him to find the most poetic equivalent.

At Christmas, after having gone to the Unitarian service, he wrote:

> Eternal Bliss
> Brought by a baby born on
> This day

On 30 December, in New York, in the crowd at Grand Central Station, he ran into Professor Hideo Kishimoto, from the University of Tokyo, who was arriving from Europe and getting ready to leave for Harvard.

> At Grand Central Station
> Like a blind turtle finding a log at sea:
> Our chance meeting.

I would like to be able to copy a lot of these haiku for the pleasure of finding them here each time I open this notebook. On Christmas Eve, at six o'clock, the full moon is rising.

> The winter Moon
> In the window—my study—lamp
> Is growing old.

On 7 October he gave his first class on Mahayana. The leaves were beginning to fall.

> Autumn leaves:
> Each with the compassionate face
> Of a Bodhisattva.

CAMBRIDGE, MASSACHUSETTS, *13 February*

Invited to dinner by A. D. Nock, at the Society of Fellows. Nock and I evoked men and places: Basel and Karl Meuli, the Rome of Pettazzoni and of Parvan, Alexandria. After dinner, in the adjoining salon with Harry Levin and some young people, we "talked literature." Astonished at the value that everyone puts on Nabokov's *Lolita.* Speaking of the nymphet fad, I submitted "my theory": it's the latest masculine reaction against the modern "matriarchate." In the USA, the wife and mother dominate. So the men get revenge by praising adolescence to prove *that* is what they like, and not mature, accomplished womanhood. *Lolita*—and the fashion that imitates little girls' dresses—demonstrates that men are attracted by what *precedes womanhood:* and although they are dominated by mature women, they feel no desire for them. I'm thinking of the crises that this trend sets off in a woman: the feeling that she is obsolete, old at thirty! . . . And the efforts that women make to appear not *young,* but still immature, still tender, still little girls. . . .

Harry Levin seems very interested by this hypothesis.

CHICAGO, *1 March*

Last night I gave a lecture at Loyola University: "The Nature and Function of Myth." Fascinating discussion. Despite all that, I fear that everything is happening *too late,* when almost nothing can be saved anymore. If the Western world and Christianity had understood these things—myth, symbol, cosmic religion—half a century ago. . . . If . . .

10 March

Perhaps that is why Americans love Albert Camus' *The Myth of Sisyphus* so much: they recognize themselves in Sisyphus. That is indeed their life: telephone calls, meetings, answering dozens of letters, and in the evening they're happy because they've done everything (the sturdy feeling of having *worked,* of having done one's duty), and the next morning they find dozens more letters to answer, more meetings, more telephone calls. . . .

17 March

Mrs. V. told us about her son. He is seventeen and is earning the money for his education himself by working in a cemetery. He's even a member of the gravediggers' union. Last week, Professor and Mrs. V. celebrated their twentieth wedding anniversary. The boy wanted to give them a surprise. This is Mrs. V. speaking: "In the bedroom there was a carpet of white roses. Splendid. But we could see that they had already been used. . . . The boy had collected them from fresh graves."

29 March

I don't know who sent me two recent editions of an occult-spiritualist magazine from England: *The Voice Universal.* (On the frontispiece I read "Our goal: Universal Illumination and Friendship.") I leafed through it with enchantment. I would love to note here some of the headlines or advertisements, but how to choose? Almost everything deserves to be cited. I stopped today at this article: "Playing with Fire. A warning to General de Gaulle." It's an analysis of Hans Georg Weidner's study which appeared in the magazine he publishes himself, *Lichthort.*

Here's what it is about: General de Gaulle is encouraging atomic explosions in the Sahara. But, says Weidner, the earth constitutes an organism analogous to man's, and the Sahara is the equivalent of the pancreas, that is, it is located in the region of the stomach. What happens to a man who is hit "below the belt"? He becomes sick, his breathing stops, and he faints.

In the same way, by atomic explosions produced in the stomach region of the earth, the vital secretions of this part of its body, secretions so necessary to the "digestion," are upset and certain reactions will be produced in the organism of the earth, as has happened in the Nevada desert and Siberia. What will happen if the explosions continue? The earth's axis could tilt, which would bring about a series of catastrophes. The warm winds from Africa would bring about the melting of the ice cap of the North Pole (the earth's "head"); inversely, the glacial regions would grow at the South Pole (the earth's "behind"). When the earth "gets sick" and has to vomit, that would be the beginning of volcanic eruptions. But Stromboli, Vesuvius, etc., are connected by a subterranean canal to the extinct volcanoes of Ethiopia and the Sahara, which, in their turn, are connected with the "Atlantic base" of the ocean of the same name, which corresponds, certainly, to Atlantis. This submerged continent is destined, in any case, to emerge some day. But if the birth is premature, it will provoke a series of catastrophes: Australia, the isthmus between the two Americas, the Sahara, and a part of Mediterranean Europe will be drowned. Other earth tremors are to be feared in Persia, Russia, India, and in the region of the Himalayas. In fact, that is why the Dalai Lama and so many other lamas left Tibet, Weidner adds. Consequently Weidner demands that the campaign against atomic explosions in the solar plexus region of Mother Earth be intensified.

31 March

India, too, "has sabotaged" history (to use Lucian Blaga's expression): Indian literature has kept no memory of Alexander the Great, nor of his prodigious military campaigns. India's historical destiny was changed by Alexander's invasion—but the Indian consciousness has forgotten him. What survives of this gigantic military undertaking is not the historical event of the invasion, but its "mythology," as it has been created by the popular imagination, namely: the so-called Alexander-romance.

8 April

On 24 October 1920, James Joyce wrote from Paris to Frank Budgen: "I observe a furtive attempt to run a certain Mr. Marcel Proust of here against the signatory of this letter. I have read some pages of his. I cannot see any special talent but I am a bad critic. Still I think a fall of mine would not altogether disappoint some admirers." The fantastic egocentricity of Joyce: his unlimited confidence in his own genius, and in the uniqueness of his work. I've gotten to page 163 of *Letters of James Joyce,* edited by Stuart Gilbert. About three-fourths of his letters are addressed to publishers, magazine editors, agents and literary critics, writer friends. He speaks almost exclusively about his work, about what is being written or has been written about him, etc., etc. A tiresome, suffocating impression of a "man of letters" and a small-time employee at the same time. The former student of the Jesuits who devotes himself entirely to a *mediocre absolute:* nothing exalting, fanatic, mystical, crazy, in the stubbornness with which he pushes his work on the literary market. He lives in his "literary universe." What seems to interest him above all is to "push" his work, just as one pushes a new invention or a new make of automobile. He is inexhaustible when it comes to the merchandise he wants to sell.

10 April

From Joyce's correspondence: "It is very irritating waiting for reviews" (11 March 1922, to Harriet Shaw Weaver). "I received M. Bennett's article and sent him a word of thanks. For the purpose of sales his article is not very useful as it does not give the name and address of the publisher. I always look for this first of all in an article, then at its length and finally at its signature" (16 May 1922, to the same). I could copy numerous other passages—but what for? Proust did the same thing. And Freud, and so many others.

15 April

I've learned from E.W. Tomlin, who has written a book about Simone Weil, this detail about her death: it is indeed a case of a suicide. Simone Weil let herself die of hunger not only because she wanted to live solely on the ration fixed in occupied France, but also because she was tired of life and fascinated by death. But Tomlin didn't dare say so in his book.

1 May

Glorious day! Not a cloud, not a shadow in this transparent sky. Cold morning. The "specialists" have come back. This time the condemned is one of the giant trees behind our little house. It seems perfectly healthy to me, but my neighbor is afraid that it will be blown over by the wind and crush his house in falling. The "specialists" go around the tree, tie ropes to the branches, then they begin to cut it apart. The piercing, exasperating cry of the machine. The branches are gathered up on the ground and thrown into the mouth of another machine, which inhales them and digests them within a few seconds. I am fascinated watching this insatiable Moloch. And the death rattle it makes when it pulverizes its victims.

Impossible to render the dissonance between the slow, well-ordered, scientific execution of the condemned tree and the divine light which seems to reach us from another world, a light glimpsed only in childhood, or sometimes felt in a dream.

3 May

The concept of Natural Law inherited from the Greeks has been abolished by Marxism. And it has been replaced by History, that is, the class struggle. Any other "universalism" than that established by the dictatorship of the proletariat is discredited; worse yet, it is considered an obstacle to the emancipation of the proletariat.

I don't think that it's been seen so far that Marxism reintroduces —in the place of Natural Law—pre-Stoic mythological provincialisms. Instead of a universal, rational structure, we now have a myth, that is, an "exemplary History" elaborated by a certain social class, at a certain historical moment, in a certain culture, and projected as *the only Truth and the only possible Destiny.* That is what I call "mythological provincialism." Primitive mythologies too, even if they are only the expression of a tribe or of a cultural province, lay claim to a universal value. All hamlets are at the "Center of the World." Every tribal chief is a Cosmic Ruler, etc. Seen from outside, these cultural expressions are provincial. But Marxists don't accept being looked at "from outside." They are sure of incarnating the only possible meaning to history.

WASHINGTON, D.C., *12 May*

Afternoon at Edith Hamilton's. She is ninety-four. A little deaf, but she looks better than four years ago (when she had broken

her leg and was in a wheelchair). Last year she published another
book. And with Huntington Cairns she prepared the complete edition
of Plato's works, using the most faithful and most beautiful translations which exist in English, accompanied with notes and commentaries. A volume of thirteen hundred pages which will appear in the
autumn.

She told me that from the age of eighty on, life really deserves to
be lived. She invited me to her hundredth birthday in August 1967
and told me about the amusing conversations she has had with
Suzuki. I'll have to write them down some day.

18 May

Tonight, while I was in my Meadville office, someone telephoned me at home. Christinel answered. It was a young man who
had read my books and insisted on speaking to me. His problem:
today I am becoming the "guru of America." All this on the assump-
tion that I *believe* in what I write. And if I believe in it, I have to "go
down into the arena," to take a position on the problem of the Amerindians, for example. The tribes that survive today in the larva state
on the reservations represent the sole archaic cultural traditions in the
USA. According to my "theories," the Amerindians are called to hold
an important role tomorrow in the culture of the United States. So
why am I doing nothing to hasten the process?

22 May

One can understand nothing of American life, culture, and
politics if one doesn't realize that the United States has its roots in
theology. "A Nation under God," they like to say of themselves. The
religious origins of American democracy—its great strength as well
as its tragic weakness—stem from that: democracy has not yet succeeded in becoming secularized; it is a hybrid political institution.

4 June

I've just learned of the death of Lucian Blaga. How long has
it been since I've seen him? Probably since the fall of 1939 or the

winter of 1940. A thousand disparate memories come to mind indiscriminately. His silences (as he admits himself in a poem: "Lucian Blaga is quiet as a swan"). I spent a week in Bern, during the summer of 1937, and I would see him every afternoon. Sometimes I felt ill at ease because Blaga would proffer a word every three minutes. And yet, when I was leaving Bern, Mme. Blaga didn't know how to thank me. "I've never seen Lucian so talkative since I've known him," she told me. From Bern, I went to Berlin. That's where I wrote "Conversations with L. B.," published in *Vremea*. It's also where I put the finishing touches on my travel notes. I hadn't forgotten to write down what he had told me about his daughter, Isidora: one day she went into a stable where a cow was calving, and the cow turned her head toward her. "Perhaps she thought I was the calf," said Isidora. Blaga was very happy that I had recorded this detail.

When I met him for the first time, in 1933 or 1934, he told me that he, too, would write a novel, but when he was forty. He went into detail: at twenty, poetry; at thirty, philosophy; at forty, the novel.

In my "Conversations with L. B.," I told how he would write his books on philosophy: each morning, before going to the Legation, he would write for two hours in a notebook. The first draft of a book would have seventy to eighty pages. Then, he would dictate it to Mme. Blaga—and in dictating it, he would add, correct, develop. And on this last manuscript he would work weeks or months. Only then would he send the book to the publisher.

He works with difficulty, very great difficulty, Mme. Blaga told me.

14 June

Why, when I was trying to rest and was dozing in the leather armchair in my study, did I remember that adventure from my adolescence? I was fourteen or fifteen, and, as I did each summer, I had left for the Carpathians with a group of friends and buddies. We had climbed the Bucegi by the classic trail, we had spent the first night at the little monastery of Ialomicioara, and we had taken off the next day toward Piatra Craiului. We probably lost our way, and at nightfall we went up via an abrupt, rocky slope. When we reached the top, it was completely dark. We realized that we were on the edge of the chasm. We barely had enough space to stretch out. Impossible to go down, and it would have been veritable madness to look for a better place to sleep at that hour. We lit a fire, gulped something down rapidly, then lay down and tied ourselves to the trees by our belts so as not to slip over into the chasm while asleep.

I don't know how we were able to sleep. But we slept, and even rather deeply. I woke up around midnight, I remember, and I gave a start at the sight of a string of green and white precious stones quite near me, a few meters into the chasm. It took me a few seconds to realize that it was the lights of the city of Campina, located several dozen kilometers away in the valley.

We weren't afraid until the next day, after we saw where we were. We didn't even dare stand up, and we descended the first few hundred meters on all fours. We recounted our adventure to the shepherds, and I'm not sure they believed us. But why did I remember this episode forty years later? (At what chasm's edge am I at this moment, so tired that I'm ready to fall asleep?)

29 June

Vaun Gillmor showed me the letter in which Aniela Jaffé gave her some details on the last months of Jung's life. After his September illness (liver, gall bladder) the old man had become frightfully thin. He hardly ate anymore. But bit by bit, during the winter, he regained his strength. He didn't dictate any more letters, but he was continually asking Aniela if he "had anything else to do." (He meant whether there weren't still certain things unfinished—articles, interviews, etc.) The last few months all his activity was limited to making the final draft of an article.

Then, last spring, he had an attack. For several days he could no longer talk. When he got a little better, he mixed up his languages— he would say a few words in German, then in English, French, or dialect—all of which depressed him terribly. He suffered from not being able to express himself normally. The doctor had assured him that he would recover, but Jung didn't want to. He didn't want to begin a "new life" again.

A few days before his death, he dreamed that he found a stone at the top of a mountain. The next morning he was happy. It was, he said, the exemplary sign that his life had attained its end. He had found the *lapis philosophorum*.

PARIS, *6 July*

Last night, at Suzanne Tezenas's, I met Henri Michaux. He talked about Padre Pio, whose Mass he had attended several times. Extraordinary impression: Padre Pio speaks with God; for him God is *there*. At the end of three days he left, for fear of being converted. "My path is entirely different," he told me. "I'm an artist. I have my personal experiences."

10 July

I'm reading *India (Journal, 1915–1943)*, by Romain Rolland. The long observations and reflections on Tagore remind me of the pages I wrote in 1929 and 1930, after staying at Santiniketan. Pages in my journal, but also a separate notebook, where I put down everything I was learning about R.T. I had promised myself that I would publish them ten or fifteen years after the poet's death, for I had written down the rumors that were circulating about him (women that had committed suicide over him, his mystico-erotic adventures). The information Romain Rolland gives about Sylvain Levy is somehow unexpected; his jealousy when Rolland published his book on Gandhi; he was furious that someone who had not been his student, had not worked with him, could write about India. S. L.'s maneuvers to prevent him from meeting Tagore, etc. All these details must be carefully read and meditated upon to understand the sectarianism of scholars and teachers. The memories of Miss Josephine Macleod, Vivekananda's friend and admirer, are just as fascinating. I myself met her during the winter of 1929, at Belur-math. She had written inviting me to go see her. How happy I was when I discovered that she spoke French. I spent a whole afternoon on her terrace looking at the Ganges. I went back to Calcutta with a young Indian student who also spoke French. I noted all that at the time in my journal. I believed that the meeting with the young student would have a great significance in my life. But I hardly ever saw him again. It was through Miss Macleod that I was later to receive Vivekananda's books. But they didn't win me over. I was already immune to spiritualistic rhetoric, to popularized, vague neo-Vedantic fervor; all that seemed shoddy to me.

11 July

I'm continuing to read Romain Rolland's Indian journal, not so much for the intrinsic worth of the text as to see how this pacifist went from Gandhiism to communism. And I've learned this purely and simply extraordinary thing: R. R. didn't know English at all; his sister would read and translate Vivekananda's books for him, the critical studies and biographies on Ramakrishna, Gandhi's texts and letters, etc. And it was in this total ignorance—of the country, the history, the languages of India, and even of English—that Rolland wrote the four volumes on Gandhi, Ramakrishna, and Vivekananda! . . . I believe the case is unique in the history of modern culture.

Concerning Gandhi's visit to Romain Rolland in December 1931, the latter gives these picturesque details: an Italian woman wrote Gandhi to demand the ten winning numbers of the future lotto; the Swiss nudists wanted to monopolize him: "Some troubled minds, 'Sons of God' are coming out of the earth, like snails. . . . The 'dairymen's association of Leman' telephones majestically that it intends to insure the 'supplying' of the 'king of the Indies during his stay' " (p. 308).

20 July

Last night, at Siegfried's the conversation slipped for a minute over to dreams, visions, premonitions. Rodica Ionesco tells this story: when she was five years old, her family moved into a new house; she went up to the attic and groped her way across it because it was almost pitch black. At the end of the attic, she suddenly found herself in front of a very beautiful garden, bathed in sunlight. She hesitated an instant but didn't go in. She went back many times, but never again found the garden. She doesn't understand what happened. At the end of the attic, there was only the wall, and no windows.

Siegfried told us about his frequent dreams, with doors and thresholds; a door which opens into an unknown room, a threshold that he must pass, etc. I reminded them of the symbolism of the threshold, the "passage to the other side," the *rupture de niveau:* the passage from one mode of being to another. Then I told them about one of the most significant dreams of my life. It was during the winter of 1930–1931, while I was at Rishikesh. In the dream I saw myself go down toward the Ganges, where a boat I knew very well was waiting for me to take me to the other side. But once in the boat, I no longer recognized it. It was much bigger than the one I knew. Tied up along its side was another boat, which I hadn't noticed at first, and of which I could make out neither the shape nor the dimensions. Almost without realizing it, I went from my boat to this other mysterious boat. And suddenly, *I understood:* everything became extraordinarily clear and simple. Everything: life, death, the meaning of existence. And even stronger than this revelation was my surprise: how had *no one* on earth yet understood this thing, *so extraordinarily simple?* Death, that was the extraordinarily simple and *obvious* thing. While getting into that boat, I said to myself: It's unbelievable that no one has yet seen it when it's so obvious. And all of a sudden I had the feeling that a message had been transmitted to me, that I should certainly remember in what the obviousness and simplicity of this beyondness of death consisted, so as to be able to communicate it to men. I woke up in my *kutiar* with this idea in mind: not to forget what I had seen. A second later, I had forgotten.

I also recounted the dream that I had ten days after the death of Nae Ionesco. I saw him come into my room, smiling. With his hand on the doorknob, he said to me: You see, Mircea, that is the whole mystery; you open a door and pass to the other side.

21 July

At Henri Michaux's for the autographed copy of *L' Infini turbulent.* I stood fascinated at the window for a few moments, looking at the great trees and the garden. From the street I would never have been able to guess it was there. I told him how much I envied him for this silence. He interrupted me: From time to time I hear a child. That's normal, I said to him without thinking. Excuse me, he cut me off once again, it's not at all normal. It would be normal if I heard a tiger, not a child.

Roland Cahen saw us in front of the Café du Dôme, just as we were getting into a taxi, and offered to take us home in his car. We invited him to have a drink and we chatted until after midnight. Among other things, we talked about the correspondence between Freud and Jung, "edited" and typed in quadruplicate, which can't be published for twenty-five years. Cahen tried a thousand times to persuade Jung to accept immediate publication. In vain. It's some 350 letters with their answers, a volume of 700 to 800 pages. The extravagant praise that Freud paid to Jung in the early years. The later letters are sorry ones: the two giants are shown to be small indeed. The true cause of the break is supposedly this, according to Cahen: during their trip to the United States, Jung and Freud told each other their dreams and interpreted them. And, as Jung was trying to draw certain conclusions, Freud reacted brutally; *he* would not be, should not be, analyzed; he, Freud, could not be dependent on another. I spoke to Cahen about the letter Jung sent to B. Nelson in 1956; Nelson had asked him if he had anything to say about the volume that he was preparing for Freud's centennial. Jung answered that it would be understood later that he was Freud's only *true* disciple, that he alone *continued* Freud's work and imitated his example.

23 July

We had dinner at the Dehollains with Father Bruno, Wilhelm Kempff, Henry Corbin, and Jean Gouillard. Kempff told us about his last visit to Sibelius, when the composer was about eighty-five. A short time afterward, Sibelius saw three herons fly over his house. They've come to take me, he told his wife. And he died that night. Father Bruno told us about his meetings with Jung, at the Avon conference in 1949, and a number of other things. At Marie-Louise's request, he told us once again about the event of which he had spoken to us two years ago. One of his friends was near death. Surrounded by his family (two of his boys were doctors) and his physician. He went into a coma. The physician asked the children with his eyes if he could give an injection to the heart. He gave the injection and the man regained consciousness. He lived another week. Father Bruno saw him every day. He was perfectly lucid, his memory unimpaired, but he always repeated the same thing: I don't know where I am. I don't *feel* at home, in my world, in the world. I recognize the family, the room—and yet I don't know where I am.

ASCONA, *2 August*

In the afternoon we went to Casa Gabriella to see Olga. We had telephoned her in the morning and she had told us that she felt very bad. (We knew from her latest letters that she had been keeping to her bed for several months.) The emotion with which we climbed the steps of Casa Gabriella; it's the first time in ten years that we've come to Ascona without staying here. Olga looked better to us than we dared to imagine. At least that's the impression her appearance gave. Her face calm, her eyes lively. Even her voice surprised us. Olga was stretched out in her bed, without moving, not even her head. Among a thousand other things, she is suffering from a generalized arthrosis. She is allergic to the classical treatments. Cortisone, for example, has no positive effect on her. Each evening a nurse comes to sleep next to her. She can't take a single step alone. She is too thin. (Her bones can be made out through the thin bedcover.)

It was a great mistake, she told us, to give up Eranos to Corti, a mistake that she paid for by this illness for nearly two years. But now she has paid and thinks that everything is going to improve. Jung, Neumann, Dr. Katzenbach—these three deaths, she said, would defend and protect her. And she quoted an English proverb: One should be afraid of two deaths, but if a third friend dies, you can be sure of being saved. Olga doesn't doubt that she has been saved, and she even thinks she'll be able to get up when the Eranos lectures open. But the women who are taking care of her are rather pessimistic. Olga often loses her senses, not knowing what she says or what is said to her. As usual, she is taking considerable medication.

We asked her how the visit of the Zuckerkandls went this winter, when they lived in the Eranos villa for four weeks. Mme. Z., Olga told us, is "extremely old" and talks without stopping. She never leaves her husband, not even for a few minutes. The reason, according to Olga, is that Mme. Z. lost four men—fiancés, lovers, husbands?—one after the other in a bizarre way: she would be speaking with the man, he would leave, and a short time afterward she would learn that he had been killed in an accident. Now she no longer lets her husband get away from her.

ABANO, *23 August*

Alexandrina Mititelu telephoned me back at midnight. She didn't want to tell us last night. She learned from Mircea Popesco that Herescu died a few days ago in a Swiss clinic.

I am prostrate. More than overwhelmed with pain. All of a sudden I'm measuring the importance of Herescu's friendship for me. I feel myself struck in the depths of my being. With him, I am losing the last companion of my youth, from the exile in Lisbon and Paris. The last witness of a quarter-century of our lives.

24 August

I'll never forget how he was when I saw him again in Lisbon, during the summer of 1944: tall, young, handsome. He had just escaped with his wife and his daughter, and an overcoat under his arm, from the bombardment of the German airport where they had stopped. All his luggage had burned—not only his best clothes, but all his money, his manuscripts, and the notes he wanted to save. He was smiling, laughing, happy to return to Portugal—and peace. After all he had seen in Germany he had become, he told me, the most sincere "humanitarian" and pacifist. He had lost everything—and he never complained.

His extraordinary discretion. No one ever knew how very little money he had. There were days, Tantzi was to tell me later, around 1954–1955, when they had only bread. Not even enough to buy themselves two eggs.

He made a religion of friendship. For his friends he would sacrifice everything: his money, his time, his tranquillity.

26 August

N. I. H. has died of an infarct in a clinic near Zurich. Tantzi and Ioana were present. He was buried in a village cemetery.

I had seen him for the last time on the twelfth or thirteenth of July. He seemed unchanged to me. As was his habit, when he spoke, he was looking at himself in the mirror and smiling at himself. Just as we were about to leave him, he took us both by the waist and told us something that made us laugh very much.

VENICE, *7 September*

At an itinerant bookseller's in Piazza SS. Apostoli I found Papini's *L'altra metà*. A shiver ran through me when I noticed the brick-colored cover, the title written in that well-known type that lets you recognize among a hundred others that it's a book by Papini. I bought it, but I didn't dare read anything but the preface to the fourth edition, written a few years after his conversion. *L'altra metà* is one of the rare books by Papini that I haven't reread, for fear of being disappointed. I discovered this book around 1924–1925. With what emotion I would read it in my garret, anguished at the idea of finishing it too quickly, and before having grasped it all, because I was absorbing page after page like a man athirst. . . . And then, with a great effort, I would interrupt my reading. I would walk up and down in front of the bookshelves of my library, and I would open other books at random. I would let a quarter of an hour go by, perhaps a little more. I would return to my study and go back to the rough, aggressive prose that so delighted me at that time. "Voi altri economi e santi compratori di felicità al minuto, che tremate a ogni malesserre e campate a forza di anestetici e di calmanti . . . !"

PARIS, *23 September*

I read in an afternoon newspaper a review of the International Conference in Aix-en-Provence "on high-energy particles." I am fascinated by this new category of nuclear particles or, as the writer put it, "physical beings whose lives are only one ten-thousandth of a billionth of a billionth of a second. It's a case of 'resonating states' which are transitorily established between two particles. In interacting, two particles seem to create a complex particle; their mutual resonating, in any case, causes a state to appear which is defined by characteristics similar to those that are classically applied to particles."

With what interest an Indian thinker would have read those lines! It is the most pregnant description possible of the transitory character of the cosmos. These "resonating states" which have a "life" of only a billionth of a billionth of a second—and which nevertheless *exist* in this unthinkable and unimaginable temporal fragment—represent for the Indian the exemplary archetype of all existence in time.

28 September

Politics, "history"—as they say today—doesn't interest me because all the problems discussed day after day seem to me already resolved. Naturally, there are still men who don't know or who don't want to know that the problems of freedom, social justice, economic planning, etc., have been resolved and that their solutions are irreversible. But what sense would it make to devote your energy and your intelligence to convincing them? It's as though, in the eighteenth century, you had struggled for the triumph of heliocentricism because in the seminaries certain priests continued to support geocentricism.

4 October

Visited Gabriel Marcel. He's leaving in two months for Harvard. Cioran told him that I lived nearby, so he asked me to drop in to see him "for a little conversation." It's about his lecture on "The Sacred in the Technical Age." He summarized it for me and asked me what I thought of it. So I spoke to him about the survival of symbols in camouflaged and deteriorated forms in modern times. If "diurnal man" is desacralized, "nocturnal man" still has a relationship with the zones of mystery. Etc., etc. (see any one of my recent studies on these problems). G. M. likes the terminology of "diurnal man" and "nocturnal man" very much. (Not long ago he was saying "vertical man.") He refused to use "conscious"–"unconscious" because these terms can mean anything today.

6 October

Since I arrived in Paris, there isn't a day that goes by that I don't window-shop in the bookstores. Sometimes I even go in to look through the shelves of books on display. And bit by bit I'm feeling a profound distaste for literature. I don't really know what its origin is. Is it the enormous number of books that are appearing, the thousands of novels translated from every language, and somewhat at random (for Eça de Queiroz, Pío Baroja, Rebreanu, etc., are still unknown)? Complete anarchy, chaos. And the artificial production of "the new wave." This too: a novel no longer interests the modern critic unless it's difficult, almost unreadable; or unless it illustrates a new theory of the novel or of literature.

One More Autumn

NEW YORK, *13 October*

We arrived yesterday afternoon. We're leaving for Chicago tomorrow night. In the morning to the Metropolitan Museum of Art to see the Chinese Exhibition. Amazed at so much mastery, and at the nobility of the worlds that a Kuan Tung, a Tung Yuan, unveil for me: dizzy, vertical universes, constructed in successive steps, alongside waterfalls, climbing until they are lost in the mountains, beyond the clouds. Splendid artistic images of spiritual ascent. Microcosm—"the world in miniature": you enter into the landscape, you discover a cavern, or a path, and you set out on your way.

CHICAGO, *29 October*

Has anyone noticed the resemblance between allegorical thought and psychoanalysis? With the help of allegory or of psychoanalysis, you *see* what *is not* apparent.

Eric Heller was telling us about the depressing impression that he got at a conference of microphysicists he attended last summer. These scientists find no meaning in the creation or in existence. Life, according to them, is nothing but simple randomness. Hence, according to Heller, their unconscious desire to put an end to life on earth; they feel guilty for having reached this point, for having completely "demystified" the whole creation, and they want to expiate their sin by destroying the world with a few superbombs. If nothing has any meaning, it's just as well to end it definitively.

5 November

The Alexandrianism of current literature and criticism. The passion critics bring to making distinctions, deciphering symbols, clarifying obscurities, identifying learned allusions. Whence the fascination for the work of James Joyce. That's why they so enthusiastically discuss the "new novel." It's a *new* way of showing off one's learning. But it's obvious that no contemporary critic would acknowledge such a portrait: on the contrary, they fancy themselves antischolars, because they believe they are enthusiastic over theoretical problems.

19 November

Some day, in a long article, I would like to analyze the attitude of historicists of all kinds, such as that of Marxists and Freudians—in a word, all those who believe that one can understand culture only by reducing it to something lower (sexuality, economics, history, etc.) —and to show that theirs is a neurotic attitude. The neuropath loses the sense of reality. He can no longer grasp a reality that is of the order of the mind (let us say art or religion), and it seems to him to be pure construction, a mask. The neuropath demystifies life, culture, the spiritual life. Not that the neurosis puts more perfect instruments of knowledge at his disposal than those of the normal man—but because the neurotic can no longer grasp the deep meaning of things, and consequently, he can no longer believe in their *reality*.

21 November

I imagine that the information is correct. I read it in *Christianity Today* (VI, no. 4, p. 31). On the occasion of the Twenty-third Congress of the Communist party, Darya Lazunkina made these avowals: imprisoned by Stalin for nearly twenty years, she was able

to survive only thanks to her spiritualistic conversations with Lenin.
But a short time ago, Lenin told her that he didn't like sharing the
mausoleum with Stalin. Here are her own words: "I still have Lenin
with me and I ask him what I ought to do. Yesterday, I again appealed
to him; he seemed to be before me as though he were alive, and he
told me: 'It's unpleasant for me to be alongside Stalin, who did so
much damage to the Party.' "

24 November

Still quite astonished by the case of Darya Lazunkina. I cannot
understand how the Soviets—materialists, positivists, etc., etc.—gave
publicity to a spiritualistic experience. The rest doesn't surprise me:
I noticed long ago that spiritualism is the "spiritual" compensation
that positivism allows itself. When one can no longer *believe* (in the
Judeo-Christian sense of the term), one needs *concrete proofs* of the
survival of the soul; it is on the basis of these "experimental" proofs
that an afterlife is constructed—with its structures and its hierarchies
—just as theologies are constructed (in a monotheistic climate) on the
basis of a few prophetic revelations and mystical experiences.

27 November

Not too long ago, I wanted to write an article for the *N.R.F.*:
"Hydrogen, Cobalt, and the Old Testament." I would have tried to
show that the "death" of which God speaks in connection with the
tree of knowledge refers to the death of the *species*—not of individuals. Today, I'm thinking of this detail: *here* too, I mean in this eventual catastrophic disappearance of humanity, the Jews were the pre-
cursors. The millions of Jews killed or burned in the Nazi
concentration camps constitute the avant-garde of humanity which is
waiting to be incinerated by the will of "History." Cosmic cataclysms
(floods, earthquakes, fires) are also known in other religions. The
cataclysm provoked by man, as a *historical being,* is the contribution
of our civilization. The destruction, it is true, will be possible only
thanks to the extraordinary development of Western science. But the
cause or *pretext* of the cataclysm is found in man's decision to "make

history." Now, one must remember, "History" is the creation of the Judeo-Christian tradition.

2 December

I don't know what made me take Sir Charles Sherrington's book *Man and His Nature* from the bookshelf today. I leafed through the last chapter and came across the extraordinary description of the plasmodium, the hematozoal parasite: how it penetrates into the red corpuscles, feeds off them, destroys them, multiplies itself, and then prepares for sexual reproduction. What a prodigious adventure! Impossible to sum up in a few lines what fabulous operations the sexed plasmodium must undertake to meet his or her partner. And, yet, all these operations finally succeed—and a third of the population of the globe suffers today from malaria. In India alone, 1,200,000 persons are dying from this disease. And how many other hundreds of millions on the earth are reduced to impotence, threatened with a slow death.

I suddenly "saw" the beginning of a play which made me shudder. On the stage a few patients attacked by malaria—not in our time, but in the near future, when men will have discovered that their true mission on earth, their *reason for being*, consists in nourishing infinitesimal bacillae-parasites, like the plasmodium. The patients await their crisis—this intermittent fever which manifests itself every three days, when a quadrillion red corpuscles explode and throw ten times the number of fresh parasites into the blood. During the waiting, each patient tries to describe his Master: he shows that it is infinitesimal, explains what the parasite does camouflaged in the red blood cells, etc. One of them theologizes, showing that man is predestined by the "infinitely small," and explains the fantastic progress this theory represents over the old-fashioned ideologies about human dependence on a macrocosm, which fed on the absurd hypothesis of an "infinitely great."

At the end of a few minutes, terrified, I broke off the vision of this scene. I have rarely known so desperate a conception of existence. By comparison, the absurd of the existentialists seems to me idyllic.

5 December

Why don't I speak more often about the Americans in these notebooks? I wondered about it leafing through last year's notebooks. Because Americans are interesting only when they do theology. Otherwise their intelligentsia is banal; they imitate Saint-Germain-des-Près of ten or twelve years ago. To know them well and understand them, it is necessary to remember what was happening and being thought in Paris around 1947–1948.

6 December

In Julien Green's *Journal* I found the four rules of life on which Nathaniel Hawthorne had settled. The fourth was, "To do nothing against one's genius." As Cioran would say, this man *has understood*. . . .

10 December

At Rockefeller Chapel, the *Christmas Oratorio* by Bach. If I had understood thirty or forty years ago the lesson of music! Classical music does not describe events; it doesn't even give their atmosphere. Nothing tragic, pathetic, or even dramatic in the melodies which accompany the burning words of prophets and evangelists. Miracles, tragedies occur—but the music of Bach unfolds itself in conformity with its own universe, which has nothing to do with the epic, religious, or moral universe of the subject. The music of Bach is perfectly *free*. It's from romanticism onward that music is concerned with "local color," with psychological or historical "authenticity."

16 December

Here's what James Redfield says about Athenian comedy: its bold sacrileges, its amoralism, etc., must be understood as liberties permitted in *dreams*. Through comedy, Athenian society succeeded in relieving certain obsessions, in violating the taboos, just as an individual can balance his daytime existence thanks to the excesses and liberties to which he gives a free rein in his dreams.

17 December

One of my students, William A. Lyell, a Sinologist, as his term's work for the course on myth, gave me the translation and commentary of the famous text of Han Yü (A.D. 768–824), entitled "Letter to the Crocodile." In 819, Han Yü was sent by the Emperor as a magistrate to Ch'ao Chou (the present Kwantung). In reality it was an exile because, in a report, Yü had advised the Emperor not to partake in the ceremonial reception of one of the Buddha's teeth (Yü was a convinced Confucian). Having reached Ch'ao Chou, Han Yü wanted to be informed about the situation in the region. He was told that the crocodiles, multiplying beyond measure, were devouring the domestic animals and that the population was seriously diminished. Han Yü brought a group of officials and subjects to the edge of the river to sacrifice a sheep and a pig, then he read aloud the "Letter to the Crocodile" and burned it. The legend claims that a terrible storm ravaged the region that night, and in the morning the crocodiles had disappeared.

The "Letter" is fascinating. Han Yü reminds the crocodiles that there now exists a true Emperor, the Son of Heaven (in other words, that the age of anarchy and confusion which allowed the crocodiles to multiply has come to an end: a new cosmos has replaced the chaos which preceded it). He also says, "Crocodile, you cannot live in this region along with the Magistrate. . . . If the crocodile is wise he will heed the words of the Magistrate." Han Yü advises the crocodiles to withdraw into the south sea of the province. He accords them a grace period of three days to evacuate the river. If they can't do it in three days, he will give them five days, and even seven—no more. "In the eventuality that the crocodile should arrogantly disdain the representative of the Son of Heaven; or if he does not obey his injunctions; or if he does not move, no more to be seen; or if he continues to be confused and stupid and to attack men, then he must know that each of his crimes deserves the penalty of death." Han Yü threatens to exterminate the crocodiles by shooting them with poisoned arrows. And the magistrate concludes: "Crocodile, beware, don't give yourself cause for regret!"

20 December

Fascinated by the secret meaning of the American suburb. Those charming little houses, each having its garden and its lawn, located ten or twenty kilometers from the center of the city. Since everybody, or almost everybody, in America works, that implies long car trips or hours spent in the train in the morning and, again, in the evening. And why all that? To get back the lost paradise of the pioneers, or nature—but also to defend themselves against racial integration, to recover the obvious prestige of the landowner, etc., etc.

The terrible sadness which is revealed in this slogan: "Return to nature." The guilt complex: we Americans have betrayed our forefathers ("the pioneers"), we have destroyed "nature," we have believed too much in skyscrapers and reinforced concrete. Whence all our difficulties and disappointments. But if we return once again to the source, everything can once again become as *in illo tempore....*

22 December

A few days ago, I finished reading *The City and the Stars,* by Arthur Clarke. I've never been able to read a science-fiction novel, but it seemed to me that I *ought* to read that one, because it's a masterpiece. The action takes place a billion years after the catastrophic wars that put an end to man's domination over the whole solar system. A billion years after man has been thrown back onto the earth, in circumstances so terrible that he has since decided never again to leave it. Reading the early chapters, I was a little depressed. This improbable "humanity" whose structures—anatomical, physiological, mental—had been fixed once and for all according to indestructible models, kept by some electronic brain, this humanity had thus managed to conquer not only longevity (a normal existence lasted about fifteen hundred years) but even a sort of immortality: souls were reincarnated at certain intervals and progressively recovered all the memories of past existences (memories kept in a "Memory Bank"). I have never felt more heavily the weight of arrested time; it is actually an eternal return.

The novel is not without merits. I read it with a growing interest:

I wanted to verify in what measure the universes imagined by the author corresponded to symbolic archetypal structures. And then this extratemporal world is abruptly thrown into all sorts of crises, solely because a single inhabitant refused to accept it as an absolute principle.

26 December

Burton Feldman gave me *Religion of a Scientist,* a selection from the works of Gustave Th. Fechner, translated and commented on by Walter Lowrie.

I remember the mortal boredom I felt, in the distant past of my student life, when I tried to read Fechner's *Zend-Avesta.* I don't think I got past the book's halfway point. And I haven't read it since. And, yet, six or seven years ago, Henry Corbin spoke to me enthusiastically about Fechner's angelology; he was especially intrigued by everything Fechner wrote on "the Angel (of the planet) Earth."

It's only just now that I've learned certain details on Fechner's bizarre illness. Around the age of forty, after an extraordinary activity as a scholar, teacher, and writer, Fechner became blind. For three years a blind invalid, unable to digest the least bit of food, to sleep, and even to think (he couldn't even follow his wife's reading, and he quickly gave up readings done aloud); he survived by I don't know what miracle. He became almost a skeleton. And, at a certain point, a woman friend of the family *dreamed* of a food made from raw meat, minced and soaked in Rhine wine, lemon juice, and aromatic herbs. To everyone's astonishment, Fechner managed to digest it. Little by little, he regained his strength. And one day he recovered his sight and his intellect. He lived about another forty years, and wrote a whole shelf of books.

Naturally I must read the biography written by his nephew, who was beside him (and kept a journal!), and especially what Fechner himself wrote about that mysterious illness. But what struck me is its *initiatic character:* blindness, physical torture, mental death (his incapacity to think); endurance, insomnia, and all that lasting for three years (cf. shamanic initiations), and when Fechner recovered light and awareness, he was a changed man. Another personality. Afterward he had much more courage: he finally wrote what he thought about religion and immortality.

1 January 1962

I remember the meetings and conversations with Ortega y Gasset in Portugal, in 1942–1943. I regret not having written them down. The interest aroused on Ortega's part when I told him that for years I wrote articles in newspapers. What you've just told me is very important, he exclaimed. That means that you have the vocation of an authentic philosopher.

4 January

Readings and meditations on the pre-Socratics, Democritus, and the relativism of human experience. For Democritus, everything is a question of the *temporary* combination of atoms. That is, for me, "historical context." (That's why I italicized the word *temporary*.) Democritus anticipates—from a different viewpoint—the relativism of the historicists.

Socrates tried to learn the essence of virtue. Examples of different virtues didn't satisfy him—he asked his interlocutors for a *definition* of virtue. He forced them to observe that the multiplicity of virtues doesn't mean that there doesn't exist an element that is common to all. (I think of my controversies with the historicists, who refuse to accept structures and believe only in the "concrete," isolated and defined by its own historico-cultural context.)

6 January

It's snowing, and the snow is being changed imperceptibly into frozen pellets. Evening is falling. I'm beginning chapter 7 of *Myth and Reality*. I'll be able to talk about the Platonic anamnesis and the gnostics; I'll be able to bring out certain similarities, so far unnoticed, between certain Indian legends (especially the Matsyendranāth and Gorakhnāth cycle) and the gnostic myth (the hymn of the Pearl). I have the feeling that I've perceived some interesting things.

15 January

Yesterday it snowed all day and continued snowing slowly until midnight. Again our neighborhood seems to be a landscape come from another world. The trees and shrubs are laden with snow to such an extent that one is astonished to see the branches resist— and the pale, pure light of the street lamps which seem higher and thinner under the snow. And then, later, after midnight, this supernatural silence.

20 January

Lately I've been reading the French philosophers a great deal: Merleau-Ponty, Jean Wahl, Sartre, Ricoeur, Gabriel Marcel. Pages and pages, often read with interest, but at the end of several hours I close the book and realize that I haven't benefited from it at all. Remarks, nuances, suggestions—yes! But drowned in an interminable, wordy, sticky prose. The detestable influence of phenomenology —especially that of Jaspers and Max Scheler (of the *Ethics*)—on the French philosophical style. Sartre writes "philosophy" (a "philosophical work") as if he were writing a political article or a novel. Without any plan, without controlling his "inspiration," like a faucet that you no longer know how to turn off. The obsession of contemporary philosophers (this is also an influence of phenomenology): to grasp "the concrete" with the greatest precision possible. Whence these interminable descriptions and analyses. Philosophers behave today like "writers": as close as possible to "life," and all full of the "concrete."

What is even funnier: "writers" imitate philosophical style (or what seems to them to be that style): pretentious, technical vocabulary, a passion for the abstract, a horror of *facilité,* that is, of intelligibility and of narration (the *bête noire* of the post-Joycean novel is narration: if you write a novel which tells a story, and if you write it in an intelligible way—it can't be a good novel!).

23 January

Zwi Werblowski wrote me recently that messianisms feed on historical events; he even wondered if Judaism will survive, now that there is an Israeli State; and if religion would not be ultimately an aspect of "society." For example, Judaism desacralized would become the Israeli State and people.

These remarks don't bother me. I say to myself: If, due to one's desiring a woman, one begins to live more intensely, if one becomes a poet, or if one rises to a level inaccessible up to then, etc.—it is a matter of indifference to know that all this is due to physiological or psycho-mental processes. What is of interest is to be able to rise to a level never attained, to live as a mature and responsible man, to write poems, in a word, to participate in the life of the Spirit. The "causes" which have helped us to open ourselves to the Spirit are unimportant. It doesn't matter to me to know what path you took to climb to the top of a mountain, from where one *sees* a landscape invisible from the plain. Nor does it matter to know whether you came to the concert by subway, taxi, or on foot. The only important facts are being in that hall and listening to Bach or Bartók, and that this encounter with a musical genius opens you to the Spirit and, indirectly, changes your life.

25 January

In *La Tribune de Genève* of 6 January, a report from Liverpool carries this headline: "Was a Young Woman Sacrificed to the God Tiki?" The woman, aged twenty-seven, was killed with fourteen knife wounds. It could be, according to the suspicions of the police, a sacrifice in honor of Tiki, the Polynesian divinity of fertility. The woman was killed two days before the full moon. "The full moon is the period of ritual sacrifices for the adherents of the God Tiki, whose cult, transplanted by Polynesian emigrants to the great industrial port of Lancashire, is supposedly practiced by numerous intellectuals and academics of the area." The police are looking in the city library and the bookstores for "all the works treating Polynesian religions."

If this information is correct, I am confirmed once again in my conviction that the history of religions, from the Paleolithic age to Gnosticism, is still contemporary for us. No religious behavior, however archaic it may be, is ever definitively abolished. An in-depth crisis, a syncretism inspired by despair, can make any divinity real, whether it be exotic or peripheral.

26 January

In a book on the religious situation in Communist Russia, this quip is found, which has, it seems, become proverbial: "God be praised, God doesn't exist, but, God forbid, what if God exists anyway?"

In the latest issue of *Christianity Today,* on a half-page, two photos —a young man and a young woman smiling, happy, glamorous—and the advertisement for a "new way to make money," for pastors, teachers, "evangelists," and "housewives." Here's how it begins: "New! Opportunities unlimited *for Christians to serve the Lord and make more money. . . .*" I prefer the Russian quip.

28 January

The child whom Marcel Proust meets on the Champs-Élysées, where he had gone with Gilberte Swann to buy something, and who was crying, "I like the other plum better because it has a worm" (Pléiade, I, 402). Obviously it wasn't the fruit that interested him (he had eaten so many plums)—it was *the spectacle* that fascinated him: that "living" fruit, transformed into a sort of stage, with a single character, a mysterious, disgusting character, but full of mystery and unforeseeable possibilities.

30 January

In the contract signed for his tomb, Louis XI specifies that he wants to have the handsomest face possible, young and full—and don't make it bald ("le plus beau visaige que pourrès fere et jeune et plein . . . et ne le faicte point chauve"). Louis XI was right: the face sculpted in the stone should correspond not to his earthly person, at a certain age, but to the form that he would have at the resurrection of the dead. It was not a portrait, but a paradigmatic figure: that is how bodies should appear at the Resurrection; they will be Jesus' age and, in a certain sense, they too will be transfigured. Louis XI wanted to anticipate and see the face that he knew he would have on the day of the Resurrection of the Dead.

31 January

The images and associations used by Marcel Proust, when he tried to situate his love for Gilberte within the perspective of the renewal of time at New Year's, should be analyzed. "I suddenly felt a presentiment that New Year's Day was not a day different from the rest, that it was not the first day of a new world, in which I might, by a chance that had never yet occurred, that was still intact, make Gilberte's acquaintance afresh, as at the Creation of the World, as though the past had no longer any existence, as though there had been obliterated, with the indications which I might have preserved for my future guidance, the disappointments which she has sometimes brought me; a new world in which nothing should subsist from the old—save one thing, my desire that Gilberte should love me. I realized that if my heart hoped for such a reconstruction, round about it, of a universe that had not satisfied it before, it was because my heart had not altered. . . ." [*Within a Budding Grove*] The text seems confused because Proust was attracted concomitantly by two intuitions of time: irreversible duration (which he could not give up because it was connected with Gilberte) and the cyclical regeneration of time proclaimed at the beginning of a new year, which he desired in the depths of his heart ("if my heart hoped for such a reconstruction, round about it, of a universe that had not satisfied it . . .").

What is astonishing is that Marcel Proust uses the images and expressions that had been dictated to me by the behavior of archaic man studied in *The Myth of the Eternal Return:* "new world," "destroyed," "renewal" of the "universe," "a new world in which nothing remained of the old."

2 February

I'm reading with a great deal of interest the letters written in prison by Dietrich Bonhoeffer *(Letters and Papers from Prison)*. I have finally encountered a theologian who accepts the evidence: the modern world, says D. B., has "come of age"; it no longer has any need of God's supervision; contemporary "areligiosity" is a sign of maturity, man has definitively left adolescence behind, and, adds Bonhoeffer, it would be ignoble on the part of theologians to take advantage of modern man's moments of weakness to bring him back to the faith of the adolescent. The Christians of today and, in fact, all men must live *etsi Deus non daretur,* "as if God were not presupposed." (This expression returns often to D. B.'s writing, especially from the time that he knows that his days are numbered.) The radical secularization of life must not be done *against* Christianity but *in its name.* Christians have the duty of accepting and taking this secularization upon themselves. But then, in what would their "religiosity" consist? Here is B.'s answer: "To participate in the suffering of God in a world without God."

In summary: humanity come of age renounces God; in such a world, God suffers, undergoes innumerable humiliations; the only authentic experience of Christianity (but of Christianity only?) would be to participate in this suffering.

Bonhoeffer's desperate attempt to find a religious significance in everything which is "natural, "profane," "rational." To be compared with my reflections in *The Sacred and the Profane* on "the second fall" of man. The religious life of modern man, I said, is now "unconscious." The unconscious alone is still "religious."

4 February.

Today the end of the world was to have taken place according to the forecasts of Hindu astrologers. But someone showed me a newspaper in which I read this item: following the fervent prayers of men, the world will not end today. The astronomical crisis that the earth has just gone through, on the contrary, marks a new birth. From today on, we are entering into a new world: fresh, pure, luminous.

What a strange impression to see enacted before your eyes, *today,* the religious conduct, fears, and beliefs of the archaic societies that you have studied all your life.

5 February

I don't read the *Observer,* so I wasn't able to know, in 1956, about Christopher Mayhew's article "An Excursion out of Time" (October 28). I came across it in the anthology edited by David Evin, *The Drug Experience* (New York, 1961, pp. 294–300). It's excellent. He describes his experience with mescaline, but in an intelligent way; he makes an effort to present and explain what *can be* intelligible, he rejects nuances and *sfumature.* The decisive experience is the following: on Friday, 2 December 1955, between half-past noon and four in the evening, Mayhew lived outside time. No use summarizing this prodigious document. But in reading it I trembled with joy—because in so many of my studies and even in certain of my short stories ("Nuits à Serampore," "12,000 têtes de bétail," etc.) I had spoken of the possibility of abolishing time, and of putting oneself into a trans-temporal condition. What delights me in Mayhew's experience is that it helps us to understand ecstatic situations (mystical ones, post-mortem, etc.) in which time is left behind. I have no doubt that these experiences could succeed even without drugs. Otherwise I would not be able to explain why the "exist from time" motif is so constant throughout the history of religions and the different mystical doc-trines, and even in popular literature or folklore. I believe that similar ecstatic experiences base all their conceptions on the abolition of time. These are not aberrant or peripheral experiences without interest for everyday man. On the contrary, I would say that there exists in the soul of each one of us a secret longing for this sort of ecstasy. One satisfies it as well as one can by dreams, fantasies, literature. This *imaginary* satisfaction does not mean that these ecstasies are not an integral part of our mode of being in the world (cf. what I wrote on "Symbolisms of Ascension" in *Myths, Dreams, and Mysteries*).

11 February

I took Seneca's tragedies out of the library; I don't remember ever having read them (at least in their entirety). I wanted to become familiar with the atmosphere in which Shakespeare lived and wrote. "The End of the World" announced by Seneca is the same as that predicted in the Iranian and Hindu apocalypses, the same as in the Scandinavian *ragnarök*, or in the primitive eschatological myths. The poles of the earth (North and South) will collapse. The sun will fall from heaven, giving way to the reign of darkness—"and all the gods will perish and fall in the general chaos" (*Atque omnes pariter Deos Perdet mors aliqua, et Chaos; Hercules oetaeus,* Act III, 11, verses 1114–1115). The motif returns at the end of Act IV of *Thyestes* (verse 821 sq.): men live in the fear that "the entire Universe will be broken into a thousand pieces in the general ruin, that chaos will return and will vanquish the gods and men, that the Earth and Sea will be engulfed by the Planets wandering in the Heavens. . . ." Then, this cry: "Of all the generations, it is we who have been designated to merit this fate, to be crushed by the falling pieces of the broken sky."

That could also be our cry—but, in our time, no one would any longer dare shout it on a stage. We are paralyzed because we are missing the meaning of the end of the world. Like Seneca, the men of today believe that "after death there is nothing—that death itself is nothing" (*Post mortem nihil est, ipsaque mors nihil . . .; Troades,* Act II, verse 398).

18 February

Today, while leafing through my notes taken a few years ago, I came across the summary of an article, "Comment peut-on rester Polynésien?" dated 25 March 1958. I had conceived this article after having spent several weeks reviewing the materials on Polynesian religions, depressed by the opaque, frustrated mentality of the Protestant missionaries in Polynesia. The encounter, and the conflict, between the pagan concept of religion, understood as an uninterrupted feast, and Bostonian Puritanism, could have risen to the level of a tragedy. But almost no one in the second half of the last century felt the grandeur of Polynesian "paganism." There was no tragic confrontation between two religious visions of existence—but calumny, persecution, vengeance, down to the final destruction of this "orgiastic, immoral paganism."

21 February

One of the paradoxes of our time: efforts are made to structure and express a conception of man which, on the one hand, brings out the *authenticity* of the individual and which, on the other, is *democratic*—which therefore fits all men. A desperate attempt to find in the mass of ordinary people the qualities of a small number.

23 February

Delighted to find in Leonardo the old myth of the anthropomorphic earth, the myth of Purusha in Vedic India, of P'anku in China, the Germanic Ymir, etc. I don't have the original edition within reach, and I'm copying from Edward MacCurdy, *The Notebook of L.d.V.* (1938), Volume I, p. 91: "So then we may say that the earth has a spirit of growth; that its flesh is the soil: its bones are the successive strata of the rocks which form the mountains; its muscles are the tufa stone; its blood, the springs of its water. The lake of blood that lies about its heart is the ocean" (R. 1000 ms Leic. fol. 34 r.). It would be interesting to specify in what measure this image is spontaneous, or if it is dependent on something he read in his youth. But Leonardo was not a scholar. Moreover, he would have retained the comparison between the earth and the human body, if he had read it in a book, only to the extent that it corresponded to his own scientific conceptions. Leonardo was not a mystic, but a scientist of genius; he not only had a great faculty of observation, but also of imagination; he saw structures, wholes.

26 February

In the fifth century, certain exegetes made a great effort to render "the impossible" at least a little bit possible. In *Tractatus de divitiis* we are told that *camellus* means not only "camel" but also a rope similar to that used by sailors. In other words, there would be the possibility that a *camellus* could pass through the eye of a needle.

Excellent example of what can come from the rationalization of an image or a symbol. One begins by taking the image *ad litteram*—then one makes an effort to show that, ultimately, it's not so absurd as it seems at first glance. An image seems absurd when one takes it in the literal sense. The camel that passes through the eye of a needle should not constitute an impossibility for the one who believes that "all things are possible with God" (Mark 10:27 and 14:36), and that "what is impossible with men is possible with God" (Luke 18:27).

1 March

Sa'îd 'Aql, the well-known Lebanese poet, writes in the Introduction to his tragedy in verse, *Qadmūs* (ed. II, Beirut, 1947, p. 22), "Six thousand years of patience, thought, contempt for the material self-denial, aspiration, and careful examination of each point before accepting the whole have led us to (become the custodians of) this mission—a unique mission which qualifies us to 'Lebanize' the world."

A splendid example of cultural provincialism. I remember the Portuguese patriots who wanted to introduce the Lusitanian dimension into universal culture. Or V. H., who, in one of the articles written in his youth, defined the mission of the Rumanian writer in approximately these terms: to inject the azure of the Rumanian sky into European culture.

When certain great Englishmen or Frenchmen in the seventeenth and eighteenth centuries began to speak of *civilization,* as a true ideal of modern man, they proposed to "civilize" the world, not to Gallicize or Anglicize it. It is evident that the civilization they represented or conveyed was French and English, but that was not the criterion of their appreciation. Those men believed in civilization because they esteemed it *universally valid,* and as a creation of the *European* mind.

16 March

Yesterday afternoon a Japanese student came for a work session. I was surprised to see her wearing a black hat and a leather coat, also black. She sat down in an armchair and, after a few embarrassed gestures and with an equally constrained smile, she told me that after having left my class that morning, she found a letter at home informing her that her father had died on the eighth of March. She kept smiling, but the tears were running down her face and she was drying them timidly with her hand. Her father was seventy-six and had been seriously wounded during the war. But she didn't expect this news. He died suddenly.

After five minutes, she took out the manuscript from her briefcase and began to read. She would stop often to ask me questions. She is preparing a thesis on the funeral beliefs and customs of Shintoist Japan.

20 March

In St. John's Gospel (14:26), Jesus announces to the disciples that after the resurrection, the Holy Spirit "will teach you all things, and bring to your remembrance all that I have said to you." Memory will function due to the Holy Spirit and under his control. The decisive importance of memory: those who *have seen* and *heard* the Savior will be witnesses: that is why it is necessary that they forget nothing.

23 March

The history of religions gathers and preserves the mythico-religious traditions, currently disappearing *throughout* the world, already understood with difficulty—or understood the wrong way—even by those who still have them. This mysterious and absurd discipline which is the "History of Religions" could have a royal function: the "scientific" publications constitute a reservoir where all the values and traditional religious models could be *camouflaged*. That is why I always make an effort to put forward *the meaning* of religious facts. The meaning is no longer obvious; it must be established by exegesis

5 March

Dr. Hsu read a paper today in my seminar. He is small, shrunken, rather bowed, his legs half-paralyzed, and one wonders how he manages to write.

He presented and commented on a neo-Taoist text of the tenth century, of which the title, translated approximately, would be *The Sacred and Precious Matter of Accomplishment.* It was fascinating. It begins with the well-known homologies of body-cosmos and annual-daily temporal cycle (morning = spring, etc.) and the specific mystical physiology of neo-Taoism and alchemy (the inner "fields" of the body, "the respirations," etc.). What particularly interested me was the technique of the creation and growth of the "secret embryo" in the lower "field." After the appearance of this embryo, the adept must conduct himself like a girl. At the end of three hundred days the embryo becomes a sort of golden kernel (orange color). And at that point, it has three possibilities of development: the adept can obtain (1) perfect health; (2) longevity (earthly "immortality"); or (3) immortality in heaven. When he is on the point of obtaining earthly immortality, he dreams that he is carrying a child on his back—or that he can fly. With the saliva that he swallows during certain exercises, he washes "the immortal embryo." There is also a whole series of semiyogic practices that I'll pass over here. I come to the final result: the adept can rise in the air and abandon his physical body. He has a new body, a spiritual one, which looks like a child; his true body resembles a mummy, the skin aged and wrinkled. Settled into his new spiritual body, the adept can withdraw to one of the mythical isles or can rise to heaven. But, for a certain length of time, he keeps his former body, which he can visit at irregular intervals. Finally he settles definitively into the spiritual body.

Note that freedom is conquered neither by going beyond psychosomatic conditionings (as in India) nor by the regeneration of the body —but by the creation and perfectioning of *a second body* of a spiritual nature.

and comparison. And if our generation does not record (in the "scientific" publications) the meanings of religious phenomena, this operation will become almost impossible for future generations.

27 March

Impressed by the immense critical success—and public success, for it has surpassed sixty thousand copies—of *Finnegans Wake*. One of my colleagues affirms that, in the United States alone, ten to fifteen volumes come out per year, in addition to a considerable number of articles, on James Joyce, of which the majority concern *Finnegans Wake*. One of the causes of this frenzy is the extraordinary difficulty of the text. You read the same page ten, twelve times, and certain passages a hundred times, and you reread the book untiringly for several years and then, obviously, *you have to have gotten something* out of this considerable effort. Concentration, detailed attention, reveals to you meanings inaccessible to the ordinary reader. It's like a mechanics of divination via rereading. That's why so many critics and historians of literature exploit Joyce with delight: all that is being required of them is to persevere, to reread, to have patience, to look for "sources." All these people contend—it is obviously in their interest—that *Finnegans Wake* is the most important book that exists. Since they have become specialists on this unique work, they would be ashamed to say that they have wasted their lives studying just an ordinary book.

But there is also something else that seems essential to me: the mythology of *literary difficulty*, that desperate belief that only an unintelligible text could reveal the true situation of man.

Must come back some day, perhaps in an essay, to the art of creating monstrous difficulties (in the hope that the semantic opacity will be able to facilitate the comprehension of the essential).

2 April

How deeply the superstitions of the rationalists of our century are rooted! The famous psychosociological theory of fifty or sixty years ago that claimed that the Australian aborigines had not yet understood the relationship between the sexual act and impregnation; that they explained impregnation by the introduction of an ancestral spirit into the womb of the woman. True, that is the belief of adult Australians (that is, the initiated), but they believe it not because they are incapable of perceiving the causal relationship of sexual act–fecundity, but because they were *taught* to believe in a spiritual paternity. Initiation consists, among other things, in the revelation of this mystery: impregnation of the woman is a spiritual act (the spirit of the ancestor penetrates into the womb of the woman). This is not a case of ignorance of physiology, but of transcending the *natural* knowledge through the revelation of the mystery of spiritual paternity. The proof: children already know that impregnation is the result of sexual relations (they have noticed the causal relation in dogs). In fact, children represent "the natural stage" of knowledge. But through the initiation they *forget*—or transcend—this stage and understand that it is not a case of a natural act, but of a mystery.

13 April

For the first time I'm reading the integral text of Kierkegaard's tract *The Point of View for My Work as an Author*. What he says of his "duplicity": author of aesthetic and moral works in appearance, but in reality an exclusively religious author, camouflaged, a "double agent," for it was the only way for him to make contact with "the individual," with the man in the street. If I wrote some day a similar interpretation of my books, I could show: (a) that there exists a fundamental unity through all my works; (b) that the body of scientific work illustrates my philosophical conception, namely that there exists a profound and significant meaning in everything called "natural religion" and that this meaning directly concerns modern man. S. K. tries to show that Denmark, although "christianized," was not "Christian." Today this is obvious. No point in trying to prove it once again (as so many contemporary theologians do). For me, the important point is elsewhere: modern man, radically secularized, believes himself or styles himself atheist, areligious, or, at least, indifferent. But he is wrong. He has not yet succeeded in abolishing the *homo religi-*

osus that is in him: he has only done away with (if he ever was) the *christianus.* That means that he is left with being "pagan," without knowing it. It also means something else: an areligious society does not yet exist (personally, I believe that it *cannot exist,* and that if it were achieved, it would perish after a few generations from boredom, from neurasthenia, or by a collective suicide . . .).

3 May

Around 1890 the fashion was begun, in distinguished circles in England, of greeting one's friends by the following question: "How is your karma today?"

10 May

Bultmann's "demythologization" corresponds to the absolute domination of nonfigurative art. It is the same style of thought, the same fundamental experience of the world. The "mythology" that annoys Bultmann in the Gospels, the images and symbols which are part of an archaic cosmology, definitively bypassed (says B.) by the scientific discoveries pursued since the Renaissance—all that corresponds to the worn-out, antiquated images which survived, inauthentic, in the academicism of the beginning of the century, and which were to be abolished so that the artist could be confronted with the freshness of a new world, not yet perceived, the world as it was presented on the first day of creation. And what is even more interesting: the artist of today sees only the freshness of the first day of the world—he does not yet see its "face." The time of the epiphany has not yet arrived, or does the world *truly have no face?*

13 May

Fascinated by the biology of parasites. Parasitism is reduced to the radical simplification of the organism. A parasite gives up everything which is "useless"—that is, everything it can acquire via the organs and activity of the being at whose expense it lives.

That is how I would see the extreme specialization of philologists: absolute simplification, the reduction of intellectual work to the sole effort of assimilating the discoveries, the efforts, and the risks *of others,* the creators of culture, artists and philosophers of genius, etc.

23 May

I'm resuming the writing of my little book on myth. I still have to write the end of the last chapter, notably "the survival of mythical behavior" in modern societies. I would like to emphasize the mythological function of literature and, in general, "the exit from historical time" facilitated by the reading of novels.

But several other aspects of the problem will not be brought up. Thus I should have devoted at least several paragraphs to the situation of myth in contemporary Oriental societies. "The Oriental myth" was killed by technology, by the process of Westernization and industrialization. This phenomenon will have incalculable historical consequences. It should be compared with the death of myth in Antiquity. But technology, Western civilization, is the indirect result of Christianity, which replaced the myth in Antiquity. The Orient accepts and assimilates not Christianity, but the most important of its desacralized creations.

ROYAUMONT, 19 June

Dr. Servadio—the Italian psychoanalyst whom I had met here at Royaumont, in May 1956, at a conference on parapsychology—tells me that Freud was interested all his life in occultism. He didn't dare admit it because, he continued, the theory of sexuality was sufficiently "compromising" for him to add the risk of compromising himself with "ghosts." Dr. Servadio cited me the name of an American psychoanalyst who has some letters of Freud on the subject. When this psychoanalyst met Ernest Jones, Freud's biographer, and asked him why he hadn't referred to it, Jones interrupted him with a short gesture: "It is all rubbish."

25 June

In dreams man rediscovers his "ahistoric" existence. In the oneiric universe, "the political" is surpassed or transfigured. Likewise with the sick man; he no longer is confronted with political problems.

To be compared with religious experience: if it is authentic and deep, religion rediscovers the elementary, the fundamental, the primordial, in a word, the "ahistorical."

10 July

I'm reading the manuscript of Ionel Jianou's book on Brancusi. How much I regret now the timidity which prevented me from visiting him in 1945–1950. C.V.G. had gone to see him in 1948, and had spoken to him about my *Yoga* and the years I studied in India. Brancusi had told him that he would like to meet me. I didn't make the venture, and now I regret it. I would have liked to hear him talk about his life, especially about his artistic concepts. A half-literate person who revolutionized modern art! That seems unbelievable. And, yet, if my point of view is accepted—namely, that Brancusi was a peasant who managed to *forget what he had learned in school* and thus rediscovered the spiritual universe of the Neolithic age—this exceptional creativity finds its explanation.

I'm learning all sorts of things in Ionel Jianou's book. I didn't know, for example, that Brancusi defined Wagner's music as "a beefsteak in delirium." He didn't like Michelangelo. He used to say of the *Moses,* "We ought not to be brought to feel like atoms before a work of art."

Some day I must write an article on the "Column of Heaven" in Rumanian folklore and the megalithic concepts of which it is a part, and Brancusi's *Endless Column.* That of Targul-Jiu thirty meters high. It "supports heaven," Brancusi used to say. Thus it is an *axis mundi,* a Cosmic Pillar. What I would like to know is how he managed to rediscover this megalithic concept, which disappeared from the Balkans more than two thousand years ago and survived only in religious folklore.

17 July

Today, on the Place du Trocadéro, an extraordinary old lady; violently made up (1920 style), bleached hair, hat thrust down over her forehead, a dress that came down to her ankles. She walked leaning to one side, and as though broken in two. She would stop in front of the cafés and, with an avidity tinged with irony, she would look at the young couples, the noisy groups. As though, even while drinking in their youth and their beauty, she were flinging at them, "Don't believe that it will last forever. . . ."

ABANO, *4 August*

I'm writing, as I do every year, seated at this little table on the balcony, with a view of the park of the Hotel Megiorato. In front of me, surrounded by giant cedars, a huge magnolia without flowers. It will flower for the second time toward the end of the month.

Where is this sudden feeling of beatitude and serenity coming from? As though I had rediscovered something precious that I had mislaid long ago. I'm looking at the magnolia with fascination and trying to understand what is happening to me. Some sparrows are chirping in the branches. On the top branch, two sparrows are facing each other for an instant. One is moving about, pecking; the other is calm, motionless. Could it be the well-known image of the Upanishads, the Tree of Life with the two birds, one "active," the other "contemplative"? But this theme is more ancient, it is Indo-Iranian (from Iranian iconography it extends into popular European art as much as it does into the traditional ornamentation of Oriental rugs). Moreover, the motif of the tree with the two birds is found in protohistory. I've been intending for a long time to write a study on this archaic symbolism. But why was I so deeply moved by the image of the sparrows on the magnolia? What secret meaning did it unveil, without my knowing it, for the revelation took place in the very depths of my being? I suddenly remember Hindu texts that I haven't thought of for thirty years. I note once again how concrete Hindu speculation was, at its beginnings, indissolubly tied to images and gestures.

VENICE, *20 August*

I saw Verdi's *Otello* in the Cortile of the Palazzo Ducale. Extraordinary impression. The beginning of the first act and the end of the third (the arrival of the dignitaries from Venice) were presented with so much display that the audience burst out in applause. Dimitru Ustinov as Otello and Tito Gobbi in the role of Iago, admirable.

And some inexplicable stupidities—could they be due to the librettist alone? In the last scene of Act III, for example, Iago comes up to the Doge's envoy and greets him: "Messer, son lieto di vedervi." The Doge's envoy replies: "Iago, quali nuove?"

9 September

We're leaving very early in the morning for Treviso, to visit the exhibition of Cima da Conegliano.

Two Italians, rather poorly dressed, are arguing with passion, competence, and precision in front of the *Madonna* from the British Museum. I perceive them as so indifferent to all worldly temptations and superstitions—that I suddenly feel that *all is not yet lost.*

We're having lunch in Louise Lebreton's country house. Giant trees, hundred-year-old poplars—and the little stream that goes through the end of the garden. To be able to stay for a summer month in this house, in the shelter of these great trees, far from the motorbikes and Vespas. After lunch, by car to Asolo. I had no idea that the place could be so beautiful. Browning's villa. The chateau. Then to the cemetery to see the grave of Eleonora Duse.

ASCONA, *15 September*

At Casa Eranos, to have tea with the Ritsemas. Profound sadness. R. told us how the Eranos sessions went. Bettina, Olga's daughter, was there too. In the morning, during the first lecture, a terrible storm. The lightning striking the lake, a few dozen meters from Casa Eranos. Bettina was saying, It's Mama telling me: Go away, leave this area. Olga's funeral urn, hidden in the bushes, behind the rock consecrated to the "genie of the place."

Casa Gabriella will be made over into apartments. The members of the group, and other artists or scholars, will be able to rent these apartments during the year.

16 September

Lunch with Mihalovici and Monique Haas. They told us how Beckett works: he writes without stopping, all day; then he takes scissors, cuts sentences or halves of sentences, and pastes them in a new, artificial order.

In the evening, we met Corinna, Olga's confidante who took care of her up to the end and was at her bedside when she passed away. Olga knew that she was going to die. The last two days, she would take no more shots. On the whole she retained a big appetite. She would no longer receive anyone. Nonetheless, Christina Bühler came to see her a short time before her death. When Olga saw her at the door of her room, she began to cry. It's the only time anyone saw her cry.

PARIS, 1 October

Siegfried told me about his trip to China, five or six years ago. There was also an orchestra of Tzigane musicians in the Soviet airplane. They wouldn't take seats. They sat right on the floor. (I'm not very clear as to how.) Siegfried was accompanied by a Tzigane "artist." When the airplane was flying over Mongolia, the Tzigane, pointing to the desert a few thousand meters beneath, said to him, "If we fell now, we wouldn't find a single tree to hang onto. . . ."

In China, the Tzigane said to him, "What are we doing here under the earth's arse?" And when he saw the Chinese peasants—poor, loaded down with children, buying hot water for tea—the Tzigane burst out in sobs. "They are even poorer than we, comrade," he declared out loud.

12 October

A few days ago, we had dinner at Marie-Louise's with Father Daniélou. Cioran was also there. A conversation on Teilhard de Chardin, brought about especially by Cioran, who is exasperated by Teilhard's naïve and elementary optimism. I agree with Daniélou on this point: Teilhard reacted, quite rightly, against "angelism"; he showed the importance of the Incarnation. We have a body and we are here, on earth; we must therefore accept life as it is, as a natural mode of being. We must also accept "progress"; no use complaining of having been born in an industrial society; we must try to live as *free beings* even in the midst of the most terrible social, technological, psychological conditionings.

But Cioran cannot believe in the intelligence and maturity of someone who talks about what man will be in a million years—when we have so many reasons for doubting that man can yet survive for a few hundred years.

Mythologies, Old and New

CHICAGO, *2 November*

    How the Italian humanists were thirsty for a sacred and very ancient teaching, for a primordial occult tradition, earlier than the Mosaic revelation! The exaltation over "Egyptian Wisdom," as it had been transmitted by the *Corpus Hermeticum,* constitutes in itself a whole mythology. For the primordial Egypt that the Italian humanists found in *Poimandres* in reality only reflected the Hellenistico-Christian syncretism of the second and third centuries of our era. But what is significant is the thirst among the humanists for a primordial revelation which would permit them to welcome Plato and Hermes the Egyptian into the bosom of Christianity.

    When Cosimo de Medici bought the Greek manuscript of the *Corpus Hermeticum* around 1460, he asked Marsilio Ficino to translate it immediately. Ficino had not yet begun translating the manuscripts of Plato and Plotinus that Cosimo had given him. He abandoned them to begin on the *Corpus Hermeticum.* He translated it in a few months, in 1463, just one year before Cosimo's death. It wasn't until afterward that he undertook the translation of Plato's dialogues. The *Corpus Hermeticum* was therefore the first translation done and published by Marsilio Ficino. Old Cosimo insisted on knowing this "revelation" before dying.

These details are generally passed over in silence. And yet the *Corpus Hermeticum* played a considerable role for two centuries. The whole Italian Renaissance was impregnated with hermeticism, occultism, and Egyptianism. When I was studying Giordano Bruno and Campanella in Rome, thirty-four years ago, for my *diplôme de licence,* I wanted, as a matter of fact, to bring out that the hermeticism of the Renaissance ought to be understood as a reaction against medieval rationalism, which sprang from Aristotelianism, and that this passion for occultism and magic reveals the dissatisfaction of the humanists with Christian provincialism and their thirst for a primordial, universal teaching revealed several thousand years before Moses, Pythagoras, and Plato.

All this deserves to be taken up again and elaborated.

6 November

I had a visit from a young girl who is in her last year of high school. Next fall, she is going to the university. She doesn't know which major to choose: literature or philosophy. Because, she admitted to me, she wants to study . . . sorcery, *witchcraft.* She is fascinated by medieval witchcraft. She has read everything she has come across, and she is (unfortunately) taken with the fantastic hypotheses of Margaret Murray. She wants to study witchcraft in the texts and to discover "the secret of the witches." These women who let themselves be burned at the stake without recanting or denouncing had a "great secret." The girl is neither beautiful nor ugly; she has an extremely soft, weak voice, as if she were afraid of losing it if she forced it a little.

7 November

I wanted to read the records of Giordano Bruno's trial. A copy of the whole dossier exists, discovered by Angelo Mercati in the personal archives of Pius IX, and published by him in 1942. But the original has disappeared; this is how: the manuscript was part of the archives taken to Paris by order of Napoleon. And there, these thousands of documents laid around forgotten in some basement, and one day they were sold by the kilo to a paper factory.

8 November

I've received a long letter from a stranger, H. W., who wrote from New York. He studied at the Chicago Divinity School to become a Baptist minister. But a short time afterward, he came to realize that that was not his true religious vocation. "I am convinced that the true problem is not what the world will do with Christ, but what it will do with Aphrodite." Christianity does not respond to the question: how to succeed in divinizing physical and romantic love, and thus, in founding an ethic and an aesthetic of pleasure and of the noble cult of the body. H.W. rejects the Judeo-Christian patriarchal religious tradition. "Why should the concept of a divine Sovereignty based on force and judgment be nobler than the concept of a divine Sovereignty based on love and beauty?"

In his letter, two pages long, he wrote me, among other things, that he has published a book, that he was one of the associates of the founder and priest of the Church of Aphrodite—from whom he later separated. Since he has read my *Yoga* and discovered that sexuality was still sacralizable in Tantrism, he asked me if I couldn't put him in touch with a Tantric yogi. "I am prepared to become the yogi's disciple, but I cannot pay any fees." Moreover, he is sure that the resurrection of the cult of the Goddess will have to take its inspiration from the Near East, rather than from India.

15 November

I'm reading *Le Piéton de l'air* [*A Stroll in the Air*], Eugene Ionesco's last play. I wonder if the scene with the ferocious, masked judges exists, as the little girl persists in thinking, only in the mother's imagination, and if it exists only *because the mother is afraid*—I wonder, therefore, if this scene doesn't derive indirectly from reading the Tibetan Book of the Dead. If Eugene knows this book, it's odd that he guessed its essence. . . .

Even in the pessimistic, tragic end of the play, one can detect a certain "Buddhist" influence. But who spurred Eugene to read and accept such texts? The end contrasts strikingly with Bérenger's optimism at the beginning of the play. To be able "to rise," to be able "to fly"—that is the source of unknown blessedness. Then, Bérenger returns from these transcendent worlds—depressed by what he has seen: the cyclical creation and destruction of the worlds. But that is an Indian, Asiatic vision. I wonder how Eugene was able to arrive at it.

20 November

I'm going to have to think about the lecture that I'm to give at Princeton at the beginning of January. I would like to bring certain symmetries to light: in the age of positivism and until "the death of God" proclaimed by Nietzsche, the Western world discovered (thanks to Orientalists and ethnologists) *the reality of cosmic gods* and *of cosmic religions;* Christianity's decline was accompanied by an "opening" toward other religious forms, archaic and traditional. How did the West defend itself against these discoveries: *by making them banal,* as it had learned to do during the last two centuries (when it had made nature banal in order to be able to know and dominate it).

29 November

I spent the day writing my lecture for Princeton. I've tried to bring out the religious symbolism (obviously unconscious) of the love for nature in the nineteenth century, as well as that of the different "materialistic" ideologies for which everything will be resolved when science has deciphered the enigmas of nature. This thirst for going back to the source of sources, to the beginning of beginnings, to penetrate to the depth of matter and to identify the "seed," the atom from which everything has sprung—is an extension of the thirst of the humanists and philosophers of the Italian Renaissance for the *primordial* and the archaic.

Interesting synchronisms that I noticed since my youth and to which I returned numerous times in my Bucharest classes and in Chicago. This, for example: the phenomenon of mediums is known in the West from the Old Testament onward—but it isn't until around 1850 that spiritism was born, that is, the technique (and ideology) *of proofs* that there exists a life after death; the axiom that these proofs must be *material* (tables which move, noises, "materialized" objects, ghosts which can be photographed, etc.), the establishment of a means of communication with spirits based on numbers and noises. The immortality of the soul was a philosophical problem. Spiritism introduces the criteria of the experimental sciences, to demonstrate the survival of the soul, by physical manifestations. The obsession for tangible proofs, a superstition of scientific origin.

Likewise, how far Mme. Blavatsky is in synchronism with the positivism and evolutionism of the second half of the nineteenth century. She introduces evolution into the allegedly secret Eastern doctrine—when it is known that Indian thought, and Oriental thought in general, rejects the idea of evolution. The messages that the mysterious Mahatmas transmitted "materialized" instantaneously before the eyes of the adepts. It is amazing that these materializations contributed considerably to the conversion of an Olcott or a Leadbeater to theosophy.

2 December

I'm reading the biography of Wittgenstein by Norman Malcolm. The man fascinates me. His hatred of academic life, his scorn for the profession of teaching. And this detail, which brings him even closer to me: W.'s inability (like mine) to prepare a lesson and to read a written text in front of students. Georg Henrik von Wright describes him thus: "He *thought* before the class. The impression was of a tremendous concentration." And Norman Malcolm gives this further detail (in which I recognize myself entirely): "His lectures were given without notes. He told me that once he had tried to lecture from notes but was disgusted with the results; the thoughts that came out were 'stale,' or, as he put it to another friend, the words looked like 'corpses' when he began to read them" (p. 24).

I remember how awful I was when I had to repeat my lectures on Freud and Gandhi; they had been such a success within the framework of the *Criterion* in Bucharest, around 1932–1933, that the several hundred persons who hadn't been able to get into the hall had demonstrated in front of the Carol Foundation, and the organizers had to promise that they would be given again a few days later. I was "inspired," and I had spoken with enormous success. The second and third times, I felt constrained, I had lost my fire. I had the feeling that *I was repeating myself,* that I was no longer authentic. Only the few fragments that I improvised then, the thoughts that I hadn't had the time to develop in the first series, saved me.

7 December

On the thirteenth of July 1511, the Italian humanist Girolamo Aleandro gave an account to a friend, in a letter, of the lessons that he was giving in Paris. He was dealing with Ausonius. There were more than two thousand listeners—rectors, theologians, directors of colleges, professors, councillors, royal lawyers, etc. The lecture lasted two and a half hours, and, writes Aleandro, despite the suffocating heat, nobody seemed tired. On the contrary, when the lecture was over the audience didn't move, as though it were waiting for the rest.

And all that to listen to an Italian humanist talk about a third-rate Latin poet. But that is what the elite of that time were interested in. Just as, in 1945–1946, the young were interested in Sartre's existentialism.

17 December

Reading a letter from Nietzsche to Erwin Rohde of the fourth of August 1871, I learned of the existence of one Otto Ribbeck, professor of philology at Kiel. I must remember this name. It will be of use to me in my discussions with "scholars." Actually, Ribbeck had read *The Origins of Tragedy*—but in a letter to Rohde he had refused to take it seriously, on the pretext that the book wasn't based on "evidence or proofs."

The most amusing side to this story is that Ribbeck was perhaps right, but *in culture* it is Nietzsche who triumphed. It is not the philological mind that was a creator of culture, but divination, pathos, imagination—in a word, *Error* (in capitals and underlined).

3 January 1963

I am continuing my discussions with Tom Altizer. To his objection that I'm not writing the book in which "I hold a dialogue with the representatives of modern consciousness (Nietzsche, Freud, Marx, etc.)," I reply: All these famous authors that Tom admires so are *Westerners*. That is, they attacked problems and crises belonging to modern Western spirituality. Personally, I think that these cultural horizons are provincial. The crises and problematical issues of a Freud, Nietzsche, Marx, etc., have been left behind or resolved. As for me, I'm trying to *open* windows onto other worlds for Westerners —even if some of these worlds foundered tens of thousands of years ago. My dialogue has other interlocutors than those of Freud or James Joyce: I'm trying to understand a Paleolithic hunter, a yogi or a shaman, a peasant from Indonesia, an African, etc., and to communicate with each one.

8 January

To meditate and philosophize on "primitive" mythologies and religions as Nietzsche and Rohde philosophized on Greek beliefs and creations—that is the hidden meaning of my book.

Ultimately, Western culture must rediscover and proclaim all of man's modes of being. My duty is to show the grandeur, sometimes naïve, sometimes monstrous and tragic, of archaic modes of being.

26 February

I've received Christinel's telegram. Mamy died today. I expected it, I even told myself that death would come as a blessing, and yet I am very sad. Still another part of my life has gone.

27 February

I remember: Bois-Colombes, spring of 1948, when I met her for the first time. She had arrived from Rumania, a few months before, with Oani. Beautiful, gentle, with silvery hair. Then in Capri in July-August 1949, when she told me: A man comes from this vast world and takes away your child, what you hold dearest and best.

In October she had been seriously ill. As I left, she said, "I leave them all under your protection, look after all of them, all of them. . . ."

7 March

The Australian myths have a great simplicity. For a Western reader, they're monotonous, boring, insipid. One has the impression that nothing important is happening; in any case, nothing calls to mind the pathos and grandeur of Polynesian or North American myths. The theme is almost the same: an ancestral Hero comes out of the bosom of the earth and goes off in a certain direction. He walks and walks, and from time to time meets other mythical personages, he celebrates certain ceremonies (extraordinarily simple) that the Australians still repeat today, he civilizes the tribe (he introduces the rules of matrimony, the rites of initiation, etc.), and one day he disappears beneath the earth or is changed into a rock. What is characteristic is that these mythical heroes are continually moving, traveling in every direction and leaving the traces of their passing. These primordial itineraries constitute the foundation of the tribal mythology. They are revealed, in great secret, to the neophytes during the course of their initiation.

And suddenly I recall that that is how things take place in James Joyce's *Ulysses*. Bloom, or Stephen Dedalus, only walks, stops here and there, has dialogue, remembers, satisfies his physical needs—but nothing grandiose or dramatic happens. The fantastic adventure of the Homeric Ulysses is reduced, in turn-of-the-century Dublin, to commonplace strolls, without anything dramatic. And yet, for James Joyce, and certainly for his readers and admirers, these nothings take on gigantic proportions. A whole universe is imperceptibly constructed from all these wanderings, dreamings, and conversations. Each detail acquires significance and "weight." I feel that the analogy between the poorest archaic mythology and the most significant novel of the twentieth century has a deeper meaning than I realize at this moment. I would compare the Western novel (from the epic point of view)—Balzac, Tolstoy, Dostoevsky, Dickens, Proust—to the great mythologies of Polynesia, India, Greece, etc. The decline and disappearance of these mythologies opens the way for philosophy and literature. It would have been expected that the "decline and disappearance" of the epic novel would also lead to philosophy. But James Joyce returns to the monotony of the wanderings of Australian Heroes, filled with religious significance. We are filled with wonder and admiration, just like the Australians, that Leopold Bloom stops in a bistro and orders a beer.

10 March

About two weeks ago I received a letter from L.P., dated from Paris. He has returned after having spent five years in India. (I had learned certain details about his life in Benares via one of my students, Frederick Streng, who would meet him at Professor Agrawala's.) He is asking me to help him get a Bollingen grant. He tells me that, during his absence, a friend would come regularly to his home and carry off sacks of books that he would sell. Several thousand volumes from among the most precious.

I am as distressed as if it were my own library. I had been familiar with L.'s library since the winter of 1946, when I lived on the rue des Saints-Pères. It contained perhaps one hundred thousand books. He bought ceaselessly, everywhere, and he bought everything. One day when he had invited me to lunch, he served me tomatoes in oil . . . , that day he had bought several thousand francs' worth of books. He lived only for books and reading. In 1952–1953, since he couldn't work at home, because of the children, he would go to the Bibliothèque Nationale or the Musée Guimet. He would go every day. It seemed tragic and paradoxical to me—to work in a public library, when one had a hundred thousand volumes at home.

11 March

Morning—it's snowing like in the dead of winter. A soft, supple snow. I'm rereading *Agamemnon*. Memories: first time I read it in French, in the third year of the lycée. Haig Acterian had been so enthusiastic that he had made up his mind to learn Greek. He would say to me, "You should do the same. Read only in Greek and books on Greece."

That same week, urged on by him, I had read *Apollo,* Salomon Reinach's manual of the history of the arts. Haig would say to me: "We should write together a history of all the arts, in Greece. I'll write the history of the theater and of architecture. You should begin with Homer."

On Homer, I answered him, I'll have to write a whole book. A volume of five hundred pages. Maybe even two volumes.

We would make those plans, in the garret on Strada Melodiei, forty-two years ago.

13 March

For so many weeks I've been living exclusively with the Australians, from morning until evening. (At home, at night, I'm reading other things: Aeschylus, Henry Miller, G. Meyrink.) How can I best point out the Platonic structure of Australian spirituality? For the Australians, to know means to remember. Initiation unfolds a long process of anamnesis: the neophyte learns not only the secret myths that explain and justify all existence, but he discovers himself, he *recognizes* himself in the mythical ancestor of whom he is the reincarnation. For Plato, philosophy helps you remember the Ideas; more precisely, to remember the situation of the soul in postexistence and preexistence when the soul contemplated the Ideas. For the Australians, initiation reveals to you that you *were already here,* in these places, in the dawn of time, *in illo tempore:* you were such-and-such civilizing hero. This mythical personage serves as a model: the initiates must repeat what he did in the beginning. But, through the initiation, you discover that this mythical personage is *you yourself—* as you appeared for the first time. Ultimately, you are a repetition of yourself—as you were in the beginning, *exemplary.*

15 March

We must not forget that the Americans as yet have no history, have no roots. From the cultural point of view, they are still in the pioneer and immigrant stage: free, available. It is their great good fortune: although they are descendants of an Occidental culture, they can take everything back to the beginning and create something new.

21 March

Last night's dream: I had various precious objects, I remembered that I had carried them into the bedroom, but I no longer remembered what objects they were. I left the bedroom and tried to remember; I walked in the streets, I recognized a church (I said to myself: I've already been here, I know that there is a garden in the neighborhood)—but I constantly had this distressing feeling: I'm threatened with totally losing my memory. Christinel was with me. I knelt before her and said, Help me! Only you can save me! . . .

3 April

I read in an article on Father Desmond Chute that an Italian peasant, on his deathbed, had asked for the communion in these words: "I don't want doctors, bring me the King of the universe."

5 April

I'm beginning the second volume of my autobiography. I will try to summarize my years spent in India by emphasizing certain events exclusively and by omitting all the others. I must keep certain secrets for myself. Moreover, I've written about India so many times that I no longer have any desire to return to the subject.

However, I think that this book—the autobiography—is the only one today that must be written at any price. All the other works can wait.

9 April

Every day I've written three to six pages. Astonished to discover that I remember so well the first year spent in India. It's true that sometimes I verify certain details and certain dates in *Chantier* and *India*. But what I wouldn't give to have at hand the journal from 1928 to 1940 and the letters I received when I was there (1929–1931).

Moreover, since it's a question of recollections and not an objective and systematic biography, the absence of documents leaves me a certain freedom: I will write only what has remained in my memory, what has contributed to shaping me, what seems to me essential. Thus, I will be free to comment on the events and discoveries of those years.

Certain things will obviously be passed over in silence.

18 April

I've had a visit from Garma Chang, the translator of the poems of Milarepa and, just recently, of certain Tibetan yogi texts. He spoke to me with praise for *Yoga* and especially for *The Myth of the Eternal Return*. He is astonished that I have understood so well the three spiritual universes: the world of the primitives, the East, and Western traditions.

He suggested a Formosan publisher to do the Chinese translation of *The Myth of the Eternal Return*.

21 April

Dumfounded over the "discoveries" that I'm making about my novels: *Isabelle* and *La Lumière qui s'éteint.* This latter, unreadable, monotonous, botched, seems to me today to be an unconscious reaction against India, a desperate attempt to defend myself against myself—for during the summer of 1930 I had decided to Indianize myself, to lose myself in the Indian multitude. The "mystery" of *La Lumière,* this incomprehensible fire that catches one night in the library and brings on, among other things, the blindness and breakdown of the librarian, was really only the mystery of my existence in Dasgupta's house.

There are many things I do not have the right to make public. Nonetheless I can annotate a typed copy—specifying that these annotations are never to be published. Merely information for the eventual readers of the *Souvenirs* manuscript.

ROCHESTER, *29 April*

About an hour by plane from New York. I was met at the airport by Gerow, the young Sanskritist from Chicago, now a professor of Sanskrit at Rochester.

We had dinner at Norman O. Brown's, the author of that fascinating book *Life Against Death,* who had told Gerow that he was "my disciple from the extreme left." A large country house, about ten kilometers from the university. N.O.B.—a man difficult to describe, whose age is hard to tell. Enormously cultivated. Although a Hellenist, here at Rochester he is giving a course on "cultural archetypes." Still enthusiastic over Freud.

In the lecture hall where I'm speaking, he is the one who introduces me. I'm content that he emphasizes my biographical and cultural trajectory: Bucharest, Calcutta, Lisbon, Paris, Chicago.

30 April

In the morning, conversation with about ten faculty members. Then, lunch at N. O. Brown's. We talked about books and authors —but I learned little about him. He has told me only that he has been working for several years on a book on political life and the Greek *polis.*

At 2:00 P.M., back at the university. N.O.B.'s seminar. The students ask me questions—and I try to answer them. I don't know how pleased N.O.B. was. I emphasized, once again, the distinction between *Madame Bovary* and adultery, forgetting at that moment that for a Freudian like N.O.B., this distinction doesn't exist, or is insignificant.

I was to take the 5:00 P.M. plane for New York, but because of the storm all flights were suspended. I spent my evening with Gerow and his wife talking Hindu philosophy.

At 10:30 P.M. to the railroad station. I'm writing these lines in the train to make the time pass. And this detail: this afternoon, at

N.O.B.'s seminar, one of the students asked me what I thought of "original sin." I answered him that it is one of the problems that does not interest me. Astonishment from Brown and the whole room. Brown told me that some psychoanalysis could explain this indifference to "the central problem."

HARVARD, *1 May*

Invited by the president of the university, Dr. Pusey, to be on the ad hoc committee which was to designate Slater's successor (at the Institute of World Religions). Having been put up at Dana-Palmer House, I had dinner at Slater's, with the dean of the theology faculty, Dr. Miller, and the Thorkild Jacobsens.

Slater told me that Harvard University wanted very much to have me; even now there are some professors who hope that I will accept in the end. I repeated to him what I had already said at Princeton: although I like Harvard very much, I cannot disappoint Jerry Brauer, who did so much for me. Moreover, I don't think I would have the freedom that I enjoy at Chicago. What is more, I'm not a good administrator, and the Institute has to be administered.

2 May

The ad hoc committee: Pusey, Miller, myself, the professors from Yale, from Columbia, and Ingalls from Harvard. Again the question: Am I willing to accept, etc.? I explained why I cannot. When the experts came to debating the merits of another candidate, each one began by recognizing that "the best one" would obviously be "Professor Eliade." I blushed and lowered my eyes. And, yet, I have a feeling of pride, and so much nostalgia: everything began forty years ago in the garret on Strada Melodiei. Today people talk about "the famous scholar," "the greatest . . . ," "the only one who. . . ." I remember the reaction at home, to my first publications concerning the history of religions. Many did not take me seriously. Terrible spell of melancholy, the source of which I'm not able to discern.

WASHINGTON, D.C., *4 May*

I arrived last night, with Christinel. In the morning to Meridian House, where the Conference of the John Nef Center (a Center for Human Understanding) is taking place. It's the third and last day of the conference. Chagall spoke—more precisely, he read a short autobiography, full of surprises—and I opened the series of commentaries. I emphasized this point: although Chagall was the contemporary of so many "destructions of aesthetic universes" (cubism, etc.), although he too had painted (he even brought it up in the text he had just read) persons floating in the air, their heads not in the right place, etc., *in his work the world is not annihilated,* it does not return to chaos. And yet, the world of Chagall is transfigured, filled with mysteries; the animals, for example (the ass, especially), in which I recognize a messianic or paradisiac syndrome. The painting of Chagall is impregnated with the longing for paradise; etc., etc.

The discussion over, Chagall congratulated me, hugged me in his arms. He confessed to us—to Christinel and me—that he was a little afraid of what I was going to say. "I'm afraid of scholars," he added.

5 May

Last night, we went with the Reichman couple and the Hindu writer Raja Rao to Mrs. Watkins's, in Maryland, about fifteen kilometers from here. I had read the beginning of Raja Rao's novel *The Serpent and the Rope,* and had liked it. Delighted to learn that he was familiar with *The Myth of the Eternal Return, Birth and Rebirth, Yoga.* He even wondered how a Westerner had been able to understand the symbolism of Indian initiations. I sat in the front, with him, next to Reichman, who was driving. Pastoral countryside: forest, hills, a herd of cows—then Mrs. Watkins's house, on the edge of the woods.

Raja Rao made dinner: peppered curry, made as it is in Madras. At table, general conversation. This remark of Rao to be noted: India is quite near the West, it participates in the same culture in a sense

—it is Islam which broke the unity of the world, it deepened and aggravated the differences. Today, after centuries of isolation, India seems far from Europe, foreign, exotic.

Raja Rao's remark, yesterday afternoon, at Meridian House, as he was commenting on the observations of a young physics professor, a student of Fermi (it was Anderson, from the University of Chicago): there exists an essential similarity between Western scientific thought and Hindu thought: neither one takes account of forms and appearances; they seek the fundamental and invariable. *Objective approach*. When he arrived for the first time in the USA, he asked to see a single man: Oppenheimer.

After last night's long conversation (I had to answer questions drawn from the whole history of culture, from the Neolithic to Byzantium), Rao told me that I absolutely had to return to India. The Hindus would learn from me how they should understand their own culture.

6 May

Interesting comment by Morazé, during yesterday's discussion: tools, he was saying, are not man's creation; they are part of nature, even though they are the result of human effort and intelligence. The scientist studies the laws of nature, and, to the extent that he understands them, he produces instruments, but he does not create them. Scientific objects and discoveries are part of nature.

If Morazé is right, the conception of today's man of science about his instruments and his discoveries is close to the significance accorded by the man of traditional civilizations (paleo-Oriental and primitive) to tools and, in general, to the totality of objects which made up his material culture. Cf. what I said in *The Forge and the Crucible* about the ores considered to be embryos in the womb of the Earth Mother and the metallurgical rituals by which the embryos come to the light and are helped to grow, to mature, that is, to become metals.

CHICAGO, *15 May*

Even now, reflecting on my "secret" life in India, I hardly grasp its meaning. Ultimately, my existence in India was changed (not to say abolished) by my meeting with two young girls: M. and J. If I had not met them, or if, despite these meetings, I hadn't let myself be drawn into irresponsible adventures—my life would have been entirely different. Because of M. I lost the right to become an integral part of "historical" India; because of J. I lost everything I believed I had accomplished in the Himalayas: my integration into spiritual, transhistorical India.

I understand, nevertheless (and scarcely even today!), that it had to happen that way. It is maya that put these two girls in my path, to force me to recover my wits and to find once again my own destiny. Which was: cultural creation in the Rumanian language, and in Rumania. It wasn't until after the period of intense and frenzied activity, from 1933 to 1940, that I had the right to detach myself from the Rumanian context—and to begin to think and write for a larger public and from a "universal" perspective.

17 May

"To carry Christ . . . to the heart of realities considered to be the most dangerous, the most naturalistic, the most pagan, that is my gospel and my mission." Teilhard de Chardin wrote that; he saw himself as "the evangelist for *Christ in the Universe.*"

What a joy to rediscover in a Western theologian and "man of science" the optimism of Rumanian peasants, they themselves also being Christian but belonging to that "cosmic Christianity" which has long since disappeared in the West. The peasant believes that the world is good, that it returned to that state after the incarnation, death, and resurrection of the Savior. My basic optimism probably finds its source in that certitude. If, some day, someone intelligently studies my theory on *hierophanies* and the progressive "hierophanization" of the world, life, and history—he will be able to compare me to Teilhard de Chardin. With this exception, nevertheless: he came to this theory by the discovery of Cosmogenesis, and I, by the deciphering of cosmic religions (in which must be included, despite all its differences, the peasant Christianity of eastern Europe which is, in fact, simply a cosmic liturgy).

What is significant is not only this conception of Teilhard, but also his extraordinary success with the public. The vigorous reaction of the European elite against the "provincialism" of the Christian Churches.

22 May

I'm reading Claude Cuénot's book on Teilhard de Chardin. Especially interesting for the considerable number of quotations and extracts from letters (for the most part unpublished). Teilhard's vision is comforting: Creation, Life, Man, Mind—all these realities not only have a meaning, but this meaning is revealed *at the same time*. If I understand correctly the thought of Teilhard de Chardin, I would say that Goethe's work, for example, is interdependent on the structure of the oceans, the morphology of pluricellular organisms, the cranial capacity of the prehominids, etc., etc. Interdependent in the sense that it presupposes and extends all these "creations." Obviously, Teilhard could not accept the hypothesis of a catastrophic destruction of the earth and humanity. He could not conceive that a work begun several billion years ago, and perfecting itself by a mysterious process of selection and by qualitative leaps ahead, such a magnum opus, in which a cosmic Christ is implicit, could be stopped by a thermonuclear accident.

20 June

Yesterday and today—splendid weather. I'm working on the short story. I tell myself that what I'm doing is absurd: losing these last few weeks of freedom writing a short story and without even knowing how it will end. But I feel that I must write it, for my moral health. How right G. Bachelard was when he spoke about "the function of the *unreal*"; which, if it is not satisfied, leads to neurosis and sterility. . . .

22 June

I don't know why I've been thinking so much today of Walter Otto. When I met him in the garden of Casa Gabriella in the summer of 1955, he was eighty years old. I addressed him in English, but he insisted that we speak in French, a language that he spoke rather poorly, moreover. Extraordinary vitality: during the break after his first lecture, which had lasted an hour, he turned down the sandwiches Olga had made; he asked for some champagne and smoked a cigar.

He told me that in a hundred or two hundred years, his pages on mythical Greek thought would become as important as the classical Greek texts.

23 June

Papini wrote in his *Journal,* for 31 January 1943: "The liturgy is a funeral banquet during which man eats his own God before a crowd of starving people."

24 June

A young student of social thought, Botinovici, came to see me. He had read *Andronic and the Snake* in the German translation and had been enthusiastic. He would like to read more of my "literary" works, but I didn't encourage him. Nevertheless, we spoke about my conception of the fantastic in literature. I reminded him that this conception has its roots in my theory of "the incognizability of miracles"—or in my theory that, after the Incarnation, the transcendent is camouflaged in the world or in history and thus becomes "incognizable." In *The Snake* a banal atmosphere and mediocre characters are gradually transfigured. But what came from "beyond," as well as all the paradisiac images of the end of the story, were already there from the beginning, but camouflaged by the banality of everyday life and, as such, unrecognizable.

26 June

I'm beginning to have a more and more favorable idea of "men of science." Lately I've met five or six young people—they studied physics, mathematics, biochemistry, etc. One was mad about music and knew Mozart admirably well. Two others were readers of poetry, and poetry of the best quality (admirable comments on *Four Quartets,* etc.). Another, I would say, was an excellent Kierkegaard specialist.

(What is significant is that Chuck Long had discovered Kierkegaard thanks to a physicist ten or twelve years ago.) Finally, another was interested in the "new wave" novel, in Camus and Merleau-Ponty, in painting ("tachism," "pop art," etc.). At all events, each of them goes beyond the universe of his own studies.

And when I think of the "humanists," of my colleagues who are anthropologists, Orientalists, theologians—let alone sociologists! You would think that they were ashamed of admitting that they read poets or mystics. They try to appear "serious," "scientific." They imitate the objectivity of the scientists. Actually, they are timid and sterile. Their absence of curiosity is a proof of impotence and mediocrity.

27 June

I'm returning to the short story begun ten days ago. I will probably call it "Les Fossés." At first, I wanted to give it a title that would fool the readers: "La Bataille d'Oglindesti." In point of fact, the battle took place a few dozen kilometers from the village where the last survivors are busy digging ditches to find the treasure. It was a way of showing how "the Rumanians sabotaged history." On the eve of the catastrophe, when everything was crumbling and other masters were getting ready to occupy and dominate the country, my village was listening to the counsels of an old man and looking for the treasure of which he had been dreaming for nearly eighty years.

28 June

Windy City! How well I hear the wind from my office. I listen to it, fascinated. This metallic litany transports me far back into my childhood. Summer in Tekirghiol: we would leave, in the beginning of the afternoon, for the sanatorium, for the sea. After an hour's walk, at the edge of the lake, under the burning heat, struggling against the dust that we found even in the poppies and the wild flowers, we would reach the sea pines of the sanatorium. When the wind blew, I would hear it as I hear the trees of Fifty-seventh Street today. We would penetrate into the half-light under the pines, already feeling the sand under the soles of our feet. And then, abruptly, in front of us, the sea.

Why am I writing here this uninteresting and insignificant detail?

Perhaps because, for the last half-hour, I've only been remembering little nothings, connected to my first summers in Tekirghiol. Details, faces, words that come back to me as I listen to the wind. (Obviously, Proust and the madeleine, etc., etc.—but it's not that. Purely and simply the happiness of *listening* and *remembering*.)

29 June

I haven't lived such a summer for a very long time, since Rumania. And even in Rumania, the sky was perhaps not so blue.

What a strange genius Papini had, so profound and so naïve, so childish sometimes. . . . Today I opened the *Diario,* and for 13 May 1946, I find this notation: "The latest information on solar storms confirms the law that I had discovered of the influence of the sun on the events of human history. Astrology is false concerning individual destinies, but it is true for peoples."

2 July

Gide's fear, and that of so many writers at the beginning of the century, of becoming "literary men." That's why Gide looked for life and later discovered the social dimension. J. P. Sartre continues the same tradition: literature must reflect the historical concrete, that is, the social and the political.

My emancipation from literature by the history of religions and ethnology corresponds to the same tendency: that is what is real for me—not literature. A critic who saw a penchant for scholarly learning in my scientific work would be gravely mistaken. It's a matter of something else entirely; it's a matter of a world which seems more real to me, more alive than the characters of novels and short stories.

4 July

I had forgotten the sonnet of Michelangelo with this giant

d'altezza tanta
Che da'su'occhi noi qua giù non vede,

> E molte volte ha ricoperta e franta
> una città colla pianta del piede.

Rereading it today by chance, I rememorized it. I had last thought of it in Portugal, when I was visualizing Adamastor,

> Al sole aspira, e l'alte torri pianta
> per aggiungere al cielo e non lo vede
> . . . e'l capo ha fermo e prossimo alle stelle. . . .

I would like to know more about this giant who "ardently desires the sun" and wants "to reach the sky." What impresses me is the force with which a protohistorical image reappears in the middle of the Renaissance. This giant who touches the stars is a new variation of the "Column of Heaven," of the *axis mundi,* of the *Irminsul* column which supports the sky, etc. All these columns which join the sky to the earth and which, at the same time, hold up the sky and keep it from falling, were extremely common in the megalithic age. By what chance did Michelangelo discover them? What did he mean—describing the giant? Was it his own image projected dizzily to the stars?

PARIS, *17 July*

Bernanos gave up writing novels after the Spanish civil war broke out—and he suffers for it because he sees himself as a writer above all else. But he is making this sacrifice because he wants to witness, to judge the so-called Christian world in the light of the conscience of a Christian.

I realize that, for nearly ten years, I too have sacrificed "literature"; I gave up writing novels (the only literary genre that satisfies my talent). I did it to try to lay down a new way of understanding *homo religiosus.* In a certain sense, I too have "witnessed" in a religious war that I knew in advance to be lost.

18 July

Evening, with Emile Cioran, Jean Gouillard, Corbin, and Muriel and Jerry Brauer—in our apartment on rue de la Tour. Jerry

Brauer tried to explain certain aspects of American foreign policy by "the ideology of the frontier": for more than a century the Americans knew that if they didn't like their neighbors, they could go a hundred or a thousand miles farther to the West. After the Second World War, they saw that the USSR was still there: they could neither destroy it nor forget it by going farther away. They no longer know where to go. Whence a feeling of frustration and despair.

26 July

O., who will be twenty-one in January, proclaims that Michel Butor is a genius of a writer—"greater than Ionesco." Getting him to talk a little, I've learned that he knows well neither Balzac, Stendhal, Tolstoy, Dostoevsky, nor even Proust, and he has never heard of James Joyce. But Butor is *their* discovery, the discovery of those who are today twenty years old: that is why he must be greater than Ionesco, Camus, etc., discovered ten or fifteen years ago by others, those who are now thirty or thirty-five.

I'm fascinated by this problem of the generation gap, approached from an entirely different perspective from the one we had thirty-five years ago. Certain values—or behaviors, allergies, color blindnesses— impose themselves with fatality, solely because you are *younger* than everything that was young before you. Nae Ionesco was in the habit of saying, "The young are always right." Or: "I agree with what you say because you are young."

I only wonder whether this enthusiasm for Butor and company isn't a little artificial with the very young; whether "the new wave" wasn't imposed first by the critics, and then adopted by the snobs, by the elite and finally by the youths of age twenty. At all events, the enthusiasm for a new literary formula, and its success with the critics and the public, proves nothing. It is possible that this novelty is really creative and significant and that it will remain. It also could be that this whole "revolution" is an imposture, or the result of a misunderstanding. I can't forget that between 1895 and 1910 Maeterlinck was considered, throughout Europe, as the great, brilliant representative of the renewal of the arts—whereas Gide, Claudel, to say nothing of Rimbaud and Mallarmé, were almost unknown. What an excellent subject for a doctoral thesis. The presentation of new, revolutionary values, proclaimed by the supposed elite or avant-garde in 1890–1910–1930, etc.—and, by comparison, the analysis of the situation of contemporary writers who were recognized only by succeeding generations.

27 July

I visited Walter Strauss, professor of French literature at Emory University and friend of Tom Altizer. A year in Paris to study the orphic themes in European poetry, from Hölderlin to Pierre Emmanuel. Fascinating discussion. And, nevertheless, he only asserts what one would expect from an avant-garde intellectual. For example: Beckett is a genius (especially in his later works), he is superior to Ionesco, *Rhinoceros* is "conventional," etc.

I would like to have the time to write this book too: *The Opiate of the Literary Elite.* The extraordinary falsification of all artistic perspectives, the triumph of the incomprehensible as such, the confusion of values which means that today anything is possible, etc., etc.

1 August

In *L'Art romantique,* Baudelaire republishes his article (so full of praise!) on Arsène Houssaye, and the articles on Champfleury, Pierre Dupont (proclaimed a great poet!), etc., etc. Baudelaire's admiration for Théophile Gautier or for Wagner suddenly appears to me as less significant. I like to imagine a *History of French Literature* around the year 2100—in which the record of contemporary "successes" will be presented: the numbers of copies printed, for example, the translations and the bibliography of critical articles published on Robbe-Grillet, Butor, Nathalie Sarraute, etc.

LE PLAN DE GRASSE, *10 August*

I've been going through the correspondence of Hofmannsthal and of Carl I. Burckhardt, especially interesting for the letters of the latter. His judgments (in around 1920) on Jean Cocteau and Valéry are surprisingly sound. His analyses, his criticisms, and his political foresight are astounding: England and France preoccupied with what was happening (or could have happened) in Germany, and ignoring or ignorant of Russia; Burckhardt foretold the Second World War, the decline of Europe, the triumph of Bolshevism, etc. Nae Ionesco was writing the same thing, and it's what we young people were thinking also, between 1925 and 1933; it was also the cry of the European right around 1930. What was the use? Neither public opinion nor the intelligentsia nor the chancelleries were impressed. Things took place as though no one had been there to foretell them.

11 August

In Délia's library I found *La Jeune Parque,* a critical study by Octave Nadal. I've learned that Paul Valéry kept all the outlines, rough drafts, copies, all the papers or scraps of paper on which he wrote dates, words, ideas, on which he sketched or figured, etc., etc., "about eight hundred pieces of various sizes, the major part in separate sheets and the rest comprised of seventy bound pages of a large notebook" (p. 155). He kept everything. But why? Indifference or, on the contrary, the mania of the collector and archivist? Curiosity about the gestation and maturation of his own work? Or the feeling that, by keeping everything, at least some of the mysterious processes of poetic creation could be understood?

ABANO, *24 August*

With effort and repugnance, I'm writing the second Eranos lecture. And yet the theme that I've chosen is fascinating: "Paradise and Utopia, Mythical Geography and Eschatology." I have a briefcase with me stuffed with documents on the millennialist hopes of the pioneers. America was colonized by Puritans and ecstatics, who had set out in quest of the earthly paradise. In my lecture, I cite a host of astonishing examples: the colonizers were sure they had rediscovered Paradise. They wanted to build the true heavenly Jerusalem in America. It was *there,* they believed, that they would be able to continue and consummate the Reformation, aborted in England and on the Continent.

What is yet more surprising is that the same eschatological tension is found as well in the Catholic colonies, especially the Spanish ones. Columbus was convinced that he had discovered the earthly Paradise. For Columbus the transatlantic discoveries also had an eschatological function: the New World was being opened up to the gospel—consequently the end of the world was near.

PARIS, *22 September*

Meeting with Father A. S. Shortly after, Mme. Georges Bratiano arrived as well. To my great astonishment, Mme. G. B. asked Father A. to explain to her the problem of evil. *Privatio boni,* began the father. Ontologically speaking, evil does not exist. Etc., etc.

After the father left, Mme. G. Bratiano told us about the death of her husband, in prison, in 1953. He was in solitary confinement. From November 1952 to 23 April 1953, no one had seen him. It was even believed that he had died. Then, on Saint George's Day, some of the inmates saw him in the courtyard—stooped, walking painfully, his tormentor beside him. Among the inmates, there were also some Uniate bishops. From their window, they waved at him and blessed him. Georges Bratiano looked at them, but he seemed to have dead eyes. No reaction. The next day, he was again conducted into the courtyard. The scene repeated itself. G. B. lifted his eyes toward the window, he smiled—the bishops smiled also and blessed him. The guard asked him why he looked up, what he saw. I didn't look up, answered G. B. I didn't see anyone. The guard began to hit him on the head. From the courtyard to the second floor, he didn't stop hitting him. But once in the cell, the guard took fright—and the other inmates heard him run down the stairway. Sick, exhausted, G. B. had probably had an internal hemorrhage in the cell—and the guard took fright. He went to call the doctor or the proper authority. Boots were heard in the stairway. Shortly after, they went down. G. B. was probably dying. He could no longer be saved.

That day, the guard was heard every five minutes opening the peephole of the cell and looking inside. He wanted to know if G. B. was still alive. About ten or eleven at night, the guard went running back downstairs to call the others. In the neighboring cells, they had understood: G. B. had died. But it was too late for them to be able to take him out of the cell and bury him. The operation took place the next evening, nearly twenty-four hours later.

The person who told all this to Mme. Georges Bratiano was in one of the neighboring cells with five or six other inmates. The next day, as usual, one of the guards came to call roll. He seemed drunk, dizzy. He remained like that for a few minutes, dazed, before making up his mind to call roll. Then he went into G. B.'s cell and came back out with a pot of marmalade. *Pomana* [alms given in memory of the dead], he said, holding out the pot to them.

The father had left and I was regretting it. I was thinking: *Privatio boni. . . .*

I was also thinking of this: in Paris, I had heard that Georges Bratiano had committed suicide by opening his veins with ferrets that he had rubbed for months to make them sharp. But this version had been invented by his jailers. Being very cunning, they had started a rumor that could catch on because it accorded with the will power, the patience, and the heroism of the victim.

24 September

I've begun the article on "Mioritza," the Rumanian folk song. I wanted to take up C. Brailoiu's thesis once again, correct and complete it. Brailoiu tries to show that "Mioritza" is not pessimistic, that it does not contain any high philosophy either: according to him, it is only the statement of a defense against death and ghosts, therefore an affirmation of life. B.'s thesis is inadequate—because "Mioritza" cannot be reduced to the behavior and magico-religious beliefs that it implies. But the ballad is not pessimistic, I agree, and when the shepherd speaks about death as he would about marriage, as soon as he learns from the ewe lamb the intentions of his companions, he is neither a coward nor a contemplative. Actually, the ewe lamb utters an *oracle*—and fate revealed oracularly can no longer be changed. The shepherd knows that he will die whatever he does. This is not a case of cowardice or of "contemplation," but of a serene resignation in the face of destiny. I will have to explain all this at leisure. And comment on the cosmic liturgy implied in death seen as a marriage.

What is much more important is that the Rumanian cultural elite recognized themselves in the fate of the shepherd, misfortune in history, and all the rest. And their desperate attempts to reverse this misfortune in history, by continuing to create and to believe in culture as if history didn't exist, even though it was always ready to break them and annihilate them. The Rumanian creative act is comparable to the cry of the shepherd in the ballad "Mioritza," exalting his death in the language of marriage.

"Mioritza" is especially important for what Rumanian intellectuals have seen in it for a century.

CHICAGO, *12 October*

Admirable response from Heidegger to Carnap's attacks, of which I've become aware only today: *being, nonbeing,* must not be understood "logically," but in relation to the meanings they have in a human existence—for example, in the experience of anguish and finitude which causes the shock of the *possibility* of nonbeing, and the astonishment that this shock arouses, the astonishment that something *exists,* that there is not only *nothing, nonbeing.* I wonder if all these things, so well known today, bothered Carnap the least little bit; and if they bother a neopositivist or a Marxist today.

17 October

I'm beginning to put the finishing touches on the Eranos manuscript. There are a number of other things to add, notably concerning the earthly Paradise that the Puritan pioneers were seeking in America. I should point out that the phenomenon of colonization was part of the baroque style. The love of power and the frenzy to enjoy this power. Colonization and Puritanism are the two poles of the baroque. On the one hand, the slave trader; on the other hand, the Puritan—or, on the one hand, the will to gain wealth as rapidly as possible (and by all the means available); on the other hand, the mystical doctrine of the Quakers. The will to power—outward or inward.

29 October

Ultimately, from the Australians to the Vedic Indians, there is no solution of continuity concerning rites and their meaning. In India, the sacrifice repeats what had taken place *ab origine,* at the moment of creation. By identifying himself with the sacrifice, man vanquishes death and conquers immortality. The ceremonials of the Australians repeat the paradigmatic gestures of the Heroes of the "Dream Time." By this repetition, the world is regenerated and life continues, and the individual finds a meaning to existence and assures himself of a spiritual afterlife (after death the soul returns to the primordial source and there awaits, as a "child-spirit," a new reincarnation).

2 November

On "the fate of books."

During the English civil war, thousands of books and pamphlets were printed. The most famous work, without any doubt, is Milton's *Areopagitica.* But the book passed unnoticed. It isn't even mentioned among the thousands of contemporary pamphlets, where so many long since forgotten authors and personalities were discussed. Parliament—to which Milton addressed *Areopagitica*—didn't even deign to respond. The first edition was published in November 1644—and wasn't reprinted until 1738, long after Milton's death.

5 November

Some day I must reassemble all the criticisms made of reductionism. I must make up a special category: the use of images to illustrate the absurdity of "objective explanations." For example: describing the beauty of a woman by saying that she has a delightful sternum, an admirable duodenum, etc. I remember the refutation by Leo Strauss of the objectivism dear to Max Weber. Strauss asked the scholars if the exact and rigorous sociological analysis of a concentration camp expressed the deep meaning of this social phenomenon. Leo Strauss showed that the correct presentation of concentration camps also implies their *judgment.*

6 November

I was explaining to my students the necessity of generalizations: I was showing them a minuscule map of Australia. Is it true? Of course. And yet the map does not and cannot show all the places, all the bays, the rivers, the lakes, the hills. A map ten times larger will show ten times more, but it will not be able to indicate everything a military staff map can show, which, in its turn, cannot show everything.

We therefore have the right to generalize in the history of religions. On the condition that we present the *essential* on the scale on which we are working, and that we be coherent. (A map would lose its value if, claiming to be an economic map of the regions under consideration, it added extraneous and useless indications: archaeological excavations, or linguistic boundaries, for example.)

7 November

Albert Einstein used to say: "I realized a long time ago that I mustn't waste my time trying to convince my colleagues."

If I could just take this principle into account in writing *Primitive Religions.* . . .

8 November

Some day I must write a eulogy of the idealists, the "noble intellectuals," the pacifists who refuse the drama of history and believe in universal peace, justice, brotherhood, etc. I must show that, far from being inauthentic, absent, mystified, discarded in the wastebasket of history, they illustrate the secularization of the longing for Paradise characteristic of so many mystics. These "idealistic intellectuals," in a profane culture such as that of the West of the nineteenth and twentieth centuries, represent secularized mysticism. They are neither inauthentic nor facile. They are continuing a tradition several centuries long. The desire of the mystics to return to the serenity, the plenitude, the absence of tension of Paradise, has today become the ambition of the idealists to live in an egalitarian, beatific, tensionless society.

10 November

I observe this "primitive" aspect of what has been called, since Hegel and Marx, *alienation:* alienated, man feels himself to be an object, commanded by external forces, forces and influences into which he has projected all his vital substance. Now, among numerous "primitive" peoples, the *soul* (or the true soul) is imagined as being out of the body—projected into certain objects, or camouflaged by them. If these objects are destroyed, the man loses his soul and dies.

Modern alienation is, in a certain sense, a reduced form of this magical conception of the soul.

16 November

So much has been said of the absence of originality in Roman religion, of Oriental and Greek influences, without which it would not even have had a mythology, to say nothing of the Mysteries. . . . In reality, the originality of the Roman religious genius resides in the selection and interpretation of elements borrowed from the Greeks or from the East. The creativity of Rome was spent in choice, promotion, exaltation or rejection, censorship, persecution. This is not solely a matter of practice. What Rome accepted from others she changed, adapted, and, especially, reinforced (sometimes, she enlarged it).

18 November

I've begun the article "Myth" for the *Encyclopaedia Britannica.* Certainly, I'll take whole pages of *Myth and Reality* (which has just come out). But I'll have to write a good fifteen or so typewritten pages on the history of the interpretations of different categories of myths, etc. At least a week wasted. Why squander my time on such petty work? I probably don't have much time left ahead of me. Why not concentrate on really important works? I have only one excuse: I didn't want myth—as I understand it today and as I believe it ought to be understood—to fall into the hands of some mediocre type who would rehash sociological and anthropological truisms. I wanted to conquer a key position for the history of religions.

26 November

After three hours of class and seminar, when I felt exhausted and would have liked to be alone at least a half-hour and to have a cup of coffee without saying a word, F. arrived. He is returning from the Anthropology Congress in San Francisco and, on his way to Washington, stopped a few hours in Chicago. To see me. I noticed that he has a new denture. Yet I understood him with difficulty. At the end of a half-hour I could hardly control myself. The same things, always the same things that he had already told me last year and repeated in numerous letters or reports. And everything leads to the same conclusion: an Eskimology Institute must be founded, *quickly,* under his direction. He brought his wife, who is Eskimo, to San Francisco (she had been operated on for cancer last spring; he had told me so himself) to convince anthropologists that he no longer distinguishes himself from the Eskimos—and that the latter support his project.

I was hardly listening to him. And yet, if he were right? If his explanations of the metaphorical language of the Eskimo shamans, of the dualism of souls, etc., etc., had a basis? A whole archaic culture, the last one still living, would find a new and deeper explanation. This culture is disappearing under our eyes, and it will be impossible to reconstitute it, because the documents concerning it will have been incompletely assembled and without critical safeguards. The last chance to be scientifically informed would be his Eskimology Institute. But, for the time being, there isn't any money. And the Eskimos continue to be "studied" from questionnaires prefabricated in an American university.

13 December

Melvin Hill has come from the Cape to study history of religions with me. Today he brought me a very interesting term paper on the sacred dance of the Boschimans. He stayed in my office for two hours.

He told me a thousand interesting things on South Africa. Sixty or seventy years ago, the farmers hunted the Boschimans like they hunted antelope—but they did it "for fun only." They knew that at the new moon and at the full moon, and in other circumstances as well, the Boschimans would dance without interruption eight or sixteen hours at a stretch in a sort of ecstasy—and then they could hunt them easily. (Otherwise, the Boschimans would feel the nearness of the whites and would hide.)

Many of them were forced to work in the gold or diamond mines. They would fall sick and die en masse. Those who survived, back in their desert, no longer knew how to orient themselves. They no longer found the plants with edible roots, they no longer "felt" where the subterranean water sources were—and they declined without remedy.

What a Boschiman told him while hunting: that he felt the approach of the antelope *in his calves.* His flesh there contracted, shivered, it had a presentiment of the antelope—which appeared on the horizon only much later.

19 December

The novel must tell something, because narrative (that is, literary invention) enriches the world no more and no less than history, although on another level. We have more creative possibilities in imaginary universes than we do on the level of history. The fact *that something is happening, that all kinds of things are happening,* is just as significant for the fate of man as the fact of living in history or of hoping to modify it.

28 December

In the short story I'm writing ("The Bridge"), I am obsessed with getting across its secret meaning: the camouflage of mysteries in the events of immediate reality. Consequently, I want to bring out the ambivalence of every event, in the sense that an apparently banal happening can reveal a whole universe of transcendent meanings, and that an apparently extraordinary, fantastic event can be accepted by those who live it as something that goes without saying and at which they wouldn't even dream of being surprised.

3 January 1964

Jack Hayward took us this evening to the Civic Theatre to see Langston Hughes's *Black Nativity,* with Marion Williams, Alex Bradford, and Princess Steward (blind). I learned that "Professor Bradford is one of the leading gospel singers in this country." He is "an ordained minister and director of music at the Greater Abyssinian Church of Newark, New Jersey." Extraordinary *presence*—which is also found, for that matter, in each of the twelve or fourteen singers. One has the impression of being projected into the religious universe of children. The authenticity, the naïve realism of the faith that greets you in Negro spirituals—all that does not belong to the world of adults. One is ushered, as though by enchantment, into a universe that can be imagined only in a dream that certain great poets have glimpsed.

Actually, I have known this naïve religious world for a long time; it is the same as that of the Rumanian Christmas carols (the *colinde* that the children go singing from house to house). But with American blacks, it is more than a folkloric delight; this world is part of their religious experience, it is *their* Christianity. Imagine the Rumanian peasants living exclusively in the religious universe of the Christmas carols, without the teaching and discipline of the Church, without the learned traditions represented (even approximately) by the priests. There is another difference that seems to me decisive: the passion of the blacks, their nervous instability, which makes so many Negro spirituals reach paroxysms of near-hysteria. You will never see a group of male or female peasants in eastern Europe (not even in Russia) possessed by the personalities of the hymns they are singing. The restraint, the simplicity, the serenity of southeast European religious folklore, compared with the frenzy and ecstasy of Negro spirituals: here one has the impression that the discovery of the miracles of the Nativity (or of other hierophanies) is too elating for the children's souls, and that, finally, these children begin to shout, to clap their hands, to cry for joy, for sadness, for longing.

There are so many other things to add. . . .

5 January

Marx doesn't want to explain the world, but to change it.

Buddha: antimetaphysical; he was not interested in the origin or explanation of the world, nor in the origin of the human condition. He wanted to change the human condition, as did Marx, moreover, who understood by the term "changing the world" the radical modification of the human condition.

The symbiosis of Buddhists and Communists in contemporary India: both are against castes, brahmanic ritual, metaphysical speculations. Like Marxism, Buddhism is "universalistic."

6 January

I think I've gone through the majority of primitive myths relative to the creation (or origin) of man. Everywhere, the myth presents the creation (or the appearance: in a subterranean region, in the sky, etc.) of a primordial man, more or less perfect (that is, at first, immortal). But the origin of man does not explain the current situation of humanity. Man becomes mortal, sexed, in conflict with the animal world, condemned to work, etc.—following an event or a series of events that took place in the mythical epoch. That means that for primitives, as for the Judeo-Christian tradition, man as he is now is not only the work of God, but also the result of certain events that constitute a history ("mythical," to be sure, but history all the same). I must take account of this fundamental unity of views when I present the continuity of the spiritual life—from the Paleolithic to Gnosticism.

7 January

Rabbi Samuel H. Dresner, who came to see me a few weeks ago, gave me his book, *The Zaddik*. It's an extensive study of R. Yaakov Yosef (died in 1782), the spiritual head of the Hasidim of Poland. One thing strikes me from the very beginning: during the most disastrous catastrophes of the Jews in Poland, Yaakov Yosef saw the problem in spiritual terms. When he speaks of the reformation *(takannah)* of Judaism, he is not referring to the catastrophic economic and social conditions in which the Jewish communities of Poland then found themselves, but to the fact that "after a certain number of generations, respect (reverence) has diminished" among men (p. 29). What depresses and preoccupies him above all is the spiritual crisis, i.e., the spiritual condition of the people. According to the Talmud, "abandoning the study of the Torah" is responsible for the destruction of the first Temple, and "useless hate" brought about the destruction of the second Temple. R. Yaakov Yosef believed that the same sins led to the destruction of the spiritual center of the Jewish community in the Poland of the seventeenth century.

11 January

Myths on the origin of man: he was made (by the Creator or by a Supernatural Being) from a *materia prima:* clay, stone, wood. This *materia prima* is obviously connected with the structures of the respective cultures: the megalithic peoples emphasized stone (but the myth is found elsewhere also), the agricultural ones, earth or dust (the fertility of the soil, etc.). But that is not where the significance lies— it lies in the symbolism implied by these substances. Rock, stone, is the plastic expression of perenniality: when man was made (or extracted) from stone, he partook of the mode of being of rock. He endured; he did not know death. On the other hand, the perenniality of life in a periodic, eternal regeneration is expressed by the fertile earth, the wood of trees.

15 January

Yesterday and today, almost the whole time with Ed Conze. He gave two lectures on Buddhism—amusing and extremely well attended. Long conversations between us. I learned that he was, and still is, a Theosophist: he admires *The Secret Doctrine,* and believes that Mme. Blavatsky was the reincarnation of Tsonkapa. I asked him a number of questions having to do with astrology. We have entered, he said, into the age of technocracy. The spiritual centers will be destroyed. He compares the destruction of the convents in England and France in the seventeenth and eighteenth centuries to the destruction of the Tibetan convents by the Chinese. Without the destruction of the centers of medieval Christian spirituality, neither the industrial revolution, nor democracy, nor political liberalism, etc., would have been able to triumph. Likewise, India and Central and Southeast Asia will not be able to be integrated into the modern world (i.e., technocracy, materialism, etc.) until the centers of spiritual resistance, convents, ashrams, universities, are radically annihilated.

23 January

So much has been written on animism. Yet I wonder whether one fact has been sufficiently emphasized: in postulating the autonomy of the soul and its survival post-mortem, man opened to himself an unlimited perspective, thanks to which a whole "phenomenology of the Spirit" became possible. The important, decisive fact is that, by belief in the autonomy of the soul, man revealed to himself the (paradoxical) mode of being of the spirit.

24 January

I woke up late (after the fatigue of the evening), in broad daylight. The branches of forsythia that Christinel brought in yesterday have all blossomed. One would think that spring were already here.

At the office, I suddenly remembered that it is the anniversary of the Union of Principalities. I let myself be carried away by memories: in Cernavoda, in primary school; the winters under the German occupation of 1916–1918; so many speeches that I listened to ("On the Significance of the Twenty-Fourth of January in the History of the Rumanians"). A calm, serene melancholy. I heard someone knock at the door. It was my student C. B., a passionate, talkative, enthusiastic black pastor (he believes in the transmigration of souls; he wants to reconcile Christianity with India and the Greco-Oriental mysteries). But this time he seemed shy, embarrassed. He handed me an envelope. He had thought he wouldn't find me and had written me a long letter. He sat down in a chair and watched me, nervous, curious, while I read his letter.

Last night, at the seminar with Tillich, he had got up during the last quarter-hour and had spoken passionately of the urgency of a new theodicy, and of several other problems. He wrote me that, once he got home, it had seemed to him that he had been out of place—and he hadn't been able to sleep all night. His wife had tried to calm him down. She told him once more that he was too sensitive, that he thought too much about what other people thought of him, etc. In vain. So he began to write this long letter and came to bring it to me.

I reassured him as best I could. He left satisfied and smiling. And, once again, I thought of Alexander Ion Cuza, of Ion Roata, of the Rumanian Principalities, of the problems of C. B., especially of the fact that he, as an American black, realizes very well the difficulties that he will have to face in trying to convince his coreligionists of the existence of karma and of metempsychosis, etc., etc.—and all these events, these difficulties and these obstacles, these sorrows, these defeats, these victories, suddenly seem to me to be filled with hidden meanings. But how to decipher them? How?

27 January

Paul Tillich is very interested in what I've been telling him of the *deus otiosus* among the primitives, especially by the repetition of the same phenomenon of withdrawal and passivity in the religions of the ancient East and even in Greece (the castration of Uranus—the most plastic expression of inactivity and obsoleteness). We both wonder whether the same process isn't confirmed in Judaism. Yahweh becomes more and more transcendent in later Judaism. Intermediaries take his place. The powers of Yahweh appear hypostatized: his "Wisdom," his "Glory," or his "Spirit," his "Word." In the image of the Messiah, the Son of Man, we have the "intermediary Power" *par excellence*.

Tillich goes further: for him the theology of the Enlightenment represents a deistic form of the withdrawal of God from the world. As for American Protestant theology of the last fifty years, Tillich considers it "Unitarian in Christ." God is reduced to the second person of the Trinity. The demoniac elements of Yahweh disappear. God becomes the moral law.

But ultimately he isn't so pessimistic: he believes that "the real God" can be reintroduced into American Protestantism by a true understanding of the concept of Being.

28 January

Demystification: X falls in love with Y, and thinks she is the most beautiful woman of all the ones he has met so far, that she is intelligent, good, and full of fine qualities. But she isn't. Even better: since he believes that Y is so beautiful, X imagines that all the men are after her. He suffers from it; he is jealous and unhappy. To understand X's situation, one must enter into his viewpoint and take as true everything he thinks about Y, even though nothing of it, or almost nothing, corresponds to the truth. If these beliefs are "demystified," one loses contact with the concrete reality of the situation and is working in the abstract. A demystified X wouldn't have fallen in love with Y, wouldn't have been jealous, in a word he *wouldn't have existed such as he exists now.* . . .

Try to translate this situation into the terms of the history of religions, and you will understand why demystification leads nowhere.

29 January

In Hans Schärer's book on the religion of the Ngadju-Dayak tribes of Borneo, which I am rereading in an English translation, I found this detail: the worst insult for a Ngadju is to call someone "ignorant of [i.e., uneducated in] the divine commandments." That means that this man is not occupying the place that was destined to him in the divine order and that, consequently, he is not fulfilling the function that falls to him.

The Ngadju-Dayak are, among other things, headhunters, and they practiced human sacrifice until the last century. If Schärer were not a recognized authority, and if he had not studied these tribes for nine years, and had not assimilated their language and their culture, one would be tempted not to believe that the most serious insult for a Dayak is to call him "not educated in the divine commandments."

And yet it is true. A "primitive" culture can be crystallized around a superior and complicated conception of the divinity: a neolithic tribe can have at the center of its religious life the idea of the divinity understood as an "ambivalent totality" (the expression is Schärer's) and nevertheless practice human sacrifice. "Spiritual perfection" does not always imply a moral conception acceptable to the Judeo-Christian tradition or to European humanism. This independence of the Spirit with regard to morality does not necessarily mean cruelty, abnormality, or indifference toward one's fellow men.

30 January

Myers wrote of the Herero shepherds that one could say of a society preoccupied with the well-being and the prosperity of herds that it is *the animals which tamed man.* The life of these shepherds is concentrated solely around the domestic animals whose flesh, obviously, they do not eat. The Herero shepherds are as much to be distinguished from hunters as from farmers. The archaic hunter lived in a mystical symbiosis with the animals that he hunted: he recognized himself as their brother or their relative, he would take care of their bones (he kept them, he did not destroy them, etc.)—but he did not give up his freedom, he did not let himself be obsessed by the well-being of the animals hunted.

3 February

George Wheler visited Eleusis in February 1675. The village had been abandoned a short time before from fear of the pirates ("the Christian pirates, more inhuman than the very Turks . . ."). He found only ruins ("there being nothing remaining, but ruins . . ."). In the muck and the ruins he discovered the statue of Demeter: "among the ruins of old walls, we found the remains of the Goddess herself, *viz.,* a part of her statue . . . made of very white marble, of admirable work, and perhaps of no less a master than Praxiteles himself. . . . It is a colossus at least three times bigger than nature. . . ."

. . . I believe that it was in 1923–1924; I was in the sixth or seventh class when I learned for the first time of the Mysteries of Eleusis.

Probably in a book by Frazer. It was in the autumn of 1924 that I read Raffaele Pettazzoni's *I Misteri*. More than any other, this book was decisive for my vocation as a historian of religions. In the garret of the Strada Melodiei, during the cold, damp November nights, Pettazzoni's book in front of me, I would dream of one day penetrating the secret taken to the tomb by the last hierophant.

4 February

Eleusis, Orphism, the Oriental Mysteries. We will never know of what the initiation consisted, what was revealed to the neophyte. But how creative this ignorance was for Western culture! The neo-Platonic philosophers already saw in the mysteries a philosophical initiation, that is, a series of ecstatic experiences which anticipated the voyage of the soul immediately after death. Between the second and fifth centuries of our era, the Christian apologists and the last defenders of paganism rivaled in their efforts at elucidating the mysteries. The Christians, from Clement of Alexandria to Asterius of Amaseia (d. ca. 410), claimed to know what went on at Eleusis; for them, what went on was uninteresting and, what's more, grotesque or obscene. The neo-Platonic philosophers, in their turn, found comforting realities there: sublime contemplations, intelligible ecstasies, etc., etc.

The Renaissance rehabilitated these noble Platonic interpretations, and since then, each age has taken this hermeneutic and enriched it. "The Greco-Oriental mysteries" fed the imagination of the European elite for three centuries. The role of Eleusis and of Orphism in the elaboration of the imaginary universes of romantic and positivist Europe was considerable. Ultimately, we can say that the mysteries satisfied the thirst of the European elite for *myth,* all during the terrible spiritual dryness brought on by the triumph of scientism and positivism.

6 February

An article that I am reading just now by Professor John Wilson (of the African Institute of London University) shows how different are the capacities of man for seeing. Wilson tells this story: to organize the campaign against the mosquitoes in a region of Africa, he had made a film in which he showed how to go about drying up the ditches of water, how to collect the metal cans left in the fields in which the rainwater fell and caused the larvae of the mosquitoes to flourish, and so forth. The film lasted five minutes; it was simple and direct. It showed only elementary activities: a man collected the metal cans, threw out the water, filled up the ditches, etc. Wilson showed his film in a village—and when light returned to the room, he asked the village inhabitants what they had seen. A chicken, they answered. We saw a chicken flying.

Wilson and his associates were perplexed. They did not remember having filmed a chicken. They reran the film, this time very slowly. Sure enough, for a mere second, in a corner of the screen a chicken appeared abruptly and disappeared immediately. The Africans had seen only this detail. On the one hand, it was the only living thing that interested them and that was familiar to them. The story of ditches and cans full of water that should be picked up had no meaning for them. On the other hand, as Wilson explains, they were not accustomed to looking at the screen in its totality, as a visual unity. They saw the film, as it unwound, in a fragmentary fashion, bit by bit. Since they could not mentally record the film in its totality, it had no meaning for them and they could not "tell about it," or summarize it. What they had retained was the picture of a frightened chicken crossing the screen.

18 February

The Francis Bacon exhibition. Impressed, attracted, but disgusted too. Without doubt, he has, as they say, "strength." It seems obvious that being—or wanting to be—modern, he must show us the ugly, the monstrous, the repugnant. It is to that, it seems, that we are condemned: to boredom in modern literature, to the ugly and the monstrous in the plastic arts. These experiences probably have a meaning: to discourage the public, to take it away from modern art, and thus to throw it backwards toward the cheap "academism" of the past century.

25 February

It's not only the Afrikaners who used to hunt the Boschimans like wild beasts. In Amazonia, the nomads—*Indios do matto* (i.e., the Indians of the forests)—were hunted by the aboriginal populations of a superior culture who practiced farming and were, by comparison with the nomads, extremely "civilized."

The hunting of man by man does not constitute a privilege of white "colonialists."

27 February

Freud: revolutionary or democrat? Until Freud, the Oedipus myth passed for a royal tragedy, implying and confronting royal destinies. Freud unearthed this complex in *each one of us* from the beginning of time—and across all races and all cultures. An extraordinary ambition, that of recovering a universalistic vision of all humanity, from prehistory down to our time. Freud hoped to replace the unity of a biological order (Darwin, Frazer) with a unity of a psychological sort. Men are not all alike because they descend from the ape, but because humanity is the result of the same prehistoric tragedy (the murder of the father, etc.).

Freud's tendency to interject that which is extraordinary, unique, predestined, singular, etc., into that which is universal, common, daily. Before him psychopathology singled out an individual, gave him an aura of "the damned," or "the demoniac." Freud wrote the *Psychopathology of Everyday Life.*

Is he romantic or antiromantic? From Wordsworth to James Joyce, the great European writers did nothing else than uncover the sublime, the tragic, the exceptional, the mythological, etc., in the everyday life of each one of us.

10 March

This evening Jacob Taubes telephoned from New York to tell me that Anton Zigmund Cerbu died this morning. Coronary thrombosis. I'm still dazed. I knew the long and painful heart operation (twelve hours) that he had undergone last autumn. (I telephoned Elise Cerbu each evening to get news.) He was saved—but as he wrote me about three weeks ago, he was left with hepatitis (probably transmitted by the blood generously donated by friends, students, colleagues). He wrote me that he had been keeping to his bed for two months— nausea, dizziness, etc.—but that he was looking forward to Easter as "a veritable Resurrection."

He died at the age of forty, before having had the time to finish anything, to write a single book, to write at least his doctoral thesis. He knew a number of Oriental and European languages. He had read, and he read everything. He had an enormous library. I wondered how he had managed to put it together on his modest scholarship from the Centre de la Recherche Scientifique.

I remember how I had met him: one afternoon, in the Hôtel de Suède, around 1946–1947. He had been a student of Graur and of Rosetti. He had read my books and was fascinated by Orientalism. He had come to Paris to study Sanskrit and Tibetan.

When I had him read *Forêt interdite* in manuscript, after he had finished it, he wanted to reread all my novels. He found them in libraries or at friends' houses, he stretched out on his bed, and he didn't get up until he had finished them.

31 March

Noël King, from Uganda, came to see me. I had met him in Chicago, a year ago. At that time he was teaching in a seminary in Ghana. The seminary had been closed and he had settled in Uganda, where he is inviting me to come for a semester. He assures me that my books are read in the seminaries and colleges of Uganda, and in the other African countries. Especially by the young. He cited this example: because the Anglican Church wanted to assimilate certain indigenous religious traditions, it was decided to bring into the church "the sacred tree" of some local cults. The Anglican bishop, who had read Freud, was opposed to it under the pretext that the tree was a phallic symbol. At that point, a young African priest intervened: I beg your pardon, Your Grace, Professor Eliade has shown that the tree

symbolizes the *axis mundi*. . . . And the bishop accepted bringing it
into the church. . . .

18 April

I read the following in the *New York Times:* A woman was
attacked and stabbed, toward evening, in a neighborhood in Queens
in New York City. *Thirty-eight* witnesses saw the crime; some pointed
their headlights onto the scene for a few moments and the murderer
stopped, but no one intervened; each went his way. One shouted from
a window—but he didn't come down to help or protect the woman.
The woman even recognized one of her friends, called him by name,
begged him—but the man was probably in a hurry, for he went his
way. The attack lasted thirty-five minutes, and during the whole time,
the woman screamed, yelled. The police station was two minutes away
by car. Finally one of the witnesses telephoned the police. Too late:
the woman was dead.

NEW YORK, *26 April*

From Judah Goldin's lecture (excellent), I have retained this:
the destruction of the Temple in A.D. 70 truly traumatized the Jewish
people. Since that time, the Jews no longer have any place where they
can *practice* their cult. They can no longer do anything but *pray*. But
God, Goldin made clear, has no need of jabbering. He wants gifts,
offerings, a ceremonial.

30 April

Meditation on the love of the Japanese for nature: the flowers,
the yellowed leaves, the naked trees, etc., all this illustrates precari-
ousness, becoming, passingness, vanity. That is why the Japanese
accept and love nature: they understand its lesson.

CHICAGO, *18 May*

I'm finishing the chapter on death, the afterlife, the mythologies of death, etc., for *From Primitives to Zen*. About eighty typewritten pages. In order to make my choices I've lost, now, about ten days.

I've reviewed, reread, gone through several thousand pages. It's true that I've been living among these documents for about fifteen years.

I wonder whether such a source book is worth all this trouble? And this is only one of seven or eight chapters that the book will include. If I've been able to work without stopping, it's because I don't feel myself capable of doing anything more personal. According to my estimates, I'll need about a thousand hours of work to finish the source book.

23 May

I've begun writing a short text for *L'Art du XXe siècle:* "Permanence du sacré dans l'art moderne." I would have liked to take advantage of this chance to formulate, at leisure and less abruptly, the conclusions at which I've arrived on the survival of sacredness in modern art, a survival that is unrecognizable. Brancusi, who has rediscovered the sacredness of brute matter, who approaches a "beautiful" stone with the emotion and veneration of a man of the paleolithic. Chagall, who admits his longing for paradise in his donkey foals and his angels. And especially the nonfigurative painters who abolish forms and surfaces, penetrate to the inside of matter, and try to reveal *the ultimate structures of substance.*

26 May

I'm making an effort to finish the article for *L'Art du XXe siècle.* I feel that I won't succeed in saying even the essential. I have to send it off in a few days, and every time I write under pressure, I write poorly.

I would have liked to analyze especially the religious significance of the "destruction of worlds" (traditional artistic worlds). To be compared to the ritual scenarios ("primitive" and paleo-Oriental) of periodic destruction and re-creation of the cosmos. The *religious* necessity for the abolition of old, tired, inauthentic forms ("illusory," "idolatrous"). All this corresponds in a certain sense to the death of God proclaimed by Nietzsche. But there is more: the passion for matter resembles the pre-Mosaic cosmic religiosity. The modern artist who can no longer believe in the Judeo-Christian tradition ("God is dead") is returning, without noticing it, to "paganism," to cosmic hierophanies: substance as such incarnates and manifests the sacred.

6 June

While Freud was preparing his *Traumdeutung,* the English Theosophists were talking about "akashic history" and "nature's memory." According to the latter, nothing of what happened has ever been forgotten by nature. The memory of these events—cosmic, historical, personal—is conserved in different natural objects. Certain men—those who possess a "proper psychically attuned mind"—succeed, upon contact with certain tangible objects, to capture the latent history that lies there.

It's interesting to note that Freud also thinks that nothing of what happens to man in his childhood is lost, that is, really forgotten. Everything can be recovered (with the help of the psychoanalyst) from a basis not of "tangible objects" but of images.

Marx said that the great historical transformations are repeated: everything that is accomplished in a "tragic manner" is repeated in a comic form. (I don't remember exactly his formulation. To be checked.) I would add that the repetition is not always a regression from the tragic to the comic. The theory of akashic history of which the Theosophists dreamed does in fact seem a little comic and irresponsible, and yet, it corresponds in its structure to Freudian theory. Freud was fascinated with occultism. Could he have read the theosophical lucubrations in fashion after 1895, and very popular especially in 1898?

To gather material on the recovery method of akashic history, I should go through the confused volumes of Leadbeater and Annie Besant. I can't face it. . . .

1 July

In the evening, I'm continuing reading the second volume of Annie Besant's biography by Nethercot. The extraordinary vitality and energy of this woman. And during the theosophical period, her unbelievable naïveté which surpasses all limits of the credulity expected of an occultist, and reaches delirium or hypnotic stupidity.

And yet, at the time as she was letting herself be dulled by Leadbeater and company, Annie Besant was awaking India from its secular lethargy, organizing the first centers of propaganda and political education. Gandhi came *later*. He benefited from everything A. B. had accomplished—and, at a given moment, he surpassed her and concentrated in himself all the hopes and energies of India, for the very good reason that he had guessed this: in a political movement, the only leaders with a chance of success are those who know how to satisfy (or to chloroform) the extremists.

Some day I must study this paradox: the triumph of the apostle of nonviolence is due in large part to the support of *extremists*.

Interesting details: Annie Besant was the first to call Gandhi by the title Mahatma. She was also the one who created the term that was so popular during the First World War: *The Huns* (i.e., the Germans).

8 July

Van Nuffel, S.J., told me that in ecstasy one feels only oneself. One does not *feel* God. You know him before—and after. And you know him because you have been told about him, that is, because the Church has taught you about him.

We spoke about the religious situation of today. Van Nuffel is not afraid of the accelerated desacralization of the world, of life, of man. He thinks that desacralization and "demythologization" purify the structures of religious life.

23 July

My desk is disappearing bit by bit under the stacks of files and books. And the several hundred volumes recently arrived from all the libraries of the university are submerging the armchair and the two straight-backed chairs and are piling up dangerously, propped up by the shelves of my library, which they are hiding. I tremble every time I don't find a folder or book immediately, because I often lose half an hour looking for it. To say nothing of the letters and notes that I usually keep on my desk, and that disappear just as frequently, buried under folders, papers, books.

In the evening I take several volumes, with the intention of reading them or leafing through them to look for texts (sometimes only one or two pages) for *From Primitives to Zen*. I've reread *Digha Nikâya* and *Majjhima Nikâya* with pleasure and a certain melancholy (too many memories . . .). So far, I've kept seven or eight pages.

Actually, I am the only one who benefits from this routine work: I'm rereading in order to refresh my memory of the sources close to which I've been living for nearly forty years. What tires me and depresses me is correcting typed texts and putting the finishing touches on them for publication (the time I waste finding a title, writing a little introductory note five or six lines long, copying the explanatory notes . . .).

25 July

Went with the Weavers and some other colleagues to Ravinia to hear Ella Fitzgerald. Nearly an hour by car through parks and woods, not without going through little towns from time to time— "the suburbs"—which seem to me unreal, artificial, at least such as I find them among the trees and grass. How much longer will they be able to survive, hidden, lost in the midst of this mass of cheap, ugly, even monstrous houses, some dilapidated, others erected overnight on ground vacant yesterday and, it seems to me, uglier and more hideous than those built yesterday or the day before.

The extraordinary park of Ravinia with its auditorium open on three sides. Picnic on the grass, among several hundred families and groups. Then, at eight thirty, Ella Fitzgerald—and all those jazz songs from the different parts of the country and from the 1920s, 1930s, 1940s. . . . The enthusiasm of the audience, young for the greater part. At the intermission and after the end of the show we had trouble passing through the couples stretched out on the grass, in the semi-darkness. One has the impression of being somewhere in France. How the "customs" of Chicago have changed since our arrival here! Today the young people kiss on the grass, they walk everywhere with their arms around each other, or holding hands. And yet I'm not convinced that they love one another, that they desire one another. If this is how they act, it is because they think they ought to do it—and especially to prove to themselves that they are not like their parents, that they are *different,* and that they can do what they want.

27 July

From time to time, I remember—and I find myself suddenly sad, depressed: I no longer know which way to look for courage. *Whatever happens, we are lost.* Our world, my world, is irremediably condemned. This alone would be enough: every three years China increases by the population of France. In the beginning of the twenty-first century, China will constitute half the population of the globe. In fifty or sixty years, the world will not have the same face—nor culture, nor meaning of existence, nor moral values. There will be born another world which could be just as creative and interesting as the one that came into being in Greece around the seventh century B.C. But it is no less true that *our world* will disappear, and in a manner perhaps even more tragic than the way the worlds of the Near East and Greece disappeared. For example, I imagine Europe inhabited by Asiatic or African populations; intelligent and cultured people walking in the old cities or among the ruins, without even looking at them, without understanding them (like the Anglo-Indians of Calcutta who would pass Hindu temples every day without giving them a glance, from scorn or from hate).

2 August

Yesterday I began a short article: "Notes sur le *Journal* d'Ernst Jünger." Wolf had been asking me for it for a long time for *Antaios* (March 1965, when Jünger will be seventy years old). I've already written eight pages—but I know that I will have to delete, correct, add. I want to get this article over with, to become free again to be able to enjoy my stay in Paris in September.

The article on Jünger interests me. I would like to say everything I'm thinking about the interest of a journal worked out following

E. J.'s technique: that is, using rapid notes or little fragments written during the day in order to write (probably in the evening or the next day) a short paragraph which reflects the essential. In other words, the journal conceived as a literary genre—and not as a short report (the Léautaud sort). What seems important to me is this: our generation and those that have followed it no longer believe in "systematic works," but in personal creations (and, nevertheless, exemplary ones), in "free" texts (an essay that uses the technique of the novel, of drama, etc.), in meaningful fragments, etc. A good part of Jünger's work is written as a journal, or it has that structure. That's where I see its "actuality" (although Jünger seems somehow neglected in Germany). He illustrates a literary genre that will soon become the fashion.

3 August

Tom Altizer is still asking me how my autobiography is going. I regret having interrupted it three weeks ago to devote myself t   the source book (which is useful only for American students). Tom is pushing me to write about Proust some day. You are fascinated, he said, by the problem of the ritual recovery of lost time, and now that you are writing your autobiography, you will "see" things in Proust that no one has seen.

6 August

I'm rereading—perhaps for the twentieth time—the Bhaga-vad-Gita, to choose a few fragments from it. As usual, overwhelmed, carried away. What an extraordinary book! It is rare that you *feel,* as you do here, the religious genius of India; you feel even the creative act, because you have the impression that it is *there,* before your eyes that the synthesis is accomplished that was awaited and prepared for by century upon century of intellectual effort, meditation, despair.

And, as always, memories: I can see myself, for example, in my hut at Rishikesh, during the winter of 1931, translating the Bhagavad-Gita into Rumanian. Are these pages still to be found somewhere? The only direct translation from the Sanskrit into Rumanian attempted up to that date. But, in 1931, my Rumanian—which I hadn't been speaking for nearly three years—didn't permit me to render all the beauties of the Gita.

15 August

Since I am approaching (in the writing of my autobiography) the summer and autumn of 1935, when I was writing *The Hooligans*, I was curious enough to reread that novel. I hadn't reread it, I believe, for around twenty years; the last time was in Portugal. Certain episodes appeared admirable to me. But I didn't have the patience to read the pages devoted to theoretical conversations and arguments. The cruelty of some scenes exasperated me. Nevertheless, perhaps it is precisely the savagery and bestiality of these hooligans twenty to twenty-five years old that give the novel its significance and *actuality*. For these cynical, cruel, wild young men have become familiar in the western Europe of the last ten years. The *blousons noirs*, the beatniks, behave in 1960 like my hooligans of 1930.

I remember what M. was saying to me last autumn, after having read *The Hooligans*. The novel, she was telling me, is very *modern* and I ought to correct it, improve it, and have it translated into French. She was sure it would be successful. At that time I didn't believe her, but perhaps she was right. I ought to try to recast it. But when? When?

18 August

How important is *what happened after*—that is, what, in a spiritual creation, has been retained, assimilated, put to use, developed. Zalmoxis, for example, is more original, more profound, more "true" than many of the Greek gods—but we do not know what happened after him. Did he disappear? Was he forgotten? Was he transformed and camouflaged afterward into one of the figures of Rumanian folklore? We do not know. It is for that reason that Zalmoxis has not played the role that he would have deserved in the history of religions or of culture.

28 August

I don't know why I thought of Matyla Ghica today; I remembered our meetings in London, in 1940, his novel *Pluie d'étoiles,* which he had given me and in which I found once again the London of before the First World War, and so many other things. Matyla Ghica was then around sixty-five, and he would read a book every day (he was, of course, a member of several lending libraries). He believed in ghosts—once he showed me the photo of a country house, the family and friends dowirs at the front door, and at one of the upstairs windows, a blurred figure: someone who had recently died. M.G. also believed that the Second World War was really the conflict between two secret societies: the Templars and the Masons.

He knew an enormous number of things, and he expressed them well, with humor—just as well in Rumanian as in French or in English. M.G. was a famous author around 1930, after he had published *Le Nombre d'or,* with a preface by Valéry. He continued to write and publish, but after 1945 he no longer interested anybody. For a year, he was a visiting professor of aesthetics at one of the California universities, collaborated with W. Disney, etc. And, yet, around 1950 he had become very poor. Old Payot, the publisher, told me that he used to give him books to translate, for otherwise he would have died of hunger. (And his wife was an Asquith. . . .) If he is still alive, he must be almost ninety. When I met him the last time, around ten years ago, he told me that he had just written a detective novel. . . . In London, he had a collection of yataghans, sabers, and Malaysian knives. He also had an extraordinary collection of posters and proclamations from the time of the French Revolution. He had probably sold everything.

29 August

I'm reading *The American Adam* by R. W. B. Lewis. The examples that he gives of the rejection of the past by American writers of the first half of the nineteenth century—such as *Earth's Holocaust* by N. Hawthorne (written in 1844): the vision of a conflagration of cosmic proportions, consuming indiscriminately the costumes, the scepters, the symbols, the institutions, the literatures, and the philosophies of Europe. " 'Now,' declared the chief celebrant, 'we shall get rid of the weight of dead men's thoughts.' "

Thomas Jefferson: "The earth belongs in usufruct to the living; the dead have neither power nor rights over it." Around 1850, Hawthorne wrote *The House of the Seven Gables;* one of the characters, Holgrave, exclaims: "Shall we never, never get rid of this Past? It lies upon the present like a giant's dead body!" And he complains: "We read dead men's books! We laugh at dead men's jokes," etc. The same character regrets that the public buildings and the churches are built of stone or brick. He would have liked to see them be demolished and disappear every twenty years to allow the people "to examine and reform the institutions which they symbolize." (To be compared with the Japanese customs that consist in periodically remaking the temples. But how different the reasons are! . . .)

The same attitude from Thoreau: every link with the past must be severed; the past must be rejected as a "dead skin," etc. "I look on England today as an old gentleman who is traveling with a great deal of baggage, trumpery which has accumulated from long housekeeping, which he has not the courage to burn." Admirable image—and one that applies just as well to countries and to cultures, as it does to individuals.

Lewis shows how obsessive is the picture of this American Adam and how deep the belief that in America humanity has a unique chance to *begin history over.* Last year, when I was preparing my Eranos lecture, I had collected a good deal of material concerning the paradisiac mythology of the pioneers and colonists (cf. "Paradise and Utopia: Mythical Geography and Eschatology"). What is interesting to note is that the Adamic longing survives, slightly altered, among the writers of the first half of the nineteenth century. Thoreau is fascinating also as an example of Adamic life: the bath that he takes every morning in the pond and that he considers a rite of rebirth. And his love for children (so specifically American): "Every child begins the world again," he wrote. A "traditional" idea, i.e., implying the hope for periodical regeneration of the cosmos, society, the individual.

Rejection of the past, the desire to abolish it—all that reflects an archaic mentality, "pre-" and "anti-" historical. There are so many more things to say. . . .

30 August

I'm continuing to read Lewis's book. The religious vocabulary in *Leaves of Grass;* for example, the odor of the body was "finer than prayer"; in Whitman's head there was "more than churches, bibles, and all creeds." And this admission in which Lewis rightly sees an Adamic narcissism: "If I worship one thing more than another, it shall be the spread of my own body." Or: "Divine am I, inside and out, and I make holy whatever I touch." To be compared with the vocabulary of the mystic *sahajiya* that I presented (summarily, incompletely) in my book *Yoga: Immortality and Freedom.*

But Lewis also points out this theme in Whitman: the past is dead, it is a corpse, etc. All this in order to be able to affirm that *the human race is born to a new life* in America. The obsession with the dawn, the primordial, the absolute beginning. (Whitman read only Homer, for Homer was so "primordial" that he didn't constitute a past, a history. . . .)

And yet it is with the older James—the father of William and Henry—that the reaction against the paradisiac myth begins. James writes: "The first and highest service which Eve renders Adam is to throw him out of Paradise." In losing Paradise, man begins to become himself; that is, disengaged, open to culture, perfectible; he gives meaning and value to existence, to the things of the life around him.

1 September

If Freud is right (what is *essential* is unconscious), the current tendency of literary critics to decipher initiatic scenarios, myth and ritual patterns, in novels, short stories, plays—this tendency has a deeper meaning. Therefore it is necessary to apply a demythologization in reverse. Freud, like Marx, taught us to find the "profane" in the "sacred." In the case that I am considering here, it is in "the profane" (the narrative novel, everyday characters, common adventures) that the critics are finding "the sacred," implicit and camouflaged. And that is precisely what is significant in the situation of modern man: he satisfies his nonexistent religious life (nonexistent on the conscious level) by the imaginary universes of literature and art. And it is just as significant for literary critics who find religious significance in profane works.

16 September

Goethe, Rilke, and all the other great writers who took up the themes and characters of Greek mythology revalued, reinterpreted, them. Admirably. But I feel that *we* can no longer do the same thing; we can no longer return to the classic mythologies, to what refers exclusively to Greece and Europe. Our duty—as writers, scholars, and philosophers—consists of reinterpreting, for the modern Western consciousness, the *other* mythological traditions, and first of all, the archaic traditions. Orpheus and Eurydice. That's all very well. But this time the poet must also know, and take into consideration, the Amerindian, Polynesian, Siberian Shamanistic mythologies which anticipate or presuppose the descent of Orpheus to Hades to save his soul. (Cf. the pages devoted to that theme in *Shamanism.*) It's not a matter of letting oneself be inspired by these exotic myths or legends, but of creating poetically in a perspective in which the significance and beauty of the Polynesian myths, for example, are revealed to the reader with a force equal to that of Rilke revealing to him the meaning of the myth of Orpheus.

17 September

Why can "scholars"—anthropologists, historians of religions —not *look at* the objects of their study with the same patience and passion with which artists look at nature (more precisely, at the natural objects that they want to paint)? How many things a scholar would succeed in seeing in an institution, a belief, a custom, a religious idea—if he observed them with the concentrated attention, the disciplined sympathy, the spiritual openness that artists evince. What anthropologist has ever looked at the objects of his study with the fervor, the concentration, and the intelligence of a Van Gogh or a Cézanne before the countryside, the forests, or the wheat fields?

How can one understand a thing if he does not even have the patience to look at it attentively?

24 September

Santayana and the profession of teaching: Oliver (the hero of *The Last Puritan*) says he is going to become a teacher because he doesn't think he is "fit for anything else." And another character remarks: "People must teach themselves or remain ignorant, and the latter was what the majority preferred." Santayana considered the profession of teaching a means of subsistence—and especially of being able to go to Europe every year. More on Santayana and on the university: he didn't socialize with his colleagues. Here is what he said about Harvard, or more precisely about the increasing emphasis on specialization at Harvard: "An anonymous concourse of coral insects each secreting one cell, and leaving that fossil legacy to enlarge the earth."

And a legend: During his class, Santayana suddenly looked through the window, then addressed the students: "I have a date with spring," he told them, and he left. And he never came back.

25 September

An anecdote taken from the recollections of Miss Sarah Champion, who, in 1940, one year before Frazer's death, had been his secretary at Cambridge. "She describes Sir James and Lady Frazer, he quite blind and paralyzed, she stone deaf, seated in two thronelike chairs in Cambridge, holding hands. Miss Champion's principal job was reading aloud for Frazer. She writes: These readings were always from his own works, and he would listen with the greatest attention, as if hearing for the first time the words of a promising colleague. His favorite tale was that of the witch of Endor, taken from his own version of the Old Testament." [S. E. Hyman, *The Tangled Bank*, p. 192]

10 October

Next week the Faculty Retreat will take place at Lake Geneva. Brauer is asking me to comment on Gilkey's text on "The Death of God Theology." I'm beginning to read it. It is entirely devoted to Hamilton, Van Buren, and Tom Altizer. Moving, but difficult to understand, the seriousness with which these three young theologians are discussed. The death of God is a well-known phenomenon throughout the history of religions. Usually it is a matter of the "death"—i.e., of the disuse—of the traditional, *conventional expression* of a certain god or of God. Or of "God" camouflaged in apparently secular figures, images, powers, symbols.

What I do not understand is the *theology* that these three young authors are trying to build on the evidence of the "death" of God. I understand Giordano Bruno ("Dio, come assoluto, non a niente da fare con noi . . ."), I understand Nietzsche. . . . And yet, the interest that a Van Buren or a Hamilton is awakening among the young theologians is significant.

22 October

Freud had the courage to admit: "I am not really a man of science. . . . I am by temperament nothing but a conquistador . . . with the curiosity, the boldness, and the tenacity that belong to that type of person."

2 November

The acculturation of "primitive" societies upon contact with Western cultural values is not a lone phenomenon. A similar process is to be observed in the West, especially in the last thirty or forty years: one can speak of the acculturation of Occidentals under the influence of scientism and technology. Let us take as an example contemporary art and literature: their roots in traditional ideologies and their continuity with them have been broken. To be able to be the contemporary of modern science and technology, an artist must ignore the whole (Western!) history of his art.

18 November

A long conversation with Alfred Stern, philosopher and man of science, who is here for one year as a visiting professor with the Committee on Social Thought. For me, it was a stimulating and comforting discussion. Stern—who is only thirty-five—is not afraid of admitting his "universalism": in no way does he want to confine himself to mathematical physics, logic, or history of culture. He thinks that specialization means spiritual death, cultural sterilization. He especially detests "social scientists": arrogant, conceited, and, finally, naïve. He explained to me at great length how unscientific their method is. Stern has come here to be able to finish a book begun some time ago on wit and humor. He asked me for numerous items of information on humor in primitive and Oriental cultures.

6 December

In the study that I am now writing, I wonder if I should emphasize the fact that true History of Religions, that is, an authentic and imaginative hermeneutic, changes man (for reading such a book has an awakening effect). I wonder, too, if I should allude to the fact that historians risk their serenity and their equilibrium to try to understand and interpret archaic, exotic, aberrant, "terrible" religious situations. It is obvious that the majority of historians of religion risk nothing—either they isolate themselves in their own beliefs or in the most trivial materialism, or they devote their whole lives to a single sector (India, Greece, etc.) and finish by banalizing their documents. But some day I must show the seriousness of the influence exerted by meditation on archaic myths and symbols. It is a change from within which the scholar does not even realize. Compare the *memory* of such a historian of religions with the memory of a literary critic, or of a historian, to say nothing of the memory of a naturalist.

11 December

I'm reading in a single sitting the mediocre biography of Croce by Fausto Nicolini. My admiration for the man Croce when I become aware of his daily schedule: six hours of sleep, twelve hours of work —but how? Every morning he would make a detailed plan of his day, and when night had come, before going to bed, he would check to what extent he had accomplished it.

Peculiarities: while he was writing, he didn't keep a single book on his desk. If he needed a quotation, he would get up, take the book, copy the lines that interested him, and put it back on the bookshelf. Extraordinary power of concentration. How is it that he didn't lose the thread of his thought during these repeated comings and goings? (Croce would regularly quote dozens upon dozens of works. . . .) I admire—and I do not understand. And I'm ashamed of my laziness, my negligence, and my indifference: when I "work," books, folders, papers pile up on the desk, pile up around me, on chairs, on the floor, remain there for weeks and weeks, become covered with dust or discolored in the sun, because I always put off until later the long and boring task of clearing off my worktable. I prefer taking books and folders indiscriminately and putting them (for how long?) in a free spot in the room.

13 December

I'm continuing to read Nicolini's book on Croce. His enormous correspondence, and the critical editions that he published. I've learned that Croce kept a journal for I don't know how many years. Then, later, he found the time to copy it into six large notebooks— which can be published only in twenty years.

15 December

The Croce-Vossler correspondence that I had leafed through ten or twelve years ago. This time I am rereading it with care and delight. The surprising and distressing letters of Vossler in 1914 on the war: Germany, which had been attacked by an act of treason, should defend itself and will defend itself to its last drop of blood, etc., etc. "We will conquer," he wrote. "The cowardly French hide their cannon behind the Reims cathedral. . . ."

I wonder if Vossler really believed what he was saying.

Croce to Vossler, July 22, 1919: "The Italians, out of modesty, are only a little chauvinistic, and the English are only a little chauvinistic because they are superficial. It is the French and the Germans who are chauvinistic."

17 December

In *La Critica,* Croce comments on Heidegger's rectorship speech. Vossler wrote him on September 4, 1933, that Heidegger's influence is stronger in Spain than in Germany. Among Heidegger's admirers, he also names Zubiri.

Remarkable also are the errors, the resistances, and the naïvetés of Croce's obtuseness. In 1938 (cf. *Carteggio,* p. 362) he wrote to Vossler that Mallarmé "in poetry has done little or nothing and that he exerts so much ascendancy by promising something or other that he called poetry."

Winter in Mexico

MEXICO CITY, *29 January 1965*

We left Chicago this morning during a terrible cold spell (−18 degrees F.). We took off around eleven o'clock and landed in Mexico City at two thirty in the afternoon. We didn't believe our eyes: heat, cloudless sky, palm trees, flowers. It was so hot that I was tempted to take off my jacket. At the airport, Graciela de la Lama, director of the Oriental section of the Colegio de Mexico. She drove us in her car to the Hotel Luma, Orizaba Street. Bad room. We rested for a few hours, but we're both a little dizzy. In the evening de la Lama and Laurette Séjourné (with whom I have been in correspondence for nearly ten years) came to see us. At night we collapsed from fatigue.

30 January

We awoke late. Splendid sky—and it is as warm as Capri in May. I went off to visit El Colegio de Mexico, a few blocks of houses from the Hotel Luma. A new, modern, almost luxurious building. I discovered, with a sigh of relief, that I have an office here of my own where I will be able to work.

After that, we took a walk in Insurgentes y Reforma until two in the afternoon. Lunch at the hotel (excellent). They changed our room. (We now have a window as big as the wall, we are bathed in light. . . .)

At five o'clock Laurette Séjourné came by car to get us. The Museum of Anthropology, Chapultepec Park with its high, proud trees —and a strange, unknown odor, as if we were a few steps from the jungle.

We went back downtown and arrived at Zócalo Square at nightfall. The presidential palace, the cathedral, and all the other buildings are illuminated. L. S. guided us through old Mexico City. In front of San Dominico Church, an "Indian" dance. The father, mother and three children, costumed, wearing feathered headdresses, danced (I would say) with an archaic step, leaping and challenging one another. The people gathered around them threw money.

After the dance was over, a few women, some helped by children, headed slowly, painfully, on their knees toward the portal of the cathedral. There are about thirty meters to cover on a pavement of old stones. One old woman was bleeding.

31 January

Graciela de la Lama took us to Xochimilco, a village about fifty kilometers from Mexico City. It's Sunday, and the fruit, vegetable, and flower market was teeming with buyers, tourists, peasants from the surrounding countryside who have come to sell or to buy goodness knows what: some eggs, some tomatoes, a bag of grain. We threaded our way through the crowd with difficulty. Smells, colors, hubbub, and good humor as in an Indian bazaar.

The Church Del Rosario—admirable when seen from the sidewalk across the street. Then toward the lake—and of it there remain only some canals and a lagoon crowded with boats. But what sort of boats? Large, spacious (some have eighteen to twenty little chairs), covered with a flower-bedecked, highly decorated canopy, of an aggressively bad taste which, finally, saves them because they seem to be giant, cheap toys. We all got into a boat (it was called *Ofelia*), and we were rowed off. The water is shallow, not more than half a meter deep, and the rower pushes the boat from behind like the gondoliers of Venice. The shores between which we were gliding (followed by hungry dogs) were not the real shores as I would have imagined; they are rather floating islands that move slowly with the trees and houses with which they are laden. That is what the lake is: innumerable floating islands separated by canals. Tens and hundreds of bedecked, pink boats advancing side by side gliding past one another. And worming their way between them are alert, flat little boats on which all sorts of things are sold: beer, lemon soda, Coca-Cola, sandwiches, grilled meat, shawls, rugs, toys—and boats with photographers following us patiently and obstinately. In the majority of boats, bands of musicians —costumed, merry, tired, and not stopping their playing except when a more powerful band comes close to them. Families of Mexicans have lunch and throw a bone or some other scrap to the dogs on the shore.

In one spacious boat, a compact group of young people—and some couples who were dancing. We heard English being spoken, and we quickly recognized American tourists. But for the most part it was Mexicans, and this sort of diversion suits them marvelously. They are relaxed, smiling; they eat and drink without hurrying; they enjoy the light and the sun.

1 February

Bad night: insomnia. Still, I woke at eight o'clock so I could attend the opening of the new academic year at the Colegio de Mexico two hours later. The director of the college, Silvio Zavala, read the report on the current state of affairs. Then the secretary general of public instruction said a few words. The whole thing lasted less than fifteen minutes. I ran into Bosh-Gimpera (after how many years?) and met Professor Paul Kirchhoff, who is fascinated by pre-Columbian China-India-Mexico relations.

In the afternoon, in my office, I went through my files of notes on Indian religions. I'm trying to prepare my first class for tomorrow (Mohenjo-Daro and the invasion of the Aryans). Immense melancholy; all these things have been assembled, interpreted, organized for years. (I believe I've given three courses on Indian religions.) The pages I'm going through now should constitute the first chapter: India (without Buddhism) of the magnum opus. It only remains for me to go on to the definitive *writing*—and in French.

2 February

I've begun my class: from noon to one o'clock. About fifty students in the lecture room, which has at least one hundred seats. Twenty-five are registered for my course; the others are auditors (coming for the most part from the linguistic section, but also from other disciplines). I spoke on Mohenjo-Daro and the Indo-Europeans. Fairly good. Before the class, a lady, de Mora, came to invite me to give a lecture at the Jesuits' university (Ibero-Americana). I declined the proposal, but I agreed to meet a group of professors and Jesuit fathers for a discussion (on the methods of the History of Religions, naturally).

I had lunch with Professor Paul Kirchhoff. A titan. And a "concentration camp" voice, as Laurette Séjourné says. (Without making any allusion, moreover, for P. K. was not a Nazi; he has been a professor at the University of Mexico for twenty-two years. Before that, he was in the United States.) He speaks English perfectly. He is fascinated by the China–India (Java)–Mexico connections. "I am an old-fashioned diffusionist," he admitted to me. And he explains in this way the resistance of American scholars (North and South): they want there to have been, at any cost, a great *autochthonous* civilization in America too (outside the "primitive" civilizations studied by the ethnologists). Everything that is great in North and South America is of European origin. They would like the pre-Columbian civilizations of Central America at least not to depend on another culture: India, China, Mesopotamia.

In the afternoon back to the college. I like to work in this warm, light room. The purple light from the mountains that I see from the window.

I took out a pile of books from the library on the pre-Columbian civilizations; I also took out a few volumes of the *Obras Completas* of Unamuno, which I'm leafing through nostalgically, but I have to prepare my second class, look for some Vedic and Brahmanic texts, pick from my files the pages that I will read and comment on.

3 February

On his way to the capital of Mexico, Cortés stopped at Cholula, the most famous sanctuary of the pre-Columbian world, and there, in less than two hours, he killed six thousand persons gathered in the inner court of the temple. This massacre aroused the admiration of the great warrior Montezuma, emperor of the Aztecs. Which explains the welcome that he gave to Cortés. It also explains the fact that the Spaniards could walk in the streets, enter the temples, destroy "the idols." They were even able to arrest Montezuma, make him a prisoner in his palace, without provoking any reaction.

A second Cholula was necessary—namely the massacre in the Great Temple—for Tenochtitlán to revolt, and the Spaniards to have to withdraw from the capital. But they returned a few months later to annihilate the Aztec empire and civilization.

I have never read the history of the conquest of Mexico without being ashamed of being European and Christian.

4 February

At three in the afternoon, Laurette Séjourné came to drive us to Teotihuacán. Three-quarters of an hour of superhighway. Then, suddenly, we saw the Pyramid of the Sun. But the paved road (in stones!) which goes around the recently cleared field of ruins is completely absurd. Nothing can be seen anymore. L. S. told us that, to construct this road, hundreds and hundreds of houses of great archaeological interest had to be destroyed. So much so, and so well, that the road is raised by two meters and that the levels of the destroyed houses can sometimes be distinguished on the edges: the floor of the first edifices, the ruins, the floor of the habitations built on top of them, etc.

We left the car in the shadow of an administrative building and went in. The Pyramid of the Sun. Christinel and I climbed as far as the first terrace. A young boy offered us some "authentic," fired clay statuettes. I bought two or three from him to make him happy.

By car to the Pyramid of the Moon, recently unearthed. We left the car on the road and went in. The excavation work on the whole thing was finished last September. Theatrical performances are being organized. Some workmen were taking down the scaffolding which had been used for the last show.

We visited a restored house, with admirable frescoes (some authentic). Then to Ciudadela. Behind one pyramid is another one that cannot be seen from a distance, with gargoyles, threatening dragon heads which jut out. A furious wind; it is cold. And as always when, for the first time, I see monuments that I had been dreaming of seeing for a long time and that I knew only by photographs or reproductions—a little disappointed. Without knowing why.

On the way back, we stopped at Acolman Monastery—a grayish-white color, splendid. In the courtyard, a cross of stone, the head of Christ carved in the center of the cross.

5 February

At Horia and Anna Tanasesco's. A family and house fit to put into a novel. Two boys, both very gifted. (Stephane, the younger, fourteen or fifteen years old, is really a genius. Last year, like so many others, I had admired his black and white sketch book.) Horia T.'s library, rich, varied, and a little strange. His books are arranged on the shelves according to the chapters of a book in preparation (on personality, language, communication?—I couldn't say precisely). His wife, Anna, Italian, makes jewelry. H. T. was, for some years, a professer (of psychology of art) at the Ibero-American University, but his chair has just been done away with. Intelligent, cultured—but aggressive and whimsical. His long article on the Dominican poet Domingo Moreno that he had given me had especially interested me in the verses that he quoted. Everything I'm learning about this highly original mulatto poet delights me. (He recites his verse in villages, fairs; he prints them himself at obscure printing presses, etc.) H. T. thinks that, without knowing it, Domingo Moreno has rediscovered Zen Buddhism and psychoanalysis.

6 February

I woke up dizzy. We went to the Museum of Anthropology. I had noticed it last Sunday from the car, when Laurette Séjourné had taken us for a ride in Chapultepec Park. Admirable—and extraordinarily rich in everything concerning pre-Columbian civilization. One would need weeks to become familiar with it as it deserves. Dizzy as I am, I'm contenting myself with going through the rooms in a highly melancholy mood. For the first time I *feel* that I won't have enough time ahead of me anymore to become familiar with a civilization that I don't know.

7 February

Still just as dizzy. Splendid day. I went to Rio de Janeiro Park, a few hundred meters from the college. On a bench in full sunlight, I let myself be carried away by the whim of my memories. After a little time, I couldn't follow them anymore—they were running too fast. Once, on a bench (but where?), in full sunlight too, I was reading *L'Océanographie de l'Ennui,* by Eugenio d'Ors. A good many years ago. If I weren't having these dizzy spells, perhaps I'd be able to remember it more precisely.

And suddenly, images of the provincial parks in Portugal came to mind. I remember their terrible melancholy. Worlds long since dead that are waiting only for a vigorous blow of the barbarian to crumble.

Evening, at Horia T.'s. He gave a lecture for his former students at the Ibero-American University. An amusing group: a refugee Cuban doctor, and his brother, who is a painter; a young woman with a swaddled child; some female students. H.T. asked me to say a few words on Taoism and Zen, which were recorded.

8 February

In the window of an Orizaba bookstore, a couple of steps from our hotel, a sun-yellowed copy of *La Gondole aux chimères,* by Maurice Dekobra. *Sic transit.* . . . Ten or twelve years ago, a couple steps from Les Deux-Magots café, I noticed a photograph of the author in a window, and a copy of a Japanese translation; beside a typewritten page, covered with fly specks, some information on the number of copies printed and the number of the translations of Dekobra's works.

I remember: it was around 1927, in Bucharest. The Atheneum Hall, packed: Maurice Dekobra was to give a lecture there. I had gone to write the review in *Cuvântul.* Even with my press card, I had a lot of trouble getting into the room. Several hundred persons were left outside. I saw Stelian Mateesco giving a speech and explaining to those who were around him that they shouldn't go hear this third-rate author, etc. We met after the lecture, and we both wrote short, violent reviews: I *from the inside,* he *from the outside.*

Then, during the winter of 1929, I met Dekobra in Dasgupta's house. He wrote this dedication for me on a copy of *La Gondole aux chimères:* "To M.E., this gondola for dreaming of the Upanishads on the shores of the Ganges."

9 February

This morning, I gave my class. In the evening, from seven to eight o'clock, public lecture on "Yoga and Modern Philosophy." After that, an anthropology professor from the Ibero-American University took me by car to Mme. de la Mora's. A forty-minute trip. Splendid house in the university neighborhood. (It seems that Mr. de la Mora is a famous architect.) I was invited to meet some Jesuit professors from the Ibero-American University. X. tried again to persuade me to give a lecture. I excused myself as well as I could (dizzy spells, sleepiness). Interesting discussion.

Last year, on the way to Moscow, he was in Rumania and stayed a few days in Bucharest and Mamaia. The anthropology professor told me a host of fascinating details about that trip. They were with about ten Mexican students. All impressed by the Latinness and anti-Slavism of the Rumanians.

10 February

Cuahtemoc, the last Aztec emperor. The name means "the falling eagle." His fierce resistance against Cortés during the siege of

Tenochtitlán. Captured, he was tortured to make him reveal where the treasures of the empire were hidden. (They burned the soles of his feet with boiling oil.) He did not reveal where the hiding place was. They took him far from Tenochtitlán, when Cortés abruptly decided to execute him: he was afraid of the revolt of populations submissive only in appearance. The emperor was hanged by his feet in the tropical forest of Chiapas. Some claim that, hanged head downward, he did indeed look like an eagle falling. And yet . . . There is his statue in the center of Mexico City. And his name on innumerable streets, factories, advertisements, etc. And there is not a single street bearing the name of Cortés in all of Mexico. Although they speak Spanish, the Mexicans feel themselves one with their Aztec ancestors, conquered and exterminated by Cortés.

I'm thinking of the fate of Trajan and of Decebal. We Rumanians claim both of them but are especially proud of Trajan and our Latin origin (so precarious, nevertheless, from the ethnic point of view); culturally, however, that is first of all linguistically, we belong to Rome and not to Dacia.

12 February

Second "Round Table" seminar. There is also the anthropology professor, Jiménez Moreno, a specialist on Central America. He says some interesting things, but always stays on the descriptive and empirical level. Every time I tried to go further into interpretation and asked him what *meaning* all these religious facts could have, Moreno would agree with me, would seem delighted, but wouldn't continue the hermeneutic on that level. He would always go back to the "documents," to the "sources."

Afternoon. Tanasesco took us by car to the Monastery Monte Carmel. We climbed nearly five hundred meters in the "Park of the Lions," a forest of giant conifers. The monastery was burned during the Revolution. But except for some demolished rooms, the church and the adjacent buildings have remained standing. Beautiful, melancholic cloister, with all sorts of well-cared-for flowers. (The Mexican passion for flowers. Is it true that cruel people like flowers?) We visited the torture chamber: the victim was tied at the bottom of an empty pool, would hear the water running alongside, but couldn't drink. The corpse was carried away by the subterranean stream. (But what truth is there in all that? Tanasesco is the one who told it to us. It seems that there have been no studies of the "problem.") In any case, we saw the prisoners' cell—and that was enough for us. (As at Castel Sant' Angelo.)

And the inevitable legends: the subterranean corridors that connect the monastery to the town (several tens of kilometers!) and through which they took the women for the "orgies." When the women became pregnant, they walled them up alive in the corridors of the monastery.

14 February

In N. Petra's car, to Cuernavaca. As soon as we began to climb, the rocks rose up on either side of the road like fortresses. And bee hives everywhere.

After an hour we arrived at the little town of Tepoztlan. It was Sunday, and the fair was going full swing. In the shade of the walls, old women with Aztec features as if they had escaped from bas-reliefs. The church—Dominica de la Natividad—is from the sixteenth century. A wedding (some little girls were skillfully gathering up the grains of rice on the ground) and a baptism. A young man came forward on the threshold of the church and threw a fistful of little copper coins. Children, teenagers, and some big, husky fellows jostled one another. And meanwhile, a loudspeaker was giving forth Bach.

Two pesos per person to visit the *patio* and a part of the former cells of the monks. On the fourth floor, a gallery in ruins where one can gaze at the view of the valley. The cells, dilapidated, are abandoned. A poster announces that the curate—who probably lives toward the square—is available to the parishioners at certain hours.

On the *patio,* a fountain and a basin shaded by palm trees. Two young girls came to draw water in light plastic pails of the most varied colors.

The path followed its hairpin turns through the mountains. At the edge of a village, Ocotopec, the cemetery; we stopped the car and went up to the low wall to look. It looked like a village in miniature. The tombs were surmounted with (I ought rather to have said supported) little colored houses; one expected even to see dolls at their windows —or babies. We went through Ocotopec—and we noticed the churches in passing.

At Cuernavaca, in the beginning of the afternoon. We had lunch in a picturesque restaurant, evidently invaded by tourists: Las Mañanitas. Above the fireplace a strange painting—a lady of the colonial period—it looked like a painting by Leonor Fini. Beside us, at the next table, an old lady—she seemed even older when she tried to smile. She had lost her teeth quite a while ago.

We left on foot, in a burning heat, for the park and the chateau. In the Viennese café where we stopped, some little girls insistently offered us necklaces of seeds and dried fruits. Christinel bought necklaces for all her lady friends in Chicago and Paris. The park—the same; the same in the Spain of the nineteenth century, in the Portugal of yesterday, of before yesterday. . . .

The road to Xochicalco. The car climbed very high—we continued on foot to the pyramids. Not far from there can be seen the lakes, and on the horizon, as everywhere, mountain ranges. Some half-starved dogs, a few houses: in a courtyard chickens, kids. Under the arch, a Mexican was selling Coca-Cola, lemon soda, tortillas.

The "Structure C" edifice; we climbed the steps as far as the first platform; of the sanctuary that once stood there but has since burned, there still remain some walls. Not very far from here, the Pyramid of the Feathered Serpent. Admirable ornamentation of different colors. The motif of the feathered serpent, as well as that of the big-eared god, is repeated indefinitely. I bought Cesar A. Saenz's brochure, *Ultimos descubrimientos in Xochicalco* (Instituto Nacional de Antropologia e Historia, Mexico City, 1964), and looked through it right on the spot. I learned that, quite probably, a temple used to stand on the top of the Pyramid of the Feathered Serpent, identical to that of Structure

C. I also learned that, during the excavations, some anthropomorphic vases with the face of the Rain God, Tlaloc, and offerings of all kinds were found. In the neighborhood of the zone of ceremonies, the cemeteries. From the pottery, Saenz situates them between A.D. 500 and 750.

From above, other earth-covered structures can be made out, not yet explored. How much time is still needed before all the stages of this civilization are known?

We returned to Mexico City at nightfall. That ocean of lights an extraordinary spectacle.

Monday, 15 February

We woke up late, both of us dizzy. Is it because we went down to Cuernavaca and came back up afterward? For the first time since I've been in Mexico City the sky is dark. In a bad mood all morning. I worked reluctantly, trying to prepare my class for tomorrow.

16 February

Difficult day. Class from noon to one (the Upanishads). At one thirty, lunch with Jiménez Moreno. Fortunately, he did the talking most of the time. (I listened to him with interest and I learned a good many things. When people are surprised that "I know so many things," I reveal my "secret": I know how to listen, I know especially what questions to ask specialists.)

At seven in the evening, a second public lecture ("Mythologies of Memory and Forgetting"). The ambassador from India attended. He is a giant with a beard and a turban. He congratulated me warmly after the lecture. (But I wonder if he listened to it. He had probably come because he had learned that the first lecture was about yoga. He had thought that I would talk some more about India.)

Afterward, we went to have dinner at Horia Tanasesco's, and, once again, we talked until midnight. I went to bed around two o'clock, exhausted.

Thursday, 18 February

Last class. (With what clarity does the history of Indian religious thought now reveal itself to my eyes! The lecture was recorded. If it is well transcribed, I could publish it.)

In the evening at Laurette Séjourné's. Cohen, who translated my book *Méphistophélès et l'Androgyne* [*The Two and the One*] into English, was also there. Great lover of poetry. He wrote a book on Robert Graves and sent him the manuscript. Graves answered only this: "Very well done!" (Like at school, Cohen commented.) He is surprised—and delighted—that I am so "human," that I have a "sense of humor."

Finally, there was Juan Rulfo, the author of the novel *Pedro Paramo,* which many consider the best contemporary Mexican novel. Still young—perhaps forty-five, forty-six years old—but he looks worn out, tired. Unfortunately, he speaks only Spanish, but he understands French. He told me that he has read almost all my books translated into Spanish. The conversation was facilitated by a young philosophy teacher, just returned from an international congress in Geneva. Likable, intelligent; he is interested in the philosophy of religion.

After dinner, we listened to the recording (edited by Wassens) of the ceremonial of hallucinogenic mushrooms. Monotonous litanies in one of the numerous Mexican dialects that no one in our group understood. Every now and then, the words "Santo! Santo!"

19 February

Last meeting of the "Round Table." Also present were Dr. Caso (author of the book *El pueblo del Sol*) and a French ethnologist who has been working for twenty years on a thesis on the Mexican ritual of "the flying man." There was also the young philosophy teacher whom I met last night at L. S.'s. Once again the problem of human sacrifice among the Aztecs. I was asked to give a comparative exposé of all the types of human sacrifices that the History of Religions knows about. The exposé finished, I spoke of the ambivalence of this sort of sacrifice in which, in fact, the god—incarnate in or represented by a human being—is *immolated to himself.* I emphasized once again the meaning of these bloody rites in relation to agriculture. Cereals are not given (like animals to the paleolithic hunter, for example), but they are born from the body of a divine, or half-divine, being who has been assassinated. To ensure their permanent supply, human beings are sacrificed, which means that man assumes the responsibility for maintaining the cosmos alive and fertile.

Afterward, the lunch given by the director of the college, Silvio Zavala. At our table, Dr. Caso and the Frenchman spoke without stopping. I rested. Neither a speech nor a toast, fortunately.

TAXCO, *20 February*

We gave up Acapulco. We decided to rest two days at Taxco. N. Petra is taking care of both travel and accommodations. We left by car—both of us and a Dutch couple from Curaçao.

We arrived at Cuernavaca around noon. This time we stopped to visit the cathedral: a fortress of pink stone, built in the sixteenth century, in the middle of a garden with large trees, flowers of all kinds, and a pond.

Two years ago, while cleaning the walls, they discovered some frescoes illustrating the life and martyrdom of the first Mexican saint, San Felipe de Jesu. Some scenes: fish and fishing boats; the arrival of the missionaries in Nagasaki, their crucifixion alongside a few Japanese converts.

The surprise of the cathedral is the high altar—extremely modern. It was the bishop who wanted it that way. But the government supposedly forbade the modernization of the rest of the cathedral. The driver who was serving us as a guide told us that the bishop is very "advanced"; certain newspapers have supposedly even stated that he considers the Jews to be "Christians, or nearly so."

Borda Gardens—the garden of Maximilian. Mango trees and, invisible, birds with tropical cries, and parrots. The private chapel. The guest rooms. A pond, as big as a natural one, in which algae are growing—on the edge of the pond, a walk and a "place of contemplation." A young boy appears and runs past, near to us, with a bow and a quiver.

Once again in the Garden of the Heroes and the palace of Maximilian, which we had seen Sunday. We stopped to have coffee. The driver talked to us enthusiastically about the archaeological discoveries of Mexico. The Dutchman from Curaçao remembered a Rumanian jurist, a specialist in the problems of interplanetary commerce, from whom he had learned a few Rumanian words. He added, with sadness, that the jurist had just died.

To Taxco. Marcas trees (calabashes), cactus-shaped. On the side of the road, the girls were offering us live iguanas for sale; they showed them to us, tied on a cord. For about twenty kilometers we climbed up a road with hairpin turns. And then, abruptly, you discover Taxco —on the hill opposite, several tens of giant jacarandas in bloom. The Hotel de la Borda, on the edge of the town. Brand new, admirably constructed and furnished. Full of American tourists. They stay there one day and go farther on to Acapulco. Our room on the top floor, with beams in the ceiling, and a smell of wax and honey, as in Rumanian monasteries.

In the afternoon, the sky darkened and it began to rain. Like in the mountains. Like in the Bucegi. In the evening, in the lobby full of elderly Americans, we watched the fire in the fireplace and waited for the lights of Taxco to be lit. Between two showers, we strolled past store windows displaying silverware.

21 February

Sunday. A burning sun which heralds rain. We read in the garden. A huge, beautiful swimming pool that two Mexicans were lazily cleaning; they slowly fished out the jacaranda flowers which were losing their petals.

At the end of the garden, two cages; in one a pair of little monkeys from the tropical forest no bigger than a cat a few months old; in the other, another monkey just as small, from Brazil. We watched him with fascination: he had the head of an Indian.

It rained all afternoon. Around sunset, the weather seemed to be about to clear. Through the windowpanes of our veranda, we followed the flight of the colored birds (orange, blue, red) among the branches in search of some rare food or other in the half-closed corollas. Then, they disappeared abruptly, silently: they hid, became immobile somewhere under the branches. We soon understood why: from over toward the mountain the vultures had taken flight, heading toward us, gliding majestically a few hundred meters overhead. They were almost not moving their wings. Calm, proud, they glided without haste.

At night, in our almost glacial room (some covers were brought us . . .), I read *Les Mots*. I don't understand why this book is considered a "great," important book. Paul Ricoeur was telling me a few months ago in Chicago that it was "admirably written." In comparison with so many theoretical pages of J. P. Sartre, this book is, indeed, well written. But then what can be said of Emile Cioran?

I cannot manage to believe in the child that Sartre reconstructs. I constantly have the impression that he is projecting "into his tender childhood" his later philosophical conceptions.

22 February

All morning in the garden waiting for the car which was to take us to Mexico City. Then two hours of waiting in the hotel lobby. Strange sensation: dozens of tourists leaving, dozens of others arriving —they seem to be the same ones.

The car arrived just when we had given up waiting for it and were ready to hire another one from Taxco. The young driver praised the archaeological riches of Mexico.

Late, toward evening, we stopped at the Tres Marías to have coffee. An impression of great poverty—but much good will. (Which we haven't found in Mexico City. The inhabitants of Mexico City are sad, melancholy, shut up in their dreams and the balancing of their accounts.)

MEXICO CITY, *23 February*

In Dostoevsky's novels the hero reveals unexpected aspects and contradicts himself from one chapter to another in his behavior as well as in his ideas: the same thing happens to certain gods of India (Varuna, Indra, etc.). After having learned that Varuna is a celestial god, Cosmocrator (master of the universe), and so on, one learns that he is also "the brother of the Serpent," a "viper," and that he has something of the Great Serpent Vritra. After having enthused over Indra's heroism in hundreds of hymns, you learn that after his victory over Vritra, he became afraid, fled, hid himself, made himself tiny, etc.

OAXACA, *24 February*

We got up at five thirty so we could take the plane for Oaxaca at seven thirty. We crossed the city in the darkness. But on the street corners we saw children and young people shivering in the cold waiting for the bus to go to school.

The flight over mountains the color of burnt clay. On our left the two volcanoes—covered with snow. At eight thirty we landed at Oaxaca. It was warm, the sky was clear, and the city came into view half-hidden among the trees. By car to the Hotel Victoria; brand new, almost sumptuous, built on the hill on the edge of the city. Now we saw Oaxaca at our feet. All around, fields—and in the background, the mountains.

In the afternoon we went down to walk in the city. We chose at random a steep street which seemed to fall off toward the valley, with children playing in the dust and the inevitable starving dogs. We reached Calle General Garcia Vigil—and shortly after, we discovered the first church, Santisima Virgen de la Soledad, surrounded by tall trees. The church is beautiful, constructed like a fortress, according to the custom of the past. The inside lacks interest; it has been redone, painted a cheap "angelic" blue. Some women creep toward the altar on their knees.

Next to the church, the flower and vegetable market. We went on.

The houses became more beautiful—with those long, thin bars on the windows.

San Domingo cathedral is truly majestic. I read that it was built in the sixteenth century by Dominican monks: in 1862 it was converted into *caballeriza* "because of the necessities of war"; in 1869 fourteen altars and chapels were destroyed. In 1902 it was given back over for worship services—but only the church proper. (Next to it, in the former convent, there is now a military barracks.) Very gaudy, Spanish baroque, with a great deal of gold, statues of saints, ornaments. Near the high altar, on one side, is a door, today walled up, which used to open onto the convent; on the other side is the damaged wall, of which the old frescoes (or decoration) have been destroyed.

We headed toward the center of the city. The inevitable park with its bandstand for military music—and all around hotels, stores, cafés. It seemed like a fallen provincial city. We visited the square and the adjacent streets which reminded me of the Lipscani of my childhood. And the little church of Misericordia Street. When we came out of the church, the brass band in the bandstand was getting ready to begin. We waited on a bench; seated on benches, or in isolated groups, the inhabitants of the city were waiting also. I don't know why, but the band didn't play.

At night I'm reading *Cat and Mouse,* by Günter Grass. Without enthusiasm. (Exasperated too by that Canadian critic who proclaimed that Günter Grass is superior to all American novelists, including Faulkner. . . . I read such nonsense on the cover.)

It seems as though I'm starting my life over again, beginning with my childhood and adolescence. In fact, all my interests of those times are being rekindled—and in the same order. First, stamp collecting; then, entomology, botany, mineralogy. With what impatience I looked today for insects in the hills behind the hotel. With what joy I inspected unknown flowers. I close my eyes and see once again the ten volumes of *Souvenirs entomologiques* in the garret of Strada Melodiei; I leaf through them again mentally. I've promised myself to borrow them from the library as soon as I return to Chicago.

25 February

In the morning, very early, by car toward Mitla. We stopped at the village of Tule, to see the famous Arbol del Tule. A sort of cypress (*Taxodium mucronatum,* an inscription on the wall specifies), it is near a little church; it is about twenty meters in diameter, and, probably, 2,500 or 3,000 years old. (The guide tells us that "French botanists" affirm that it is 5,000 years old.) The church, commonplace. Two turrets painted white and blue. Alongside, another *Taxodium,* more modest: only about twelve meters in diameter.

We got into the car and continued our trip. Excellent (American) road through poor fields. That treelike plant with red flowers is the castor-oil plant; from its seeds is drawn the laxative oil.

We passed near the little pyramid which is almost entirely buried. They tried to excavate it, but it was so deteriorated that the archaeologists gave up.

We arrived in a village, Tlacolula. At the entrance, on the walls of the first house, giant advertisements: Pepsi-Cola, Coca-Cola. The guide told us that Tlacolula means "the twisted thing." Here a city was founded before the Conquest. In 1550 the first Dominican missionaries arrived, and between 1580 and 1621 they built the church of Santa Maria de la Asunción. It has two little towers, painted pink-orange and white. It supposedly has one of the most beautiful chapels in all Mexico; "very original," the guide explained to us. We went in. Some women dressed in black. Ornamental candles in gilded wood, and the inevitable statues of saints in front of which were other women, kneeling, dressed in black. (And again, that same impression of a pagan temple, of a polytheist cult which does not even dare admit itself and assume itself as such.)

In front of the church, a large, recently constructed school, and alongside, the square.

We stopped again, at the edge of the town of Mitla, to visit a weaving workshop: "Alberto's Handcrafts (Turistes welcomed)." Two men, one rather old, work standing at a loom for covers and carpets. The Americans photograph him, film him. (And how proud the men are, the old one especially. . . .)

Above the houses the vultures were slowly circling—and so high! The burning noon sun, and the overly blue sky—and suddenly I remembered: in the Carpathians, the same scene, I was watching the vultures gliding, after having read "La Vraie Mort de Guynemer," and i was wondering: Is that how Cesar Petresco discovered the subject of his short story by watching, as I am doing at this moment, the vultures circling in the sky?

In the courtyard of the workshop, a pomegranate tree laden with ripe fruit.

We crossed Mitla to go directly to the ruins. San Paolo Cathedral (we didn't visit it: it's from the nineteenth century, the guide told us, blasé), but right next to it, the archaelogical zone. Between the cathedral and the ruins—women cloth vendors, little bells, reproductions, figurines and statuettes.

Mitla: *mictlan en nahuatl,* "place of rest." In fact, this is where the Zapotecs' cemetery was located. It was not a city, but a necropolis, with temples, public buildings, and a palace where the king and the priests came to live a few months each year for the duration of the ceremonies. (The king was also the high priest.)

We climbed up toward the sanctuary and went into the first hall. In the middle, stone columns, three to four meters high. I began to remember what I learned. The Zapotecs were the first inhabitants of the region of Monte Alban. Mitla was probably one of the last places where they came to build. They took 150 years to finish the sanctuaries and the palaces. Around 900–950, Mitla was built. Then the Zapotecs left Monte Alban and came here. When the Spanish arrived, they were amazed. Obviously, they began to destroy, and they eventually destroyed almost everything. With the stones of the monuments, they constructed houses and the church (not the one which is alongside, but another, long since demolished).

It is exasperating to find everywhere the same cruel, stupid vandalism. But I try to understand: for the Spanish, the Zapotecs, the

Aztecs, and all the others were like the "pagans" were for the ancient Hebrews (Canaanites, Philistines, etc.); they had just about the same religious beliefs, and practiced, among other things, human sacrifice. I remember the rage with which the Hebrews destroyed the altars, the temples, the idols; I remember the Old Testament.

The great hall of the palace was decorated. In 1901, the guide told us, the government decided to reconstruct the whole archaeological complex. And in the beginning the reconstruction was badly conducted (poorly matched stones and bricks can still be seen in the walls). Mitla is a site unique in Mexico because it was never buried. What the Spanish were not able to destroy has remained as we see it today. And after the blunders of 1901, nothing more has been restored. The rooms had wooden roofs—they burned, rotted, and now one sees through to the sky.

We went through a tunnel and reached another room, square, with stone ornaments. Next to it, the apartments of the priest-king. Everything was constructed of stones—big ones, little ones, minute ones—arranged in such a way that cement wasn't necessary. (Moreover, they did not know about cement.) And extraordinary mosaics. The ornate pavement is slightly inclined so that the rainwater can drain off (one can still see the drainage holes). The guide pointed out that some half a million stones, large and small, had been used. Some transported from a distance of twenty kilometers. The architects therefore had a plan of the whole construction; they knew a system of mensuration, therefore "mathematics."

On the ornate pavement and on the walls the mosaic is a red or green color. The Dominican monks reported that there were furs on the floor; there were also chairs and low beds.

We went out and, from the top of the stairway, looked once more at the plaza where the ceremonies had taken place. Temples all around. Here the sacrifices had taken place: wild animals and, three times a year, human sacrifices. They have been described by the Dominican monks who were present at them. We went down. From the middle of the square we looked at the palace façade, with its three central doors. The wind suddenly rose. We saw an American's hat fly away—so high that we thought he would never recover it. We headed toward the tombs. Here in this public garden, on the side of the main square, there were four temples—and under each temple, tombs. We entered the necropolis of kings. The guide got the attention of those who suffered from claustrophobia, and asked them not to go in. It really seemed that each of us suddenly found himself seized with claustrophobia. It was warm, almost suffocating—and we breathed with effort, as though we lacked air. On all fours we went into a tunnel fifty or sixty centimeters high. In the center of the necropolis, which was in the form of a cross, the guide was waiting for us with a flashlight. He showed us the designs on the walls—swastikas among others. And a map of the world, a sort of ziggurat and a cross in the middle (the center of the world). The corpses were not buried but were deposited on the ground and surrounded with jewels and gifts. (I saw similar tombs in the museum at Mexico City.) The wind seemed to have frozen, we felt it slap us in the face so. The other necropolis is that of the priests. We didn't go in. It is half-open—and a stone column can be seen in it. It is called the column of death. Men embrace it, and the number of fingers which can be placed between the two hands is the number of years that they have left to live.

(Opposite us, beside us, the Dutch couple on their honeymoon, holding hands, silent, absorbed. Why? . . .)

MONTE ALBAN, 26 February

We went through the village of San Juanito. Twelve kilometers from Monte Alban. The name is Spanish (at that time, the mount was covered with white trees in the spring); in Zapotec it is called Oanidipa, "fortified place." The Zapotecs used to come up here for their cult. In the valley they built their houses of reeds, which is why nothing of them has been discovered. The first dwellings, around A.D. 800–1000. The citadel was abandoned around the year 1000 of our era, when the Mixtecs arrived.

Monte Alban was conquered late by the Spaniards. Afterward it was forgotten until the end of the nineteenth century, when Dupaix discovered the pyramids. In 1901–1905, Porfirio Díaz, from Oaxaca, began the excavations. Dr. Caso resumed the exploration in 1930; he uncovered temples and tombs (twenty-five temples so far, but there were probably many more). They all have the same form. We saw one from above. The walls were colored. Of the north esplanade (restored in part), there remain six truncated columns, two meters in diameter. We headed toward the central esplanade, carved in the mountain. The stairway by which we gained access to it has remained as it was originally. Stelae with strange designs (they supposedly represent astronomical figures). We visited an edifice with a sundial. We were taken next to another pyramid. We went in through a tunnel. Other faces, different ethnic types. In fact: mongoloid, negroid (= Aztec? Semite?). They seemed to be wearing Egyptian headdresses. Dances. Phallic symbols. On the outside, numbered stones. A piece that represented a lewd woman.

We climbed onto an immense pyramid, partially unearthed. One can see the whole city. The pyramid proper is covered again by the forest.

Afternoon in the museum in Oaxaca. Extraordinarily rich. We lingered especially in the Monte Alban hall. The corn deities in the hall of the monoliths. Then, on the floor above, tomb number VII with its fabulous treasure. In the display windows: corals, shells, enormous pearl necklaces, alabaster vases, turquoise and jade necklaces. (If Flaubert could have seen them!) In an isolated corner, a rock-crystal vase. And that extraordinary skull done in a turquoise mosaic. And the God of death; his golden mask reproduced on so many postcards. On the wall, the photograph of Caso, in front of tomb number VII, at the moment he had discovered it. (I should have written down more closely my conversations with Dr. Caso last week.)

Discoveries

CHICAGO, *2 March*

. . . And since my friend had annoyed me by telling me that these were only "speculations," I reminded him that "speculation" comes from *speculari,* "to observe." Well, then?

6 March

Blaga saw in "popular folk culture"—"more particularly in the anonymous creations born of the Christian spirit as well as those which issue from the heresies"—the source of Rumanian creativity. I think that he is not mistaken—but for reasons very different from those he advances. Folk culture is fed on what I have called "cosmic Christianity," that is, a Christianity in which the historical element is ignored, and in which the dogmatic element is scarcely manifest. On the other hand, all nature in its entirety is transfigured by the presence of Jesus, who participates in the mysteries and the sacraments. *The world, life, living matter* acquire religious dimensions. Christianity in general, and "Christian philosophy" in particular, are capable of renovation if they develop the cosmic Christianity in which the Rumanian people matured. The considerable success of Teilhard de Chardin is due notably to this fact: he "resanctified" and re-Christianized the world, life, matter.

PRINCETON, *4 April*
As it is, half demolished, Pennsylvania Station is depressing. And by chance we found the dingy train, worn, dirty seats—a train such as I didn't think still existed in America. Fortunately, it was a warm, clear Sunday—and the blue sky, the budding forests, consoled us on our misadventure.

At Princeton Junction, Professor and Mrs. Ashby were waiting to take us by car to 130 North Stanworth Drive. A little apartment belonging to the university where we will live for six weeks. Absolute silence—we hear only the whistling of the blackbirds at nightfall.

I took out my folders and put them on the desk. I could work profitably here if I weren't continually traveling (beginning next week . . .).

5 April
In the morning, I visited the university. My office is in the library. (It's Ch'en's office; he has gone to Japan for a year.) It's as if I were once again at Oxford. (The Oxford of the summer of 1936, not the one that I knew four years later, in the middle of the Blitzkrieg.) How well I could work here!

7 April
Surprise at the seminar of the other evening: those with a certain artistic experience (notably in painting and architecture) understood what I meant when I spoke about the morphology of sacred space. They understood because they knew how different "artistic spaces" are from Altamira to cubism, from megalithic constructions to baroque architecture. On the other hand, they had difficulty following me when I talked about the "space" of the novel *Finnegans Wake* —which the listeners with psychological concerns "understood" so well (they had certainly read Piaget, Minkowski, Erikson).

However that may be, the interest with which I was listened to, the questions that were put to me, convinced me once again how timely is the analysis of the symbolism and the morphology of space, such

as I understand it myself; that is, by referring to archaic and traditional cultures, in which "to exist" means first of all to exist in a world
constructed in conformity with the exemplary model (the cosmogonic
myth). Thence, the indissoluble bond between sacred space and mythical, primordial time, that is, the time when the world was created.
I illustrated this space-time unity by Indonesian examples, but it
seemed so logical that most of them accepted it as being obvious.

Another surprise: all the listeners agreed that the two types of space
—"chaos" and "the world," that is, ritually constructed space—are
still valid for the experience of man today.

19 April

Did I write down the conversation I had with R. Bultmann in
Marburg, during the winter of 1955–1956? The meeting had been
organized by E. Benz. All the questions I asked Bultmann were so
many blunders. First on Rudolf Otto (his *bête noire*), then on Van der
Leeuw, finally on Barth. But when I explained to him that the "demythologization" of the New Testament did not always seem justified
to me, that was the last straw. For example, that *raptus mysticus* of
Saint Paul reported in the Second Epistle to the Corinthians. Why
"demythologize" the "third heaven" solely because it does not exist
as an astronomical reality? I spoke to him about the reality of the
imaginary universe based on ecstatic and oneiric experiences, about
"magical flight" and about all these images which manage to communicate transcendence, absolute freedom (the flight), the abolition of
the human condition, etc. I certainly didn't convince him. Far from
it.

NEW YORK, 21 April

Last night at Carnegie Hall, Ionel Perlea admirably directed
Lucretia Borgia. The American debut of the soprano Monserrat Ca-
ballé—sensational. She is a young woman, pretty, but rather strong.
And then, with unequaled instinct, she moves, swaying, as if she were
copying certain positions from Greek vases. It was not applause, but
ovations which lasted five or six minutes. Ionel was brought onto the

podium on the arm of the assistant. He conducts seated on a chair. But he conducts "divinely," as a stranger said in a neighboring box. He finally has this satisfaction: a triumph at Carnegie Hall, after the cardiac accident of eight years ago, which left him half-paralyzed.

Today we read all the newspapers we could buy at the newsstands in the neighborhood. Enthusiastic reviews.

PRINCETON, *5 May*

Last evening we had dinner at J. Nichols's (former Chicago colleague). An admirable house, in the forest, a few kilometers from Princeton. One of his boys, about seventeen years old, is a great lover of boas. He has had three so far. When the first two died, he put them into a box and buried them with this inscription: "Here lies my good friend, the snake X [the name], whom I will never forget." The third boa is still small: about a meter and a half. The boy came to show it to us, the serpent wound around his neck. It was sick, and an emergency call was made to a specialist from the zoo (the visit cost ten dollars). The snake is now out of danger. A cage was set up for it in the boy's room: an electric light is constantly lit to maintain the necessary temperature (on the sand, the thermometer that the boy consults from time to time). Every two weeks the snake swallows a little mouse. If it isn't hungry, it doesn't swallow it immediately. The last time, the mouse walked up and down for several days on the snake's back.

I am happy to note once again that man can love *anything*.

9 May

The sensation aroused by my statement that Buddha, Zarathustra, and the Jewish prophets are our contemporaries, in the sense that the problems they posed are still ours. When one studies these problems, one is not building erudition—but one is confronting the problems of the philosophy of *today*.

10 May

I found a note in which I had written some details (transmitted by Joe Kitagawa) concerning a Japanese who liked to raise tigers. It took place around 1938. Several tigers, big or little, were left free and walked around in the house as they wished. In the same region at the time there was a well-known thief, nicknamed Sekkyo-goto ("the preaching thief") because after having stolen what pleased him, he would leave a note in which he would reproach the owner with his negligence and with not having taken the necessary measures. The thief had become famous. Even the police who had come specially from Tokyo hadn't succeeded in putting their hands on him. One night the "preaching thief" got into the house of the man with the tigers. As soon as he saw the first tiger, he fainted. That is how he was caught and condemned to I don't know how many years of prison. But the encounter with the tigers had definitively cured him; it had been like a sort of conversion. While he was in prison he wrote "the confessions of a thief" (or something of the sort; Joe no longer remembered the exact title). The book was published, and it was extraordinarily successful.

12 May

The desire of archaic man to live in an open universe, a center which could communicate both with heaven and with the underworld regions. One has difficulty believing how general was this longing to be located in a world both *orientated* and *meaningful* together, that is, "sacred."

CHICAGO, 21 May

John A. Wilson tells this anecdote: there were two giants of Egyptology at Thebes for the excavations: Sethe from Berlin and Naville from Geneva. Although isolated in the desert with a few other scholars, the two "greats" would never speak to each other, because they didn't agree about an event from the time of Queen Hatshepsut. But this occurred: following the excavations, Naville's quarters collapsed and Mrs. Naville announced that they would return to Geneva. Mrs. Sethe, who learned of their misfortune, invited them to live with them, on a single condition (established by Sethe): that Naville never speak of Queen Hatshepsut. Naville accepted and spent several months in Sethe's house. They became the best of friends. Eventually, the Navilles' house was repaired, and they went back to their own place. From that day on, the two Egyptologists returned to the previous situation: they no longer spoke to each other, and if, by chance, they were invited to a mutual friend's, the one later to arrive would withdraw. . . .

8 June

I'm working on "Prince Dragos and the Ritual Hunt," but, as I feared, I've let myself get carried away—and the study will be twice as long as expected. I would like to have at least this understood: if in these myths and legends an animal, notably a wild beast, plays the leading role (in pursuing him the hero discovers an unknown country, or reaches the underworld, or else meets a fairy, a demon, or a Boddhisattva, or finally dies . . .), it is because in the myths and legends an archaic conception of the world survives, perhaps the most ancient: to wit, the animal *reveals* and man behaves according to these revelations; it is the animal that determines the *orientation* in an amorphous, indefinite space, it is the animal that predicts the future, and it is again it that determines the *path,* which is equivalent to breaking through to another level; the path, that is, the solution of an impasse. In Sanskrit, *marga,* "path" (i.e., soteriological solution), from the root *mrg,* "to pursue game."

30 June

I'm doing the review of Scholem's book on the Kabbala. As usual, when I'm in a hurry, I'm stating, without developing them, a good number of ideas and comments. Some day I must return to this theme: in the Kabbala we have to do with a new, real creation of the Judaic religious genius, due to the need to recover a part of the cosmic religiosity smothered and persecuted as much by the prophets as by the later Talmudic rigorists. What is significant is that the Kabbala redevelops very ancient, cosmic symbols and images (the Tree, the Sun, Fertility, etc), alongside gnostic, almost "heretical" ideas. Even better: introduced into the idea of God are feminine elements (Shekinah) and dramatic ones (God's withdrawal, His exile, etc.). It would be interesting to compare cosmic Christianity, that is, the beliefs of the rural populations of southeast Europe and of the Mediterranean, with these medieval and postmedieval Judaic religious creations. Surprising parallelisms: devotion to the Virgin Mary and the importance of the Shekinah: the Christological drama and Yahweh's exile, paradigm of Israel's exile, etc.

PARIS, *23 July*

I was telling Cioran not long ago how boring and useless the modern studies (1920–1940) on the problem of God seem to me. It is as if I were to find a pre-Socratic ontological argument one hundred or two hundred years after Aristotle. In a "world" composed of billions of galaxies, including, quite probably, a million inhabited planets (as I've read in the statements of a famous astronomer), all the classical arguments for or against the existence of God seem to me naïve and even childish. I do not think that, for the moment, we have the right to argue philosophically. The problem should be left in suspension as it is. We must content ourselves with personal certitudes, with wagers based on dreams, with divinations, ecstasies, aesthetic emotions. That also is a mode of knowing, but without arguments (of whatever nature: logical, cosmological, ontological, etc.).

31 July

Stig Wikander told us some fascinating things on the history of "Aryanism" in Europe. He found the origin of the idea of the superiority of the Aryans in the anticlericalism of Jules Michelet and Edgar Quinet. It is because they wanted to disparage Christianity (directly or indirectly) that Michelet and Quinet exalted the Vedas and "Aryan wisdom." Their anti-Semitism and that of their admirers was only a reflection of their anticlericalism. Their Aryanophilia was of a religious nature. The brother of the celebrated Sanskritist Eugène Burnouf, Emile, who was a professor at Nantes, wrote a history of religions in which he demonstrated the importance and antiquity of the Vedas. The book had an enormous influence. Even Mallarmé read it and affirmed that Homer had ruined epic poetry. But what came before Homer? He was asked. The Vedas, answered Mallarmé.

The Aryanizing anticlericalism had no connection with the political anti-Semitism that arose later. The origins of this anti-Semitic current are located in Austria-Hungary and in the Germany of the second half of the nineteenth century.

9 August

I'm reading Eugenio Garin's book *Scienza et vita civile nel Rinascimento italiano*. Admirable remarks (p. 119 sq.) on the "professors" and the "philosophers." Between the fourteenth and the sixteenth centuries, culture neither began nor triumphed in the universities. Neither Petrarch, nor Marsilio Ficino, nor Nicolas of Cusa, nor Alberti, nor Toscanelli was a university professor. In the fifteenth century, Plato, Plotinus, Proclus, and even Archimedes were being read, *but outside the universities.*

I should have expected it, and yet I am amazed. I thought that the process of the universities' becoming sterile was a later phenomenon. Only Enlightenment and romantic Germany of the eighteenth century constitute exceptions.

1 October

When something sacred manifests itself (hierophany), at the same time something "occults" itself, becomes cryptic. Therein is the true dialectic of the sacred: by the mere fact of *showing* itself, the sacred *hides itself.* We can never claim that we definitively understand a religious phenomenon: something—perhaps even the essential—will be understood by us later, or by others immediately.

5 October

I found in Junod (*Moeurs et coutumes des Bantous,* II, 346) these details which would delight Cioran. In the region of Thonga, the chief of a village "overcome with sadness and devoid of everything" shows the gods his misery by making them an offering of his own spittle. It is called "the offering of bitterness." The man hopes to arouse the pity of the gods by this derisory gift.

But, on the other hand, Leenhardt thinks that the saliva "is the true offering, *perhaps something of a gift of oneself.*" This should be followed: the process by which saliva, as a gift of oneself, therefore as an exemplary offering, becomes a "derisory gift" in Thonga, thanks to which man hopes to move the gods.

7 October

Psychoanalysis justifies its importance by asserting that it forces you to look at and accept reality. But what sort of reality? A reality conditioned by the materialistic and scientific ideology of psychoanalysis, that is, a historical product: we see a thing in which certain scholars and thinkers of the nineteenth century believed. If psychoanalysis some day accepts a *total reality,* not conditioned by its own ideology, a new stage could then open in the history of the Western mind.

12 October

After dinner, lecture of Paul Tillich at Breasted Hall. Packed auditorium. I introduced him—more exactly I said a few words on our seminar in common. Paul spoke of "The Significance of the History of Religions for the Systematic Theologian." I didn't think he would give his lecture. When he arrived a week ago, he telephoned me in despair: angina of the chest, attack after attack, the doctors forbade him all activity, except the Chicago seminar. He seemed very depressed and tired. I saw him a few days later; he was recovered, it seemed to me, but changed. This evening he seemed an old man—but nevertheless he read his lecture with vigor.

We went back afterward to Kitagawa's. Paul went to the kitchen first to ask for a glass of whiskey. He told us that he liked very much to linger in the kitchen, near the stove—it reminded him of his childhood. A long conversation with Tom Altizer—and Tom repeating to him that he was the greatest theologian of his time, and that those of the "God-is-dead theology" are his disciples, etc. Paul seemed radiant. He made a date with him for the next day, at his hotel, to continue the conversation.

Paul's extraordinary faculty of "recuperating" through the active, creative presence of some intelligent interlocutors. This man lives from human warmth, from fellow feeling, and from dialogue.

13 October

We learned that, this morning at four o'clock, Paul had a heart attack and was taken to the clinic. He is in an oxygen tent. And suddenly I feel guilty: if I hadn't insisted that he give his lecture, if he hadn't talked with such passion last night at Kitagawa's. . . .

22 October

Toward evening, we learned that Paul Tillich had a new attack. The doctors think that he won't last the night.

We were invited to dinner at Nathan Scott's. But Christinel went to the clinic with Muriel Brauer; Hannah could need them. At eight o'clock, phone call from the university: Paul had just died. Shortly after, Christinel returned. She had seen the doctor, who was so moved that he could hardly speak. Paul knew that he was going to die, the doctor said, but he was serene, at peace.

23 October

Ultimately, Paul Tillich died as we would have wished. At the age of seventy-nine, he collapsed suddenly, struck down, like an oak. After his lecture in which he said something new (he emphasized the importance of the history of religions for contemporary theology), and after having spent three hours in the company of three young, beautiful women, stretched out at his feet, on the carpet, and listening to him talk. . . .

25 November

Cocktail at Mills'. A lot of people. Richard Stern arrived and told us some juicy anecdotes about two Rumanian "princesses" ninety years old whom he had met in Venice. One of them, drinking her coffee, brought the cup too close to her face—and, Stern went on, the nose, probably restored with a wax cast, began to melt and finally fell into the coffee. . . .

1 December

I'm beginning *La Force des choses*. I am amazed, or almost, by the *assurance* of J. P. Sartre and his companion: they are always right; everyone else is wrong (Camus, Merleau-Ponty or Koestler), they alone, *never*. And the ultra-Marxist interpretation of Camus' and Koestler's political positions—absolutely astounding. There is almost nothing more to add. What fortunate people! . . .

5 February 1966

Yesterday, from seven in the evening to three in the morning with Gayle and Tom Altizer. Extraordinary transformation since three months ago—that is, since he has become famous. Apparently nothing has changed. Tom has remained the same man, "happy to be alive," who drinks and eats a lot, laughs uproariously (making the room shake), hits the table with his fist. But in his eyes, in his smile, and in his whole behavior there is something new, difficult to define. As if the *prophet* which is in him were beginning to manifest himself. They were both exhausted after three days of lectures, conversations, interviews on television—in Wisconsin, in Evanston, in Chicago. His lecture in Wisconsin: two thousand students from the college and from the different graduate schools. All fascinated by radical theology —i.e., God-is-dead theology. Tom's thesis: American youth are interested in Christianity, but can no longer be satisfied by the old dogmatic formulas. In becoming totally incarnate in Jesus, God the Father "died," he emptied himself, he became immanent, that is: body, history; he became everything that humanity does and will do in concrete historical time. But Jesus *was not* resurrected and he *did not* ascend into heaven. Otherwise the whole miracle of the Incarnation would have been canceled. We would have gone back to the transcendent, extrahistorical God. Tom claims that it was Blake who taught him all that (nevertheless, he recognizes that there was a period in which, for two or three years, he could read nothing but Nietzsche). Consequently, the true Christian has no other recourse than to live totally in history, for that is what Jesus-God became: the history of men, of all men. Therein is a curious reinterpretation and acceptance of Marxism and of Sartrean existentialism grafted onto Bonhoeffer.

Thus, the one who, three months ago, was the least known of the group of three (he, Van Buren, and Hamilton) seems to have become the most famous. He accepts all invitations, gives lectures in colleges, gives interviews, participates in contradictory colloquies. He wants to make the most of it, during the vogue of the God-is-dead theology.

8 February

At noon, while I was somewhat absently eating a sandwich and thinking of the class on Vedic India that I was to give an hour later—a telephone call from Wisconsin. A lady who had just read the article in *Time* on my book *The Two and the One* and had been very impressed by the popular legend of the consanguinity of God and the Devil. She asked me if I *believed* in it; I answered her that it is a legend, but that it is rich in meaning, etc. She interrupted me to tell me that she *knew* that it was true, that she had reached this conclusion by a whole series of meditations and experiences; she knew something else: that the Holy Spirit could be perceived concretely in the body and soul of another; that is what had happened to her. . . .

She would certainly have continued for at least a quarter of an hour if I hadn't told her that I was in a hurry and had to go give my class at the university.

11 February

The woman from Wisconsin telephoned again today, once at the house (she spoke to Christinel and dictated a long message to her), the second time at my office. In short, the woman tells me that she is God ("I am God," she says), and that she is getting ready to regenerate the entire world. (I quote: "Behold, I am making everything new . . ." = Revelation 21:5, "Behold, I make all things new.") She added that she could not answer in writing, but that if I wrote her (she gave me her address), she would answer me by telephone. She pointed out: Jesus wrote nothing. God manifested himself solely by the Word. She ended thus: I am informing the faculty of theology that God is here, on earth, in Wisconsin—and let the faculty draw its conclusions. . . .

A clear, calm, gentle voice, the voice of a woman still young.

14 February

I don't think I've written anything on him. He came to see me last spring, with two students from Detroit University sent by Charlotte Zimmerman. When Charlotte learned that he too had come, she wrote me a letter of excuse: it was *not she* who had sent him, she took no responsibility, and she didn't recommend him for the Committee on Social Thought, etc. I didn't grasp very well why so much emotion. It is true that the boy—Wichnetsky—seemed a little overstrung; he would jump from one idea to another and was obsessed by Judaism, his own tradition, which he did not accept, and with which he wanted to settle accounts. I interrupted him several times. What do you really know of Judaism? Almost nothing. I expected so.

And today I have learned that two days ago, in the Detroit synagogue, he threatened the congregation with his revolver, went up to the rabbi, shot at him, then shot a bullet into his own head. Both of them, it seems, are in a very serious condition. Of his whole family, only his sister was present. (NB: He died; the rabbi, if he survives, will remain paralyzed and amnesiac.) This is not the first case of madness, or of suicide, among the young—usually among the most brilliant young Americans. That prominent student, son of a Chicago professor, who killed himself after taking his last examination. Or that student, one of the most talented, a scholarship recipient in France, who killed herself, without apparent reason, as soon as she got back (after having taken all her examinations).

15 February

I'm reading the recollections of Nicholas Carja in *America:* in 1947 he was carried off in a street in the center of Bucharest, brought to Constantsa and "judged secretly, without defense, a bayonet in his back, by the Soviet tribunal of the southern armored division, and put into an old prison from the time of the Turks, with thick, humid walls." Twenty-five years of forced labor in the camps of Mordovskaya Republic on the Volga, "a region covered with immense forests where nothing is grown but potatoes and tobacco." Fortunately he only did nine years. The head of the Constantsa prison was Colonel Belinki, "a short, fat man with heavy movements, hairy as a bear, who would be arrested in his turn, a little later, because he took for his own use objects confiscated from the inmates." This Colonel Belinki had a habit (I've written all this so I wouldn't forget it): during interrogations, he would offer people cigarettes stuck in the barrel of a revolver.

It is also about a Captain Karagolnicov who, when the noise was heard of a motorcycle parked for that purpose in the prison enclosure, would personally execute those condemned to death. The banality of evil, as Hannah Arendt says. In fact, the condemned were killed with a bullet in the nape of the neck, their hands bound behind their backs, kneeling, with their heads against the wall. Nicholas Carja remembers that the captain "was always anxious and had his tunic spotted with blood." Is that all?

20 February

Last evening, dinner at our house: the Scotts, the Alouères, Erich Heller, Bill Earle, and Saul Bellow. The conversation could have been interesting. Erich insisted that "modern" writers, from Tolstoy to Gide, have corrupted literature and Western man by progressively introducing and finally divinizing personal autobiographical elements, and, further, by refusing to make a moral judgment on the characters. Naturally, Alouère and even Nathan Scott protested. And Bill Earle admitted that he—and he let it be inferred that man in general—does not accept the act of judging. Not even Buchenwald. There must be a perspective in which all crimes and errors are "saved," or wherein they find a meaning or at least a justification.

28 February

I've learned from Jerry of the death of Mme. Meland. She had been sick for a long time (heart, cancer) and had been considered lost since last autumn—but the doctors kept her alive with injections and medicines. A few days ago she told the doctors that her husband, a theologian and pastor, had given her permission to refuse pills and shots. Thus, satisfied, she refused medical aid, and she died the next morning. . . .

1 March

Course on Iranian religions and Zarathustra. These last few days, I've read almost constantly and I've reread my files, notes, and materials amassed over a long period. But how frustrated I feel every time I approach this fascinating problem! The most important religious tradition, after Judaism, with which Christianity, and Western civilization in general, has been confronted and from which it has drawn inspiration. We encounter the Iranian spirit everywhere, and perhaps even Zarathustra—the resurrection of the body, the myth of the Savior, gnosis, the problems of dualism, so many sects and heresies which survived very late up to the Middle Ages, the Faust myth, etc., etc. And each time I go back to the texts—how disappointed I am. Except for the Gathas, where I find once again the prophetic vehemence of Zarathustra, except for some Yashts and fragments of Bundahishh, what monotonous texts, inspirationless, full of flaws, boring!

7 March

In ancient Greece, only the *Heroes* kept their memory after death (cf. Achilles, etc.); likewise, the community preserves only the memory of their most noteworthy exploits after the death of the heroes (but not the memory of other obscure "historical events" in which ordinary people have participated). The epic begins by the proclamation and exaltation of these heroic *gesta*. In other words: what happens, *after death,* to the heroes (who keep their memory) is equally true of *the memory that they leave behind.* The epic reflects on the collective level what happens to each hero personally in his situation after death.

25 March

Yesterday I went to the Redemptorist Fathers' seminary in Oconomowoc, Wisconsin. I had long since agreed to give a lecture there, "followed by discussions." I wonder why. Perhaps because I hardly knew this order. A Canadian Redemptorist came to get me by car around three in the afternoon. It had begun to snow. On the Wisconsin road, storm was alternating with clear sky, and I saw the robins shivering, paralyzed with cold, walking, indignant, in the fresh snow.

We arrived when evening was falling. The seminary, a solid old building, dating from eighty years ago, and to which two wings have been added on the two sides. In an admirable landscape, under old trees, on the edge of the lake. I was welcomed by Brother Thomas Emanuel, who had invited me. He seemed very young. The seminarians and the teachers were at the office, in the chapel. We then had dinner in the refectory—for us, arriving from Chicago, they had also prepared grilled meat, in addition to soup, some boiled eggs, vegetables, macaroni. There are about a hundred seminarians—all religious, but about half still in the probation period—and about fifteen teachers.

After dinner, I visited the chapel, the classrooms, the library, the recreation room, with Ping-Pong tables, television, etc. If the students hadn't been wearing the black cassock, I would have thought I were in an ultramodern college. I gave my lecture, and a long, rather interesting discussion followed, which went on until ten o'clock in an adjoining room, near the fireplace. All the questions converged toward the same problem: how, in a desacralized society such as ours, can the reality of the sacred be introduced? (For notions, symbolism, theories concerning the sacred can be communicated, discussed— without the interlocutors being confronted with sacredness as such.)

2 April

Hannah Arendt tells that, during her student life, she once went, with Hans Jonas, to Bultmann's, to tell him that she wanted to

study theology, on the condition that "no anti-Semitism be practiced." Bultmann at first thought that she was joking. He didn't
understand what she meant. Hannah explained to him: she wanted to
study theology, on the condition that the theologians of Marburg not
propose, in their courses, to demonstrate the inferiority of the Old
Testament.

MIDDLETOWN, CONNECTICUT, *10 April*

Invited by Magda and Michael Polanyi, with Erik Erikson and
his wife, to the Commodore Inn, a restaurant in the middle of the
countryside two miles from Middletown. It is Easter Sunday, and the
restaurant is half-empty. Through the window, the Connecticut River
can be seen very close: blue, majestic.

As he was telling me last evening, Erikson is writing a book on
Gandhi. He has gone to India several times to have talks with the last
of Gandhi's oldest companions. He especially wants to evoke the first
attempt at civil disobedience, in 1918. A strike in a factory, the owners
of which—the brother and sister—could not agree: the woman took
the part of the strikers; the brother was against them. Gandhi was
called to arbitrate. He decided in favor of the sister—but the decision
was full of risks because the brother was one of Gandhi's warmest
defenders. So Gandhi took the decision of fasting until the solution
of the conflict. The first political fast, says Erikson. I am impatiently
awaiting his book to see why Erikson considers this episode of Gandhi's life to be capital.

Conversation in connection with this famous episode: Gandhi,
aged, in the middle of a political crisis (sharp conflict with Jinnah),
slept each night next to his niece. Erikson asked me how I understood
this behavior. I answered that Gandhi probably felt that he was losing
his political "virtue," his almost magical prestige, and so he resorted
to an initiatic trial. Sleeping naked, next to a virgin, and managing not
to be affected permitted him to acquire a power of magico-religious
nature which he projected into his political action. Desperate effort
to regain authority over the party and to ensure the success of the
action under way.

12 April

A subject for a short story is beginning to intrigue me. I see only the beginning, which is rather mysterious. A man arrives in a taxi, is in a hurry, goes into a hotel with several floors—and stops, exasperated. He has come to meet someone whose name suddenly escapes him. Impossible to remember it. In vain, the concierge tries to help him: he is to meet this person for the first time; he has never seen him and does not even know what his profession is. The concierge shows him the list with the names of the occupants. The stranger hesitates, and finally he has the impression that a certain name is indeed the one he is looking for. He repeats it several times, asks the floor, the room number, and goes up in the elevator. Having arrived on the top floor, he realizes that he has again forgotten the name and the door number. He is ashamed to go down to hunt out the concierge again. He walks somewhat haphazardly in the corridor. Time passes. After a quarter of an hour, it seems to him that he is back at the place where he started. A strange amnesia, full of surprises—for in the void left by *forgetting,* all sorts of unreal personages creep in and incomprehensible events take shape.

14 April

In a certain sense, I believe in the future of "the literature of the fantastic." For the moment, at least, the classical realistic or psychological novel is no longer interesting: first of all, it no longer interests the younger generations. But the *nouvelle vague* cannot last either. I do not very well see how such productions could satisfy the need for art and for artistic understanding, the need for growth and for metamorphosis which has been driving readers instinctively toward certain literary creations. However one examines and valorizes contemporary productions called avant-garde, I do not see therein the possibility of changing and improving, in the reader, his personal vision of the world. They do not help him to grow and to open himself toward the world. Contemporary man has learned so many things (without always assimilating them) through psychoanalysis, ethnology, the history of religions, and especially—the younger generations—through the paranormal experiences of hallucinogenic drugs, that an intelligible, significant, new literature of the fantastic could arise, availing itself of everything the last fifty years have revealed to us. I do not think this will be a literature such as the romantics of the nineteenth century practiced it, or the "decadents" or the "symbolists" of the type of Barbey D'Aurevilly, Edgar Alian Poe, Meyrink, etc. It will not be a literature of escape, unconnected with reality and history, since it will follow the same vital trajectory that the experiences and discoveries of the last fifty years have drawn. And that literature—readable, significant, fascinating—will be like a window onto meaning for all the young people enclosed today in their void. We will thus rediscover the epic quality, the narration that the *nouvelle vague* abolished. We will read fascinating, true stories, without their reflecting, for all that, immediate reality, the concrete of contemporary history and its eschatological messages. We will finally rediscover the mythical element, the symbolical element, the rites which have nourished all civilizations. Certainly, they will not be recognized as such under their camouflage. It will be a *new* mythology. It is from the longing for this that the younger generations, for example, are suffering, especially here in America.

17 April

Just now I'm reading a fascinating article on the experiments carried out in several universities in connection with the physiology and psychology of sleep (*New York Times Magazine,* 17 April 1966). One of the four phases of sleep is called REM (Rapid Eye Movement); it is the only phase during which the sleeping person dreams. The following experiments were done: Volunteers were prevented from staying in the REM phase, but were permitted to sleep. In other words, they could sleep, but it wasn't possible for them to dream. Consequence: the following night, the persons deprived of REM tried to dream as much as possible, and if they were again prevented from doing so, they proved nervous, irritable, and melancholy during the day. And, finally, when their sleep was no longer bothered, they gave themselves over to veritable "orgies of Rapid Eye Movement sleep," as if they were avid to recover everything they had lost the preceding nights.

What fascinates me in these experiments is the organic need that man has to "dream," that is, for *mythology*. (For whatever judgment one makes on the structure and content of dreams, their mythological character is indubitable. On the oneiric level, mythology signifies narrative, that is, viewing a sequence with epic or dramatic episodes. In any case, it seems that man needs to be present at these narratives, to view them, to listen to them. The original character of the epic. This needs to be related with everything I've written on the ecstatic origins of epic poetry.)

18 April

Henry Crabb Robinson, who had met Goethe in 1801, saw him again in Weimar in August 1829. In his journal he wrote down all sorts of details concerning that long and fruitful visit of 2 August. Some of them, unexpected; for example, when Robinson said to him, "The taste for Ossian is to be ascribed to you in great measure. It was Werther that set the fashion." Goethe smiled and answered, "That is partly true; but it was never perceived by the critics that Werther praised Homer while he retained his senses, and Ossian when he was going mad. But reviewers do not notice such things."

The violent reaction of Goethe against the Church: Robinson had quoted Lamennais (all truth comes from God, but it is not revealed through the Church), and Goethe, holding a flower in his hand while a magnificent butterfly was coming into the room, exclaimed, "No doubt all truth comes from God; but the Church! That is the point. God speaks to us through this flower and that butterfly; and that is a language these rascals do not understand."

I read this passage to Christinel. She fully agreed (she who, nevertheless, goes to church from time to time).

When he recounted his 1801 visit, Robinson quoted this admission from Goethe (in a letter to Lavater): "I am by no means *anti*-Christian, not even *un*-Christian, but I am indeed *not* Christian."

NEW YORK, *24 April*
I've learned through B. C. that a Lutheran pastor, Richard
Wurmbrand, has just arrived from Rumania. (He was "ransomed" by
the Swedish Lutherans.) B. tells me that he is a sort of Saint Paul. A
converted Jew who *believes* as they used to believe in the times of the
persecutions. Ten years in prison. Tortured (traces of his wounds can
still be seen), tuberculosis to boot, he survived by a sort of miracle.
He knows English fairly well and is an inspired preacher, causing
shivers. Since he was in a camp at the time of the Antonesco government, he cannot be suspected of "fascism." I almost don't dare to tell
the horrors that he recounts about what he witnessed in prison. For
example, this scene, at which he was present: On Easter, the Orthodox
priest was plunged into a tub filled with excrement coming up to his
waist; in one hand, he held a mess tin full of excrement, in the other
a mess tin full of urine. They forced him to celebrate the office of the
Resurrection in this posture before the other inmates and to give them
communion in one of the two mess tins. I wonder if he will be believed.
He also said that there were some scenes that he wouldn't dare tell
and that he would never tell. But what could be imagined that was
worse? He spoke of a priest that they had attached to a cross and that
they would bring down from the cross from time to time to stretch
him out on the ground—then they made the inmates relieve themselves on him.
He added that the resistance of the people put in prison was extraordinary. A people which had given such men could not disappear, he
said. The Communists exploited the fear of death. He admitted to
them openly, "I am not afraid. Kill me. I will be with God sooner."
During the investigations, certain priests would defy the men of the
secret police, would speak to them of God, and sometimes would
manage to convert them.
In the lead mines, otherwise so unhealthful, the inmates were better
nourished; they were even paid and could buy food from the canteen.
Once a new convoy arrived. Someone went up to one of the new
arrivals and asked him if he were hungry. Obviously, he was hungry.

The one who had asked him went to the canteen and brought him something to eat. The new arrival downed it voraciously, thanked him, and asked him why he had been convicted.

"Because I gave something to eat to a stranger who was starving. It was noted afterward that this man was part of the resistance. He was taken and convicted, and I was convicted too."

"How was such a sacrilege possible? Who was the villain who convicted you?"

"You. You were the magistrate at that time. I recognized you in the convoy. And I wanted to prove to you that I was innocent. I gave you something to eat, as I had done for that stranger: just because you were hungry. . . ."

25 April

I would still like to write down certain details of the story told to B. by Pastor Wurmbrand. A certain priest was beaten and horribly tortured by an agent of the secret police who, in turn, was arrested a short time afterward. He too was tortured and was near death. But he said he couldn't die if the priest didn't forgive him. The priest dragged himself on all fours over to him, kissed him, forgave him— and the agent died comforted. And this other detail: a peasant from whom all his sheep had been taken for a kolkhoz. They left him the little bells that he would set out somewhere. When he longed for his sheep, he would jingle the bells and would remember each of his sheep, one by one. And one day, after having rung the bells, he couldn't contain his fury: he went to find the head of the kolkhoz, the one who—he believed—had taken away his sheep, and killed him.

MIDDLETOWN, CONNECTICUT, 13 May

I've received Tom Altizer's book *The Gospel of Christian Atheism.* Each evening, I read a few pages. I don't know why, but the book isn't taking hold of me. Perhaps because it is written to provoke, arouse indignation, or conquer. There are only a few ideas that Tom takes up, repeats, and comments on over dozens and dozens of pages. Radical Christianity, he says, is not a religion like others, because it does not look backwards, it does not look at the primordial events in order to reactualize them ritually, etc. (The same solution of continuity between "religions" and Christianity as with Karl Barth or Kramer.) God having died in Jesus, and not having been resurrected, the body, the life, the totality of human experience, history, are "sanctified," saturated with the being of God. "History becomes not simply the arena of revelation but the very incarnate body of God." The death of God signifies for Tom radical Christianity: only a Christian can know this terrifying experience; he alone is therefore truly modern.

EAST HAMPTON, NEW YORK, *22 May*

Got to Meriden at eleven thirty. Overcast, it was threatening rain. We found the airport with difficulty—as small as a tennis court. We took an air taxi; the two of us and the pilot. In twenty-five minutes we were in East Hampton. We flew at a thousand meters: we soon arrived at the sound, then we flew over Long Island, the color of pale clay and of sand, with forests of conifers and beechtrees, and little towns scattered along the coastline.

Gerald Sykes was waiting for us at the airport. We had lunch at his house with Hannah Tillich. Sykes has sold his house—large, splendid, of a discreet and nevertheless sumptuous New England architecture, in the forest, near the lagoon—and he will be moving in a few weeks. The library and some of the furniture have already been sent to New York. After lunch, Hannah drove us to her house, where we are staying. When the car entered the driveway, five or six rabbits scurried off toward the forest. They come every day, Hannah told us, to eat salad and drink water. We walked in the garden; we saw and stroked with our hands the trees planted by Paul fifteen or twenty years ago.

Invited at cocktail time to Alfonso Ossorio's, a Philippine millionaire and avant-garde painter about whom Dubuffet, a few years ago, published a book: *La Peinture initiatique d'Ossorio* (which the host gave us upon leaving). Ossorio's house would have fascinated Pieyre de Mandiargue. Immense, some thirty salons and rooms, a splendid terrace on the edge of the lagoon, and an immense park. Unusual furniture, icons, strange or simply bizarre objects (a little chest for shining shoes, bought in Turkey, containing all the waxes and creams, etc.), birds and other stuffed animals, exotic, extravagant reeds reaching up to the ceiling, in enormous clay pots—and on the tables and the shelves all sorts of rock crystals, pieces of skulls, "modern" art objects. Moreover, scattered through I don't know how many rooms, an extraordinary library on the history of the arts. (Ossorio did his doctorate at Harvard; I believe his thesis was on the morphology of the Crucifixion.) Some canvases by Pollock and Dubuffet. And a good many "paintings" by the later Ossorio, when he no longer paints, but composes his picture of all sorts of objects, debris and little things (pieces of colored glass, scrap metal, etc., etc.). Some are truly extraordinary.

Buffy and Gerald Sykes arrived in their turn, and we visited the workshop, as huge as a whole building. We spent an hour among the objects and fragments from which Ossorio, tomorrow, will make his "canvases."

CHICAGO, *9 June*

The industries that live off the demand of children and adolescents between eleven and eighteen: records, illustrated magazines, objects of all kinds, etc. I've learned that some records, selling millions of copies, are bought exclusively by teenagers. And their books and their magazines. The explanation: these children want to sing, listen to songs, read, enjoy themselves *in a different way* from their parents, or differently than the latter did at the same age. They have invented ways of amusing themselves that do not at all depend on the way their parents amuse themselves. They want to be themselves. And because teenagers have money, industrialists and merchants take account of their whims. For the first time in the history of capitalism, children and adolescents have buying power and therefore succeed in influencing the world "market."

11 June

Just as the "primitives" considered themselves the result not of creation by the gods but of the activity of primordial heroes (the mythical Ancestors, the civilizing Heroes), man of Greek culture (could I really say the Greek?) considered himself to be the successor (and perhaps the inheritor) of a series of "historical" dramas: that of the Atridae, for example. The man of Greek culture did not situate himself directly in relation to the gods (or to divine providence); he depended on what had happened to certain heroes in the fabled times of the beginnings, Theseus, Oedipus, Creon, and the others.

NEW HAVEN, *13 June*

I'm so happy that Nathan Scott insisted that I take Christinel when I told him that I was leaving to receive the doctorate *honoris causa* at Yale. He assured me that the ceremonial was purely and simply extraordinary. Indeed, the more than one thousand students march in procession in their differently colored robes, with flags and music. It was threatening rain—and, yet, to the end of the ceremony not a drop of water. We mounted the platform; we, the honorary degree recipients, took our places in the front row. The president, Kingman Brewster, Jr., called us one after the other and read the brief, somewhat aulic citation. He said this about me: "You belong to the world. In early youth you voyaged from Europe into the introspective wisdom of the East, and, having probed the essence of Indian spirituality, you have worked to render the East more understandable to the West. Venerating the great mysteries expressed in myth and symbol, you have helped to find a human language for eternal truth. Yale confers upon you the degree of doctor of humane letters."

Applause—and how amusing it was to see Silone walk slowly, solemnly, and Bernstein stop in front of his chair before sitting down, and bow ceremoniously to thank the audience, like an orchestra conductor from his podium.

We took the bus for New York. Bizarre feeling. Naturally I am proud, and yet, melancholy; is it the beginning of the series of honors, the beginning of old age?

16 June

I'm reading, in an article by Jean Charon: "Man is equally in touch with another milieu: contemporary physics teaches us in fact that the elementary particles which constitute all matter must not be considered as separate from the rest of the cosmos, but as objects which, notably by what is called their 'field' (gravitational, electromagnetic or nuclear field) are coextensive with the whole universe. Man too, like all matter, is naturally 'manufactured' from these particles which are coextensive with the whole universe; and therefore man is, in a certain way, in union with the entire cosmos surrounding him. He is in constant connection with what could be called the 'cosmic milieu.' "

That is ultimately the fundamental belief of the "primitives." But not only of the primitives: Indian philosophy has been developed and articulated on the basis of similar premises (based, obviously, on a millennial experience). And what I call "cosmic religions" (down to "cosmic Christianity") imply a vision similar to the one described by Charon. That is precisely what I was saying last winter to the nuns at Manhattanville: real man is a *total* man, and the unconscious has its role and its importance; the unconscious represents *life* and *nature* in man. Symbols, images, and longings arise from the dramas and the revelations of the unconscious—and it is through these dramas and these revelations that man is in living communication with nature, the cosmic totality.

18 June

I don't know why, suddenly the fancy strikes me to reread Strindberg's *The Inferno*. In the library I found several shelves of books devoted to Strindberg, and I took some (including *Marriage with Genius* by Freda Strindberg, his second wife; she evokes the year which preceded *The Inferno* and describes the months spent in Paris from her point of view).

I have always been intrigued by this aspect of Strindberg's life and work: his absurd alchemistic operations, his certitude about having made gold, his fear of madness, his struggle against "Forces," the discovery of Swedenborg (he, a Swede, first read Swedenborg in Paris, in 1895). *The Inferno, Sylva Sylvarum,* and *Antibarbarus* were the favorite books of my student years. What especially interested me: a "naturalist" in the direct meaning of the word, obsessed by occultism, alchemy, spiritualism, black magic!

In the night, I read almost half of *The Inferno.* I wonder how it is that *this* Strindberg and *this* book were not exalted by Breton and the surrealists. Breton would have been fascinated by so many "coincidences," visions, and previsions. In 1894–1897, in Paris, Strindberg lived the life of the generation of surrealists of 1920–1925. (And even that passion of Breton for alchemy corresponds to the Parisian cycle of Strindberg.)

20 June

I've finished *The Inferno,* a little disappointed. I'm reading *From an Occult Diary: Marriage with Harriet Bosse* (London, 1965). I knew the letters to Harriet Bosse and the whole story of this third and last marriage of Strindberg. What is new and astonishing in this occult journal is Strindberg's emphasis on "telepathic" erotic experiences: during sleep, awake, and sometimes even in the course of work, Harriet—before the marriage and especially *after* the divorce—would appear and, to believe Strindberg, she possessed him. In a letter (after the separation) he implored her: "I beg you now: Leave me in peace! In my sleep I am defenseless, as everyone is, irresponsible . . . and I am ashamed afterwards—now I think it is criminal." And a few days later, he wrote her again: "Why will you not leave me go? What do you want with my old person? Take my soul, if you must, but leave me go! This will end badly!"

16 July

I'm working without enthusiasm on my lecture for the Philosophers' Congress in Geneva. I'll have to say something new about myth. I will try to specify the distinctions made by the primitives between the two sorts of *primordiality:* the *primordium* dominated by the Supreme Being (who is often transformed into *deus otiosus*) and the primordial in which the mythical ancestors or other inferior beings are manifested and created. Archaic man (not only he) is interested especially in this second *primordium:* what took place then marked him profoundly; he is the result of the events of this mythical period. It is significant that already in the archaic cultures man feels himself linked with a mythical history, and tends to forget, or neglect, the ontophanies, the creative manifestations of the supreme Gods which reveal being.

27 July

D. M. came to see me. I hadn't run into him since the day of his baptism (9 March). He admitted to me that the ceremony disappointed him. He was somber, depressed. Despite all that, when the priest made the sign of the cross with the holy oil on his forehead, he "felt" something. Immediately after the baptism, he went out alone into the street. And he felt how the cross was going down from his forehead to his heart and becoming luminous. Finally, he regained his serenity. Since then he continues to feel the cross, and can carry it from the heart to the forehead, or make it "circulate" in his body. When he is sad, irritated, or desperate, it is sufficient for him to evoke the interiorized cross to feel peace and power.

ABANO, *14 August*

The cathartic function of a technical or artistic invention, of a scientific discovery: it liberates man either on the physical level (work) or on the psychical, social level, etc. . . . As for me, I want to show the cathartic function of a correct understanding of myth. It liberates (modern) man from certain inhibitions which made him incapable of *loving* his own prehistory (and history . . .).

15 August

In the analysis of mythical thought, so popular for some time now, logical reductionism proves also to be a "scientific" reaction against humanism. Some brilliant authors begin from the following presupposition: Human existence does not have any meaning, the history of the mind does not merit being deciphered, in a word, the valid method is not hermeneutics, but the correct use of an electronic computer. But even if we wanted to, we couldn't give up hermeneutics because we are the result of a millennial hermeneutical effort. Ultimately, we are the result of interpretations and reinterpretations of life, death, consciousness, creativity, etc., elaborated since the pre-Socratics, and even before (since the discovery of agriculture and metallurgy, for example).

16 August

Still on the subject of certain interpretations of mythical thought which today fascinate philosophers and literary critics: the historian of religions has known for a long time that a theory which does not correspond to ethnological realities has every chance of interesting the philosophers (not to mention the psychologists). Let us take an example: *Totem and Taboo,* that anthropological "murder story," based on a fabled primordial parricide which philosophers have been discussing with an enthusiastic seriousness for half a century (the latest of them, and perhaps the most talented, Paul Ricoeur). Obviously the philosophers have neither the time nor the curiosity to go directly to the sources—and so they discuss the theories formulated (they believe) on the basis of these ethnological documents. Actually, mythical thought is not being discussed, but certain contemporary interpretations of that mythical thought (so fashionable today, but which few people know directly from the documents).

17 August

I should show in my Geneva lecture the importance of the creation of the world in archaic mythical thought. God *creates* the world—but afterward the world is formed, changed, actually "created," several times, and not by the creator god. Every origin myth (the origin of death or of sexuality, of the family or of initiation, etc.) is connected with the creation of our own mode of being, but also with the mode of being of all institutions (family, clan, etc.). A first conclusion: the supreme beings are not the only important ones for the understanding of a religion; they only open the way for a series of later creations and foundings. That puts the myth of the withdrawal of the creator god and his transformation into a *deus otiosus* into a different light. The god becomes *otiosus* when his example is generalized, that is, when the cosmos and man are re-created or modified continually.

ROME, *27 August*

On the inanity of materialistic explanations: a certain number of writers belonging to the same period and the same society, and equally poor, are forced to write a book in two or three weeks. One is Balzac, the other is Alexandre Dumas, or Dostoevsky and Eugène Sue. One sees the results. It is not the economic *conditioning* which is important—but the *response* made by each writer. The creativity of the responses to challenge is the only thing which is interesting for the history of culture.

GENEVA, *5 September*

This morning I read my lecture on myth. Vigorous applause, but I wonder to what extent my text succeeded in interesting the philosophers who were listening to me. Actually, I contented myself with presenting and commenting on two cosmogonic myths: the Indonesian and the Australian. I suppose it was understood why I did not take examples from Greek, Hindu, or Mesopotamian mythology: these myths do not have the central function that mythology has in the archaic civilizations. I hope that the cosmogonic myth's role of exemplary model was also understood. But from that point on, I'm not very sure. Since I was addressing myself to an audience made up almost entirely of philosophers by vocation or profession, I avoided translating into their language the lesson of archaic cosmogonic myths. It is a matter, naturally, of ontophany, for cosmogony means this: *Being which comes into being.* The birth, the creation of the world is, above all, the appearance of Being, ontophany. That is why the cosmogonic myth is an exemplary model for all types of *creation*—from the construction of a village or of a house, to the celebration of a marriage or the conception of a child. It is always a matter of a new creation of the world, that is, of a new epiphany of Being.

It is a matter, obviously, of a "primitive" ontology, of a rudimentary metaphysics, if you will—because it reveals the world as an exemplary model of all forms of reality. But I suppose that such an ontology should interest philosophers—if only because it supports and justifies a considerable number of archaic civilizations.

CHICAGO, *16 October*
Dr. Humphrey Osmond, the scientist who first recommended mescaline to Aldous Huxley, tells how he met him at a psychology congress in San Francisco: Huxley was attentively listening to the papers, "crossing himself devoutly every time Freud's name was mentioned."

11 November
What Guénon and the other "hermetists" say of the tradition should not be understood on the level of historical reality (as they claim). These speculations constitute a universe of systematically articulated meanings: they are to be compared to a great poem or a novel. It is the same with Marxist or Freudian "explanations": they are true if they are considered as imaginary universes. The "proofs" are few and uncertain—they correspond to the historical, social, psychological "realities" of a novel or of a poem.

All these global and systematic interpretations, in reality, constitute mythological creations, highly useful for understanding the world; but they are not, as their authors think, "scientific explanations."

14 December
Myamoto—lunch at the Quadrangle Club and then, conversation. He says that at the age of seventy-six he has begun to understand Buddhism (which he has been studying since his youth). "Consequently," he concludes, "I have not wasted my life."

No date (1966)
When I write my study on Brancusi, I mustn't give in to inhibitions: that I'm not an art critic, that I don't know the history

of modern art from the inside, as a specialist knows it, etc. The problems that obsess me with respect to Brancusi are of a different order. First, his passion for stone, for hard, impenetrable matter (metals belong to another class; as we know them and use them, metals are not found in nature, they are the products of man). Certainly, every sculptor loves his materials, above all, marble. But Brancusi possesses something more: he approaches stone with the sensitivity—and perhaps the veneration—of a prehistoric man. The patience, the attention, the joy with which he chiseled his works until he had transformed the surfaces into undulating mirrors—so much so, and so well, that one feels like caressing them; the time that he lavished on chiseling innumerable replicas of so many of his works, would remain inexplicable for me if I did not intuit, in this long, monotonous work, the beatitude brought by indefinitely prolonged intimacy with crystalline matter. His desire to transfigure stone, to abolish its mode of being, and above all its weight, to show us how it ascends and flies (as in *Maiastra*)—does not one intuit here a certain archaic form of religiosity, long since inaccessible on our continent?

But the most dramatic problem is the one posed by the *Endless Column*. I know very well that, from the beginning, the work was conceived as a column of steel. I also know that its model is found in popular Rumanian art, and more precisely in the structure of the wooden pillars which support and decorate peasant houses. What interests me first of all is the meaning that Brancusi himself gave to the *Column:* he compared it to the Column of Heaven, to the cosmic pillar which supports the sky and which makes communication possible between heaven and earth; in a word, Brancusi considered it to be an *axis mundi*. The idea is very old and occurs universally. This specific type of *axis mundi,* in the form of a stone column, could be the creation of megalithic cultures—but that is not so important. What matters, to my way of thinking, is that Brancusi conceived the *Endless Column* as an *axis mundi* by which one could reach heaven —and that after having achieved this masterpiece he created nothing further which was worthy of his genius. He lived on over twenty years and was content to chisel I don't know how many replicas of the works which had made him famous.

I cannot believe that at the age of sixty Brancusi's creative vigor was definitively exhausted. Did he suppose that, after having achieved his most important work, he should not attempt anything else? But while he was conceiving and realizing the *Endless Column,* another work had tempted him, at least as grandiose: the mausoleum that he proposed to erect to the memory of the wife of the maharajah of Indor. I do not have any precise information on this project; I only know some legends (according to one of them, Brancusi supposedly proposed hewing a rocky hill into the form of an egg, with a little crypt to take the cinerary urn of the maharani).

The mystery of Brancusi's "sterility" during the last twenty years of his life should be looked for: (a) either in his conviction that, after the *Endless Column,* it was pointless to tackle another major work; or (b) in his deep regret that circumstances did not permit him to surpass himself in creating the mausoleum of Indor. What impresses me in Brancusi's destiny is that the two masterpieces—the *Endless Column* and the one which remained at the planning level—belong to the same universe of spiritual creations characteristic of the stone ages. But why did he cease to create after having succeeded, by an extraordinary anamnesis, in giving life back to archaic forms, symbols, and meanings forgotten in Europe for several thousand years? Would it be that, after having erected the *Column* which led to the sky, Brancusi had nothing further to do on earth, that at least symbolically he was no longer among us?

No answer, no hypothesis, seems satisfying to me. I fear that the mystery will remain impenetrable as long as we do not know precisely how he had imagined the mausoleum in Indor, and how long he devoted to meditating on this work.

12 January 1967

N. C.: a young man with a luxuriant black beard. Not long ago, he used to attend my course on prehistoric religions. I had been surprised by his maturity of mind and by his learning (it was his last year of college). Afterward, he left the campus.

His comrade and friend, Paul R., came to see me the other day. He had spent a year in Europe. He told me, among other things, that C.

was at Stanford University, where he was studying archaeology. And today, after my course, he came back to see me and, talking, we headed toward the house. I learned that C. has given up the university forever. He feels that academic life and existence in general in a metropolis are absurd, idiotic, criminal. He has decided to *live*— and he has found a cabin in the midst of an immense forest. He will earn his living by gathering medicinal plants for a druggist in the area and by selling rare species to a botanist.

He will content himself with very little (he doesn't even smoke). In three years he will go to settle by the ocean and will live from what the ocean furnishes him.

27 January

The city is buried under snow. No cars. You can hardly walk in the street. For the first time the grocery store on Fifty-seventh Street is closed. The owner probably couldn't get there. Evelyn asked us if we had milk for Anne-Rose. Fortunately we do.

And all that for half a meter of snow. (I remember the winter of 1916–1917, in Bucharest, with snowdrifts two meters high.) Technology has its price.

28 January

In the evening we went on foot toward Grant, walking in the middle of the street. Cars buried in the snow on either side. Groups advancing arduously among the snowdrifts, but they are noisy, gay. The city has suddenly become human.

8 February

A three-hour seminar on mysticism. Despite the snow, the room was full. Two papers; the one by O. T. on Taoism, rather good. And yet, he didn't emphasize, as I expected he would, the obsession of the Taoists with reintegrating themselves into the cosmic rhythms, acquiring a physiology similar to that of the embryo of animals during hibernation. Their basic idea: *Longevity is the route to immortality;* life is prolonged by a return to animal spontaneity; the secret of spontaneity "is learned" by the imitation of embryonic physiology.

16 February

The aggressiveness of the young American intelligentsia—again a sort of parricide. These children who do exactly the opposite of what their parents did, and hate them (perhaps without realizing it), illustrate a parricide mentality which cannot be deciphered through psychoanalysis.

25 February

Ed Dimock invited us over this evening to meet Allen Ginsberg. (The poet, he told me, insisted on meeting me.) He made his appearance about eleven in the evening. Young, bald, bearded—he resembles a Himalayan ascetic. He drinks and smokes without stopping. He began immediately with having me talk about Tantrism. He said he too had practiced *maithuna* (he gave the details concerning with whom and in what circumstances).

Around us, on the floor—for we were all sitting on the floor—a whole group was assembled. Rabinow questioned him on his drug experiences. A. G. answered that he had tried mescaline, LSD, and many others. I questioned him on "poetic inspiration," if he applied a precise technique of meditation, etc. At one time while reading Blake he felt the poet's presence in the room; then he saw him. Later, he began to practice *pranayama* to be able to create and recite longer and longer verses. He recited some of them and showed me how he breathes them.

He has gone to India several times. For him, Calcutta is an "important center." He also went to the Himalayas. He met Swami Shivananda. He learned mantras with different monks. He took out of his pocket a piece of paper on which there were verses of Prajnaparamitra, and he began to recite first in Japanese, then in English, while singing and striking two little bronze bells. It was very impressive. Afterward, he recited other mantras, Shivaist ones. He showed me all sorts of objects—an enormous ring given by a lama, an oracular ring; when it is shaken one hears noises (inside there are pepper grains and other small objects). He asked me if I knew how to interpret these sounds—i.e., oracularly. I do not.

He has met Michaux. He told me that if Michaux had made the same selection in his prose written under the influence of mescaline that he had made for the poetry written while awake, *Misérable miracle* and the other books would have been much better.

Rather well informed on surrealistic literature, notably Desnos, Daumal. A significant detail: in California, thousands of students and, in general, young people of both sexes, after experiencing mescaline or LSD, turn toward tribal rites (North American or Hindu). They need something solid in the new world into which they have been projected.

2 March

The history of religions, as I understand it, is a "saving" discipline. Hermeneutics could become the only valid justification of history. A historical event will justify its appearance *when it is understood.* That could mean that things happen, that history exists, solely to force men to understand it.

4 March

Around 1911–1912, Dino Campana was selling his brochure *Canti orfici* in cafés and bookstores: he would look the buyer straight in the eye, leaf through the little book, and tear out a page here and there.

"These pages," he used to say, "don't suit you and it is pointless for you to see them." Papini writes that, in the copy sold to Marinetti, Campana had torn out all the pages.

I remember T. T.'s misadventure, around 1952, in Paris. He had written a novel. Leafing through it, P. found it so bad that he decided to destroy it. But how to be sure that not a single page would be left? Every evening, he would go into the cafés of Place Clichy, would solemnly approach each table, leave a few pages of the manuscript, and explain: "This is a brilliant writer, ladies and gentlemen. . . ." Then he would bow and go farther on.

That is how T. T.'s novel supposedly disappeared.

6 March

I'm reading the biography of James Joyce by Ellmann, in the French translation. Christinel gave it to me. Fascinated by Joyce's confidence in himself, but also by the mediocrity of his critical judgment. In 1936, he said that Ibsen "towers head and shoulders above [Shakespeare] when it comes to drama. No one approaches him there. It's very difficult to believe that Ibsen will grow stale. . . ." Joyce's resentment: "he was resolved not to find anything admirable"; "he continued to disparage Shakespeare at Ibsen's expense." *Die Meistersinger* is "pretentious stuff." B. Shaw—"a born preacher" incapable of "the noble and bare style appropriate to modern playwriting"; "a mountebank."

10 March

Fascinated, astounded, I'm continuing Joyce's biography. The most extraordinary case of self-publicity that I know. "Joyce regularly dispatched notes of thanks to the reviewers so as to impress his name even more deeply upon their memories." When he sent critics a new work, he would not forget to send press notices on the preceding book. An admirable example for young "revolutionary" writers.

12 March

Ultimately Joyce was correct to write *Finnegans Wake* as he wrote it: unreadable. "The demand that I make of my reader is that he should devote his whole life to reading my works." He succeeded. "Why did you write the book this way? To keep the critics busy for three hundred years." And that is quite probably what will happen.

4 April

Have I already noted these lines from Heidegger's *Holzwege* (p. 186) that Tom Altizer should meditate on? In any case I'm recopying them here: "Hier stirbt das Absolute. Gott ist tot. Das sagt alles andere, nur nicht: es gibt keinen Gott." (This is where the

Absolute meets death. God is dead. And this means everything except "there is no God.")

5 April

Dr. Bögers, a Dutch Catholic priest, came up to my office to speak to me about his major preoccupation: the secularization of Christianity, Bonhoeffer, and all the other problems. He has read some of my books, he thinks that I could teach him how to reintroduce rites—that is, *symbolism*—into Christian experience. He believes that Bonhoeffer and those who share his ideas still appreciate symbolism, although that is passed over in silence by many of their too enthusiastic admirers and commentators. Dr. Bögers spoke to me about the attempts at liturgical renovation in Holland, of the liturgy celebrated in a "business suit" (he asked me what I thought of that "reform"). The two great risks, as he sees them: symbolism without belief, belief without symbolism.

25 April

In the history of religions, as in anthropology and folklore, comparison has as its function to introduce the *universal element* into "local," "provincial" research. This is similar to a local or national history integrated into universal history which, finally, reveals its true meaning.

14 May

From Primitives to Zen has finally appeared. I don't dare recall the time spent on preparing this source book. My only consolation: it will be useful for students.

19 May

Goncourt wrote on 16 June 1865: "The future belongs to Russia and America, to the virgin forces."

14 June

This week, the manuscript of my work on habitations and sacred space (the six classes I gave at Princeton University) was to be ready. But I have long since interrupted the writing of the last chapters, fascinated—and at the same time, frightened—by the proportions that the Preface was taking on. I had in fact proposed to explain in the Preface the meaning of this little book, and especially to present the plan of a series of monographs which, unfortunately, I no longer hope to succeed in writing one day. In speaking, at Princeton, of the structure of sacred space, of the symbolism of houses in cities and villages, of temples and palaces, I showed the sacred roots of architecture and of urbanism. In *The Forge and the Crucible,* I brought out the prehistory—that is, the "sacredness"—of metallurgical techniques and the cosmo-soteriological function of alchemy. In other works from my younger years, I emphasized the character of qualitative science of Indian botany and of Oriental mineralogies in general. I was able to speak only in passing (in *Shamanism*) of the ecstatic origins of lyric and epic poetry. I hoped to be able one day to present a prehistory of literature: all these attempts were pursuing the same goal: to unveil that primordial world in which creations and inventions (techniques, the arts) *were not yet detached from their religious matrix.*

That is indeed what I was planning to show in the Preface that I began a long while ago; but as it was threatening to become a book, I gave it up. Thus, the work on sacred space will continue to sleep, unfinished, in the files. . . .

VENICE, *4 September*

Invited to Torcello by Ambassador Montanari. We already knew the story through Mariette Guetta: Montanari had been dreaming for a long time of buying this house—a former convent, half-ruined and abandoned, in the middle of the countryside a few hundred meters from Cipriani—and moving in definitively. Last year, an unexpected inheritance allowed him, finally, to buy it. We embarked at noon, from Harry's Bar, in two motorboats. Among the guests, Chirico, A. Moravia and his wife, Dacia Maraini, Mme. Nijinska, etc. When we arrived, under an overcast sky, a heavy, humid heat announcing a storm was suffocating us. The ambassador greeted us in Cipriani. His wife told me that she knew my books and wanted to talk with me about comparative religion and mystical doctrine. She invited us to spend a weekend on Torcello. We accepted because the ambassador has a very rich collection of African masks. Moravia, who has gone to India, to China, wants to know a little more about Tantrism. He knows everyone, but for him everybody is "right-wing" or "difficult." He spoke to us about *Desert People,* a film about an Australian tribe that he had seen yesterday, and he promised to arrange for us to see it also.

We stayed in the garden until the first drops of rain. We were to have left at four o'clock, but at three the ambassador took us to the motorboat. Scarcely had we embarked than the storm was unleashed. The lagoon was drowned in mist. The lightning chased us from behind, but we found it again in front cleaving through the tropical rain. Unusually high waves in the lagoon. I remembered the storm I encountered on the Black Sea as a youth, and I had a presentiment of adventure. It wasn't until we disembarked at Harry's Bar that the storm subsided a little.

8 September

I met P. He is a grandfather. He told me that his library was rifled a second time. He gives no more lectures and sees almost nobody. He hopes to write a book which will also be accepted as a thesis at the Sorbonne, so as to be appointed professor (at over sixty-five . . .). He is still the same, he talks ceaselessly, he asks questions but cuts off your answers, he opens a notebook and writes down the title of a book or an article. He is against Vedanta (which supposedly destroyed India) and more and more for ritual. Here, in Venice, at the library, he is studying the history of the Compagnia della Calze, which used to organize entertainments.

On the way to Carbonari, where I invited him to dinner, a terrible storm. We took refuge in the Rialto bar while the storm was raging. P. described a very popular professor's course for me. The hall was packed; not a fly could be heard. The scholar strode onto the platform, absorbed, without uttering a word. Then he turned toward the auditorium, looked at the audience almost angrily, and shouted, "I'm going to teach you to fuck!" He repeated several times, "Yes, to fuck!" Then, he added, ". . . but according to the rules of the Golden Mean."

If I had a little more time, I would write down the details of P.'s conversation with Father H., whom we also met on Torcello. I chatted a little with him, knowing only that he was a great specialist on medieval music (he has published five or six volumes of texts and studies on Aquileus, etc.: he is editor of a review of religious music). He told P., who has met him several times, approximately this (I'm summarizing as best I can): with some specialists in electronic music, Father H. succeeded in recording on tape the voices of Demosthenes, Julius Caesar, Joan of Arc, Saint Paul—but they haven't yet been able to record the voice of Jesus. The scientific justification: nothing is lost in the universe, not even a syllable uttered several thousand years ago. It is necessary to know only how to reach—through "waves"—that point where the sounds are today to be able to recover them. Father H. has not let anyone listen to the voices recorded, except his own technical collaborators. For the reason, it seems, that he would have difficulties with the hierarchy.

9 September

Today, P. told me some Parisian anecdotes. For example, the premiere of a "happening": a nun appears on the stage, goes into a striptease, and when she is naked, begins to put carrots into her vagina, then throws them to the audience. The show wasn't forbidden until the third presentation. Some existentialist philosophers attended with emotion and piety, because it was something "new," "free"; they were witnessing the beginning of a "new style of culture," postbourgeois. Etc., etc.

In the evening, at La Fenice, the Thirtieth Modern Music Festival opened. For the first time I heard Stücke für Orchester, op. 6, by Webern. The surprise of the evening (for me, at least): "Épiphanie," by Luciano Berio, for voice and orchestra, with Catherine Barberian interpreting texts by Proust, Joyce, Brecht, etc. I realized once again the immense possibilities of the human voice for the music of tomorrow.

10 September

This evening at La Fenice—"Scenes from the Mahâbharata" with the Kathakali company of Kerala. A little disappointed. The gestures *(mudra)* and the dances—admirable; but this marvelous, traditional archaic symbolism was contradicted in an almost ridiculous fashion by the naïve, vulgar realism of the artist who interpreted Draupadi; pathetic movements reminding one of the silent films; it seemed like a melodrama introduced into a Karaghioz spectacle. The costumes—in the tradition of the seventeenth or eighteenth century —heavy, grotesque, seemed Levantine (and sometimes Tibetan) rather than Indian. General impression: rococo, decadent syncretism. I would really like to know the meaning of that long hair, really horses' tails, that all the male characters wore; the meaning of their costumes (those caftan robes over puffed-out pants, like those of the Balkan boyars who imitated the Turkish fashion in the eighteenth century). I had the impression of witnessing now a Karaghioz spectacle in a village of Anatolia, now a demoniac Tibetan dance. Moreover, the final scene, the struggle danced between Bhima and Duryodhana, admirable—it reminded me of a Tibeto-Himalayan shamanist dance.

14 September

A little before noon Petru Comarnesco arrived, accompanied by Ionel and Marga Jianu. After twenty-seven years, he is still the same; scarcely thinner, the hair turning gray—and he smokes fifty cigarettes a day. We went to a café on the Zattere, then to the Carbonari restaurant. We chatted until four in the afternoon. What to write down first? Petru C. is as voluble as in our youth. He tried to convince me to participate in the colloquium on Brancusi, at least one or two days. He said that *something* has changed in Rumania these last few years, but that one must not have too many illusions.

As he has not had a chair at the university and is not part of the academy, he works twelve hours a day in order to live, he writes hundreds of articles and monographs on artists and actors, on monasteries and painters, and on a good many other things.

15 September

Morning in San Marco. I met Countess Trevisan (short, accompanied by an enormous and splendid dog), Horia Lovinescu, and his wife. H. L., too, insists that I visit the homeland. The youth of today, much more courageous than they were themselves, that is, those who are today fifty or sixty years old, are not paralyzed by terror. They are reading authors strictly forbidden. That is how it was that the young read my books when I had not yet been "rehabilitated." If I went back to Rumania, he adds, I would perhaps be able "to have accepted, through my scientific authority," the studies on the history of religions and symbolism, forbidden today.

CHICAGO, 10 November

A woman who is preparing a thesis on the psychology of education told me some astounding things on "the religion and the mythology" of youth groups; not only the hippies, but all sorts of other sects. They represent what American sociologists call "the Youth Culture." Children born after the atomic explosion. An abyss between their generation and the other generations, such as had not been known in the past. They cannot "believe in," they cannot "adhere" to, "old" values. And despite all that, they live an authentic religious life—although they do not call it religious and are ignorant of its implications. A new way of "loving one's neighbor," a new valorization of "freedom" and of life.

3 December

For months, in the window of the university bookstore on Fifty-seventh Street, books against the war in Vietnam have been on display, beginning with B. Russell, *The American Crimes in Vietnam,* an inexpensive paperback edition. For several weeks, in another window, we have been seeing the works of Mao Tse-tung, in English translation.

Naturally, all this seems difficult to believe in Europe. But I wonder what sign is to be seen in this excess of tolerance: strength, self-confidence, and confidence in the American destiny, or indifference, fatigue, the first symptoms of decadence? To what limits can tolerance be stretched, politically speaking?

15 January 1968

I've discovered a text of Saint Augustine (*Sermo suppositus,* 120, 8) in which the death of Jesus on the cross is conceived as nuptials. "Like one betrothed . . . Christ came to the nuptial bed of the cross and, in ascending it, consummated the marriage. And when he heard the sign of the creature, he offered himself with love to the agony in place of the betrothed and thus united himself forever to his wife." Is this interpretation the invention of Augustine, so tormented by carnal temptations? Or could it be a more general motif? In the latter case, the symbolism of the Rumanian folk song *Mioritza* also has—or could have—Christian valencies. *Marriage assimilated to death* is therefore not a pagan motif, superficially Christianized.

26 January

I'm having talks with the students from twelve thirty to four in the afternoon. Half an hour with each. How much I can learn from the young people in the college. Bearded, with the hair of nomadic Tziganes, dressed in a manner which is both eccentric and poor, hippies, specialists in LSD and mescaline, etc. The same general impression that I have got from the others, the twenty or thirty that I have seen this month: they are all in revolt against the ideologies of parents and institutions, especially academic institutions (the Establishment). Certain themes return like a leitmotif: antitraditionalism, antireductionism (they are for Jung and against Freud), they are interested in mystical doctrine but not in religion as an institution; they like life, they are optimistic, and they find that everything that happens to them has a meaning and a significance. Of the ten or eleven that I have just seen today, they were all antiexistentialists (especially anti-Sartre), and a single one (anthropology) was interested in structuralism. The others—"mystics," rather. The last: black hair falling onto his shoulders in braids, glasses, girlish face. He is a sociology student, but all the professors seem to him "stupid, childish, *irrele-*

vant. " An LSD experience with his girlfriend: they held each other's hands and could no longer realize, she, which was his hand, and he, which was that of his girlfriend. Then they said *we*—and each time they pronounced the word "we," the three cats that he had came up to them, jumped on them, stroked up against them as if they too were part of this plural: *we.* The feeling that life had no more "limits."

30 January

Morrissette introduced me to Borges—almost blind, his face lined with wrinkles, changeable, innumerable tics. Borges remembers *The Myth of the Eternal Return,* and he called my attention to the fact that the problem was discussed by Hume (naturally Hume, speaking about atoms, had been inspired by Lucretius, which I did not tell him).

Strange lecture: Borges spoke for almost an hour on *Leaves of Grass,* without pause, without searching for a single word, without hesitation, keeping right up to the microphone. I did not grasp whether he had improvised or had recited a text learned by heart. A lecture full of interesting remarks.

SANTA BARBARA, *5 February*

In a text by Corbin (his intervention at the Congress of Geneva, in September 1966), I have found these quotations: "Recite the Koran as if it had been revealed only for your own case" (Sohrawardî). "If the meaning of the Koran were limited to the circumstances and personalities to whom it was revealed, the Koran would have died long ago" (Bâgir Iman, eighth century). These two texts alone could justify the historico-religious hermeneutic which certain of us are trying (Corbin, myself, Ricoeur—and who else *for the moment?*). Point of departure: a revelation, although brought about in a well-defined historical moment, is always transhistorical, "universal," and open to personal interpretations. In fact, the term "interpretations" is not precise enough: it is a matter of a transmutation by the person who receives, interprets, and assimilates the revelation.

For my part, I am going even further: the creative hermeneutic of which I have been speaking in so many of my recent studies provokes equivalent transmutations even when we are confronted not with a "revelation" of the type of that of the Koran, but also with exotic (India, etc.) or archaic ("primitive") religious forms.

8 February

- The second class. I have been speaking freely, I have been improvising before a hall just as packed. (But the student's dog is no longer crossing the room to the lectern to look at me!) A long discussion, but very commonplace. A little disappointed. But I say to myself that I'm taking no notice. These are not "my students." Some students came to see me afterward in my office. One of them, with long hair falling onto his shoulders, suggested to me that I speak about Yoga, about mysticism, and that I connect the archaic world, the Oriental world, and the "modern world." He is certainly right. But I'm not speaking here as a guru; I've come to give a history of religions course. . . .

28 February

Christinel is reading *The Quest for Corvo,* by A. J. Symons, that I found in Jonathan Smith's library. I don't dare leaf through it for fear of being hooked—and of rereading it just at this time when I have so many other things on my hands. An admirable book! And I'm suddenly remembering that night in January 1941, in Oxford, when I had discovered that book. I was living with D. Danielopol, at Mme. Sassoon's (or, more precisely, we had rented a house together). We were invited once to the home of a distinguished woman whose name I forgot long ago. But I can still see the villa, the park, and the Chinese servant—and so many shelves laden with rare objects. That night, the author of *Bengal Lancer* was also invited to dinner (a film had also been made of it some years before). Although very near-sighted, he wore only a monocle which fell by chance into his soup, and he wasn't successful in recovering it (he looked for it, of course, with his spoon). Danielopol helped him fish it out.

We heard the German airplanes flying over Oxford—to "rest," it was said. (Here they escaped the antiaircraft.) The mistress of the house, seeing that biography and fantasy literature interested me a great deal, gave me *The Quest for Corvo* before I left. I don't believe I've seen that lady since.

3 March

More and more under the spell of the "hippie" phenomenon. I remember what one of my students said to me: hippies constitute a sort of secret society of a religious type. Young people who come from all parts of the United States, they are taken in by strangers (also hippies), they eat what they are given; they have "stores" where each chooses what he needs: a shirt, a piece of clothing, a pair of sandals —and leaves something in its place, if he possesses anything. In the places where they meet—the forest, the hills—they live in a sort of primitive Christian community. They all have an occupation, listen to music, "meditate," etc. They practice "free" love—but no promiscuity or orgies; the nudity of girls or women, they say, helps "camaraderie."

Why do I call this "movement" religious or quasi-religious? Because it is a reaction against the absence of meaning and the vacuousness of an alienated existence known especially by the new American generations (in revolt against the values and the ideals of their parents). These young people believe in life, in liberty, in *agape,* in love. They have found a meaning in life, they believe in an absolute reality which can be accessible to them. Finally they live in freedom, spontaneity, detachment from everything.

5 March

Some day I ought to write a critical commentary on the articles which have appeared on "With the Gypsy Girls." I have the impression that the essential has not been grasped: this story does not symbolize anything, it does not transform immediate reality by a cipher. The story *founds* a world, a universe independent of the geography and the sociology of the Bucharest of 1930–1940. One must not look for what the different episodes refer to in the reality which is accessible to us, nor what this character or that one represents. It is the presentation of a *new* universe, unprecedented, having its own laws—it is this presentation which constitutes an act of creation, and not only in the aesthetic sense of the word. In penetrating this universe, in learning to know it, to savor it—something is revealed to you. The problem that poses itself for the critic is not to decipher the "symbolism" of the story, but—admitting that the story appealed to him, convinced him—to interpret the *message* hidden by the reality of the story (more precisely the new type of reality that the adventure of my hero, Gavrilescu, unveils).

10 March

Still on "With the Gypsy Girls." Such a literature as this founds its own universe; just as myths unveil for us the foundation of worlds, of modes of being (animal, plant, man, etc.), of institutions, of behavior, etc. It is in this sense that one can speak of an extension of myth into literature: not only because certain mythological structures and figures return in the imaginary universes of literature, but especially because in both cases it is a matter of *creation,* that is of the creation (= revelation) of certain worlds parallel to the daily universe in which we move. In my story, as in a Polynesian or North American myth, there is and there is not a "real" world, that is, a world in which everyday man lives or can live. But, as in a myth, "With the Gypsy Girls" (and other stories of the same genre) reveals unsuspected meanings, gives a meaning to everyday life.

CHICAGO, *21 March*

I'm happy to find in an article by a specialist what I suspected, or rather what I intuitively perceived: to wit, that electronic computers are admirable when it comes to "ideal languages" and abstract logical relations—but that they are impotent in simulating that sort of intelligence that even animals possess, that is, above all, the perception of forms and structures ("pattern recognition").

16 April

Husserl has said: The philosopher finds himself in a state of perpetual recommencing. Philosophy can never be considered as definitively established in any of the truths it reaches; it is an experience continually renewed from its own beginning.

On an entirely different level, one finds here the necessity of periodically recovering the "beginnings," the return to the "origins" which characterizes the archaic world.

19 April

I've learned of a strange event which took place in Bengal during the last war: a rich man died and his body was transported to Darjeeling to be incinerated. But a storm extinguished the pyre, and the man was found, living, by a group of *sannyasi,* who, according to their custom, wander about the "cemeteries," the places in which the dead are burned. The rich man had completely lost his memory and he remained with this group of ascetics. He was called *sannyasi* Bhowal. After twelve years, during which he lived like any other *sannyasi,* he suddenly recovered his memory. What happened then seems very strange to me: he went back home and began a long series of trials to recover his fortune. But according to tradition and archaic Indian civil law, a *sannyasi* who returns to civil life must be treated as a *candala* (a sort of "untouchable"). From the legal point of view, the great difficulty was not that he was "resurrected," but that in becoming a *sannyasi* he had given up his civil status.

What confuses me in this affair is that, after twelve years of asceticism and contemplation, the man, recovering his memory, wanted to return to his first identity—as if his recent spiritual experience had not existed. . . .

21 April

Very interesting, this remark of Fingarette: "In psychoanalysis Freud brought into the most intimate partnership a science of human change and the art of self-liberation" (*The Self in Transformation,* p.

67). I attribute a similar function as well to the history of religions. To the degree that you *understand* a religious fact (myth, ritual, symbol, divine figure, etc.), you *change,* you are modified—and this change is the equivalent of a step forward in the process of self-liberation. If you have truly understood "renunciation of the fruit of action," the keystone of the Bhagavad-Gita, you become different; and if you compare yourself to the person you were before, you realize that you are more free, that you are delivered from an illusion, from a weight, from an inhibition, that you get rid of "something which oppresses you" (without knowing what, without having *known* befor~ what was oppressing you . . .).

NEW YORK, *26 April*

What does Ignatius of Loyola propose in his famous *Exercises:* to reactualize in a concrete manner the Passion of Jesus by going back from the forms and mental images to their sensory content: the monk in meditation sees colors, feels, smells odors, etc. Thus, *that time (illud tempus),* the time of the Passion becomes real once again. That is indeed what also takes place in archaic religions. Consequently, one can say that from this point of view, there is no solution of continuity between "primitives" and Christians.

27 April

The events at Columbia University. Pointless to summarize them. As usual, a handful of professional agitators have managed to fire up a few hundred naïve, ambitious, or eccentric people. They occupy one or several buildings. They are presented on television, photographed, interviewed by journalists—and the propaganda picks up another hundred or two hundred students, but also several hundred curious types or onlookers. What do the "students" want? Something which finally is accepted by the university. But they do not yield, because they demand something more, or at least to receive amnesty. (That is what happened at Chicago and elsewhere.) Thus, ultimately, "revolution" without risks. And if, at the final limit, the police intervene to evacuate the premises, the students are again televised and they become famous (as victims of police terror). And all that because of a tiny dynamic minority, well trained in civil or guerrilla warfare.

This evening I was at Theodore Gaster's. His wife, an emigrant of German origins, gave me her impressions: "I seemed to be seeing the same film for the second time." From the S.S. to students ravaging in the name of democracy (we were shown the offices of the university after the students were evacuated), there does not seem to have been a gap of twenty-five or thirty years. And several million dead.

5 May

The extraordinary Hindu mythology of sperm! Shiva and Parvati copulate for a thousand years. When the act is interrupted (brutally, by the intervention of the other gods), only half of the seminal emission remains in Parvati; the other half is poured out on Agni, who gives it to the gods, and they swallow it or vomit it, and the sperm thus spilled becomes a lake. And other myths in which the gods swallow sperm, or Brahma (and other gods) who at the view of a goddess ejaculate their sperm on the earth.

11 May

Exhausted by so many letters to write; sometimes I answer ten or twelve letters the same day. Redfield tells me he has seen Shills come into his office and throw into the wastebasket a whole pile of letters which have just arrived, without even looking at where they came from. There were perhaps some checks among them, adds Redfield.

17 May

With what melancholy I have finished reading the excellent biography of Macedonsky by A. Marino. It is not Macedonsky's megalomania that disturbs me, or the absolute confidence that he had in his own genius, his egocentrism. My melancholy is especially aroused by Macedonsky's illusions in Paris: he hoped to conquer Paris through his "connections," by the publication of his novel or of some articles—by him or on him—which had appeared in third-rate magazines. And the insane publicity that he made for himself—he would write notes about himself, very laudatory, and would proclaim that all Europe was at his feet, etc., etc. Almost unbelievable. He supposed that this ballyhoo was going to launch him in Rumania. What sadness to see how a great poet aspires to Parisian glory and hopes that two or three little notes signed by some unknowns will make of him a second D'Annunzio.

7 June

In the literature and in the plastic arts of the second half of the nineteenth century, works were to *resemble* reality; after 1890–1900, literature was to *symbolize* something. Latterly, it is understood that art—literature, painting, music—must *create* autonomous universes. (Bach had realized it long since!)

BOSTON, *23 June*

Around noon, when I was waiting for the taxi which was to take me to the airport, it was already 95 degrees F. At the airport the heat was suffocating, and the clouds were banking up. Surprise, when I arrived in Boston, it was nice weather, cool, a lazy wind coming from the ocean. Rasmussen and a professor from Boston College who is a specialist in Heidegger were waiting for me. Father Lonergan, the much-discussed author of the book *Insight,* arrived from Toronto. We all had dinner with the head of the philosophy department in the restaurant on the top floor of the Prudential building, the new skyscraper. A walk at nightfall in this plaza where there are so many majestic, serene new buildings. I no longer recognize here the Boston of five or six years ago.

Afterward, in Charter House where I was staying, I talked with Rasmussen until midnight about the choice of the problem to present tomorrow and the next day at the colloquium on "Methodology in Religious Studies."

24 June

About seventy or eighty people present, of which half were teachers and monks (some of them having come from Europe or from India for the colloquy). I spoke freely, rather slowly, so that the lecture could be recorded. First argument: "The sacred" is an element of the *structure* of consciousness, and not a moment in the *history* of consciousness. Next: The experience of the sacred is indissolubly linked to the effort made by man to construct a meaningful world.

I emphasized this: hierophanies and religious symbols constitute a prereflective language. As it is a case of a special language, *sui generis,* it necessitates a proper hermeneutics. In my work, I have tried to elaborate this hermeneutics; but I have illustrated it in a practical way on the basis of documents. It now remains for me or for another to systematize this hermeneutics.

6 July

I regret not knowing how to find what is called here "the underground press." From time to time, magazines and little sheets of this underground press fall into my hands, brought by some of my students. One thing strikes me from the beginning: despite the excesses of sex, of nudism, of orgiastic freedom, etc., the tone of these texts, apparently lewd or even pornographic, is religious; yes, religious. Every expression of love, especially of physical love, is accepted with emotion and deference.

As I have often repeated, it could indeed be that even the uninhibited sexual life that this young generation of rebels praises is part of the (unconscious) process of the rediscovery of the sacredness of life.

30 July

The longing to *remain:* Karl Barth is always accompanied by his old secretary, who writes down in a notebook all the conversations of the Master with the different persons whom he meets, important or not. (I saw her at work when he was in Chicago.) A new Eckermann? I doubt it. Barth said everything in his massive, prolix works.

I hope that the old secretary writes down as well the remarks *of the others*.

1 August

The joy of the spirit so sensually expressed in the Song of Songs and in all mystic and spiritual poetry. Since when has understanding, at least in Western culture, become an equivalent of sadness?

21 August

Intriguing coincidences in the history of the spirit. For the Kogi of Sierra Nevada, perfection does not consist in doing good, but in acquiring a balance between the two antagonistic forces of good and evil. That reminds me of Goethe and especially of C. G. Jung, for whom the ideal of man is not *perfection,* but *totality.*

PARIS, *20 September*

F. O. came to see me, and we chatted for two hours. He told me how he was condemned to five years in prison for having read a "manifesto" written by several monks; in reality, it was a text destined for the West in which the persecutions of the Catholics were discussed. He told me many other things about culture, notably Rumanian literature of today. The interest of the youth in poetry, metaphysics, mystical doctrine. Suspicion and refusal toward all the authors who were protected by the regime. Whence the passion of the youth for us who are in exile, who for fifteen years have been the target of all the insults of the official powers, from the literary critics to the political police.

2 October

I met Harry Brauer and Lena Constante, his wife, both convicted, around 1947–1948, at the time of the Patrascanu trial, and freed only a few years ago. Lena spent eight years in a cell. Alone. She saw no one, spoke to no one. In order not to go mad, she wrote plays for children. She didn't hurry; she "wrote" mentally, one play in several months. She had been convicted because, after 1945, she had founded and directed, with Patrascanu's wife, a marionnette theater.

Both of them extol the existence which they discovered in prison. They admit that they do not regret those fifteen or sixteen years in prison. Brauer learned by heart the mystical poetry that N. C. transmitted to him in Morse code by knocking with his fist on the wall of the neighboring cell. And Brauer composed the music for these poems. Mentally, of course. The return to the primordial function of the memory thus rediscovered. . . .

CHICAGO, *27 October*

The day before yesterday, in Kalamazoo, I was saying in the course of the conversation that today we are not in the Alexandrian age, as is erroneously thought, but in the age of Herodotus: we are discovering and taking seriously exotic, "barbaric" cultures.

14 November

Today in the "joint seminar" that Paul Ricoeur and I are conducting. We are discussing Jung. At the remark, made by a student, that Freud is "urban" and Jung "rural," I remembered that sex and eroticism play almost no role in folk cultures. On the other hand, sexuality, for desacralized, urban populations, represents the last source of the "numinous": it is life, mystery, sacredness, all in one. Freud, of course, did not judge sexuality to be the last chance for modern man to meet with the sacred—but to be a delusion which must be demystified. Freud was the last Puritan. But, without realizing it, for him sex was everything, because, for an urbanite, it was the last organic link with life. I remember, among other examples, the symbolism of climbing steps and of ascension in which Freud saw the sexual act, although that is only one of the meanings of the symbol. The total meaning, which gives a significance to the whole and to the parts, is the following: the modification of the mode of existing (passage from the profane to the sacred, from life to death, etc.).

21 November

As at each occasion that I feel tired, sick, depressed (and how not, since I don't yet know what sickness I'm suffering from?), I pick up *Gespräche mit Goethe* by Eckermann and I begin to read, some-

what at random, for hours and hours. And I find that, later, I am
calmed, comforted. The mystery of this *total* attraction felt for Goethe still fascinates me. A thought or a page of his, any work in
connection with him, projects me into a sthenic, luminous, familiar
universe. I feel like shouting: That is my world, that is the reason that
I was created, etc. And every time I visibly betray this vocation and
let myself be sidetracked by work and obligations which are not my
destiny—I fall sick. Before the sickness properly so-called arrives (like
the one today), I am weakened and sterile, enervated, in a bad mood.

23 November

In the second volume of his *Autobiography,* Bertrand Russell
speaks of his nightmares at the beginning of the 1914–1918 war. And
he adds: "I spoke of them to T. S. Eliot, who put them into *The Waste
Land*" (p. 7). I wonder how true that is. And if it is true, I am still
more fascinated by *The Waste Land* into which Eliot put the nightmares of Russell, and *The Golden Bough* and everything he had
learned reading *From Ritual to Romance* by Jessie Weston, and many
other things still—and from this chaotic manuscript Ezra Pound
extracted one of the great poems of the century.

No date (1968)

The exasperation, the rage of G. after having read some book
or other on the end of the world. I measured how humilated he felt,
he, the rationalist scientist *par excellence,* believing only in science
and the unlimited progress of technology, when he discovered the
Indian myths of Kali Yuga and of the destruction of the earth by a
gigantic incineration. All these myths and legends, he told me, are
only, and are nothing more than, the lucubrations of a sick imagination, obsessed by the apocalyptic prodrome: the more and more accelerated decadence of human societies, universal anarchy, the triumph of evil, and, finally, the cosmic catastrophe, the incineration
and the burning of the earth. But, he added, none of these horrors is
inevitable; none enters into the price that we have to pay for the
prodigious progress of the sciences and of technique in the last half-

century. (I had known for a long time what G. meant by "the price that must be paid": the mutilation and devastation of nature, the disfigurement of the cities, the pollution of the atmosphere, etc.). If the incineration of the planet now seems to him inevitable, that derives exclusively from the incapacity and the ridiculous ambitions of the political leaders who govern. But that is only an accident! he exclaims, emphasizing the words. If we are condemned to a collective incineration, that has nothing to do with scientific discoveries or with the fantastic progress of technology. The very opposite could have happened: governed by intelligent and responsible leaders, the planet would have been today on the threshold of a new stage that G. does not hesitate to call "paradisiac."

He is humiliated because a few hallucinated persons from India and Persia, who, some two or three thousand years ago, announced the end of the world with such off-handedness, could be proved correct by a future which is more or less near. And yet they have no merit, he never ceases repeating, and their prophecies are absurd and ridiculous. If we blow everything up, it is not because *they* were right, but because *we* are such imbeciles!

After he left, I had to open the window. It is the first time that I've come across, here in the USA, the odor of a filthy body, clothes rough with dust and sweat mixed. I had been told that many hippies didn't wash, but I believed that it was a legend cleverly maintained for propaganda. But this time I am convinced that filth is also part of the ideology and practices of "the rebellion." It is the expression of the same desire to protest against the opulent society and to break noisily with the moral, political, and aesthetic ideals of the parents.

Actually, this ultimate, insolent refusal of the values cultivated by preceding generations only continues the tradition of the 1950s, when exegetes of all opinions were demonstrating that it was not by chance that the ugly and the deformed were triumphing in the plastic arts, that so-called narrative literature was boring, if not downright unreadable: that was part of the *Zeitgeist*. Our age quite simply did not permit another type of creativity. The ugliness, the boredom, and the exalting of the insignificant of which the artistic creations of the last twenty years make a display are, with nihilism in philosophy, anarchism in social ethics, and violence in political activity, the expressions of a single, specific, existential situation of man in Western societies. The unprecedented success of hallucinogenic drugs among the young illustrates the same syndrome.

Torn jackets, pants and shirts in tatters, provocative negligence, and filthiness tend, to a certain degree, to cancel "the glory and charm" of the human body discovered and idealized by the Italian Renaissance. Many times in the recent history of the plastic arts, the human body has been "demythized," mutilated, transformed into geometric figures, and finally abolished. But certain hippies experiment with this process—that is, the cancellation of the Renaissance ideal—*on their own bodies*.

What is more significant still is that this is happening at the same moment in which, for the first time in the history of Christian civilization, liberated sexuality is triumphing everywhere and the almost ritual beatitude of nudity is being rediscovered.

SANTA BARBARA, *2 February 1969*

In the morning, in Chicago, the weather clouded over, the fog lowered, and we weren't sure we would be able to depart. Our plane was about an hour late. Then we waited our turn on the runway at least half an hour. Finally, we took off. After an hour, the weather was so nice that we saw the Rocky Mountains bathed in the sun. We arrived in Los Angeles somewhat late and missed the connection for Santa Barbara. We waited patiently for about two hours more. The plane—small, low, containing only eight seats—that took us flew slowly over the gulf. Florence and Bob Michaelson were waiting for us in Santa Barbara to take us to Bonnymede. We were glad to return to our apartment from last year, 1363 Plaza Pacifica. We opened the windows and went out onto the terrace. The ocean was still raging. Bob Michaelson told us about the consequences of the flood of ten days ago—the mud that had penetrated into so many houses built on the side of the hills, the mud and the streams that had invaded the gardens of the Biltmore Hotel and even here in Bonnymede.

3 February

The beach has been swallowed up by the ocean. The rocks are black, oily, and the waves push ceaselessly onto the bank of algae soaked with petroleum. We saw the six or seven tankers on the open sea. A few days ago a pipeline broke, and since then, 21,000 liters of oil are cast up onto the coast every day. The kingfishers of last year are no more to be seen. We took a walk on the dune that dominates the beach. A strong odor of petroleum.

8 February

Purely and simply splendid. We walked for an hour toward Montecito under the giant eucalyptus trees and the mimosas in bloom. On our return, we passed near that beautiful noble old house in the forest with its terraces facing the beach—quite probably the property of the one who later sold the lands on which Bonnymede was built.

In the evening we had dinner at the Comstocks'. We found out that the city of Santa Barbara asked for one billion five hundred million dollars in damages from the oil companies.

11 February

In the morning the beach was covered with workers. They came, armed with helmets and tools, to clean it. First they picked up the wood and the algae sticky with tar and loaded it into a truck. These workers, I was to find out later, were "delinquents" furnished by the local jails. The work was paid by the hour, at the union rate. I can imagine their delight: being able to work at the seaside, in the open air.

In the afternoon, a seminar on *Birth and Rebirth*. How enthusiastic these young students become over "initiation"!

13 February

At the beginning of the afternoon, one of my students came to see me. Young, bearded, he resembled a postcard Christ. He told me the story of his life (he is twenty-two years old). Until last year he was an "existentialist," an atheist, a Sartrean nihilist, Camus and company. He was studying drama and dreamed of becoming a director. In the spring of 1968, he read some books: *Tao-te-ching,* Aurobindo, *Tertium organum,* and these books led him to alchemy, mysticism, astrology, tarot. Now, *he knows.*

I have learned many things about "the mythology" of California. A "renaissance," for example, is about to descend on Santa Barbara (it was also announced by the Dalai Lama!); Los Angeles is "submerged in matter," and San Francisco is "decadent."

27 February

With the students from two to three in the afternoon, then a seminar until five. In the evening, at a student's, in an elegant, almost luxurious apartment in Isla Vista, the section in which ten thousand students live, and where there is only a single movie theater and a "cafeteria." (And it is wondered why student revolts break out so savagely. What can all these students do, *alone . . . ?)*

CHICAGO, *no date*

A long time ago I received a tragic, pessimistic letter from a young Rumanian: he succeeded in getting across the border for the first time when he was thirty years old. The destiny of this generation of persecuted youth who cannot believe in Marxism and who are prohibited from reading philosophers, mystics, and theologians, the only authors in whom they are interested. "This whole dictatorial, humanistic lie has disgusted us beyond all measure," he writes. He believed in philosophy, but after having read the Bible (in a foreign land) he realized that "only the living God can occupy this central place. It is He alone who gives hope and peace in the poverty and agony to which these hostile times have brought us. That is the path which most of the young people worth anything in the country have taken. What a shame that gifted young people cannot enter the convent. If that were possible, I think that today, in Rumania, many of them, perhaps the best, would opt for the life of a hermit."

I've learned some names borne by American Puritans in the seventeenth century. I must write here at least the following: *Praise-god-avoid-fornication Bearbones.* Anything could serve as a given name among the Puritans. But *avoid-fornication* seems to me to be truly exceptional. And I'm told that this man was married, and had children.

How the German writers who emigrated to the United States were "saved": they worked and pursued the creative activity begun in Germany. The case of Thomas Mann is exemplary: even before emigrating to the United States, when he was changing residence all the time, to Switzerland, to France (then to Princeton, to Los Angeles), he could stand anything because he was writing the *Joseph* tetralogy. That saved the inner unity and continuity threatened by exile.

This interesting detail that I got from a famous Catholic publisher: theology books are no longer selling at all; here is the cause: after the *aggiornamento,* the position of the Church on the various problems is no longer known, and so neither theologians nor laymen are reading anymore. They are waiting.

On November 9, 1824, Goethe spoke to Eckermann about Klopstock, whom he had very much admired in his youth and whom he considered a "grandfather." But he said that he never had the idea of reflecting on Klopstock's work, discussing it or comparing it with the work of other authors: "I let his best part act on me, and I continued on my way."

That is exactly my position toward the writers, scholars, or philosophers whom I have admired, who have taught me something, who have stimulated me. I do not discuss them. I assimilate what I need, and I go on my way.

I am continuing writing, well or poorly, a little or a lot, the chapter on Iranian religions. But the effort that I am making to be brief, not to throw myself into exegeses and illustrations—I wonder if this effort is worth the trouble. Finally I will perhaps make up my mind to write according to my heart—and the subject—even if striking, abridging, summarizing afterward.

Seminar. An anthropology student who is also an actor (he is playing in *Don Carlos,* "based on Schiller," he adds—for this is a new play), spoke about Antonin Artaud. Simple pretext for confiding to me what the actors do when they play *Don Carlos.* How can I summarize what he said? It seems that for them—the actors—the theater, the play, is a "spiritual exercise," but it more resembles an ecstatic dance, controlled "by a sort of Yoga." All that to obtain—before the play —a "psychophysiological communion" of the whole troupe. But, he added, they do not succeed in obtaining through the play the same communion with the audience. Very much to the contrary, they feel the aggressivity of the audience—because the spectators react instinctively before the selfish, beatific isolation of those who are on the stage.

My comments on the formula: "Artaud wanted to write a theater which put an end to the Theater." I spoke to them of the "concentrated time of the play": how one leaves the historical time (the chronological present), to penetrate into another temporal rhythm. I spoke to them about karma in the theater: the actor "purifies" himself when he incarnates and existentially actualizes so many human types, so many destinies. I spoke also about Gordon Craig and about Stanislavski, about Artaud's "solar" or "lunar theater," and I asked them this question: What can be done today in theater knowing what we know? Enthusiastic discussion, although very few of them were familiar with the theater of the avant-garde. But I felt that at that moment they were no longer participating in a scholastic, academic exercise (as they say here in the United States). They felt themselves involved in something real, living, authentic. The questions they asked me about Ionesco, for example, and the contemporary French theater. . . .

The undergraduate—he is a drummer, a hippie, and, as he says himself, a "shaman mystic." He came to see me, almost two months ago, to tell me about his "initiatic experience." On the coast, near San Francisco (where he spent almost three years, with an amateur band —a pianist, a guitarist, and he, the drummer—all three lived off the charity that they could receive in churches, bars, and restaurants, wherever they were permitted to play; but sometimes, he adds, they couldn't even get the price of gas), on the coast, then, one morning (after having smoked marijuana), while taking a walk, he found a red paper kite on which a winged devil was drawn. He took it and went home. (On the way, he remembered that it was Good Friday and that, consequently, he was carrying "the cross" of the kite.) Then a rehearsal with his band which three other young men had joined—a trumpeter and two clarinetists. And suddenly, while he was beating the drum harder and harder, he raised his eyes and saw the devil (the kite) coming down and penetrating into him. He fell to his knees—but the others continued playing; they thought it was the result of the marijuana. He had the impression that he was dead, but he felt himself on the ground and he felt at the same time that his strength was multiplying and that he would henceforth be able to help men and to communicate his strength to them with his drum. He does not know how long this "death" lasted (and it was not until later that he "understood what had happened to him," when someone had him read my *Shamanism*). Since then he feels in himself a supernatural strength and he is happy to communicate it to others through the rhythms of his drum.

He stayed half an hour. Today, at nine o'clock, he is leaving for New York, and after a week he is returning to California. As a term paper for the winter trimester, he wrote the account that I have just told (with his "shamanist" initiation), and some other adventures that I regret not being able to recount here in detail. This one, for example: in his LSD beatitude, he talked with a cat, without saying a word, of course, but the dialogue was interesting. The cat was speaking in a coherent manner, asking intelligent questions, answering his questions correctly, etc. Until the moment when this idea went through his mind: This is what I've come to, I'm talking with a cat. And at the same moment the cat looked at him, surprised, offended—it turned its head and ran away.

And his stories about E., a legendary girl from San Francisco, in whose apartment, if I understood correctly, all sorts of extraordinary things took place: orgies, magic, endless music sessions, "psychological nudism," Zen meditations. In the basement of this apartment lived her friend, a pianist. He never read the newspapers, but once he saw a newspaper protruding from a wastecan, and he stopped and read the headline of an article. It was an interview with a famous clairvoyant from San Francisco. The clairvoyant said: Search hard in the city, and if you find an electric piano in a basement lived in by a pianist, know that this pianist will one day become famous. . . .

Paradisiac experiences must not be translated in quantitative and temporal terms (the *permanence* of certain *objective* physical realities). One can "dream" or anticipate paradisiac beatitude a fraction of a second, or one can live it a few minutes or a few hours—but then one comes back into the world.

On the subject of the "Women's Liberation Front," an old psychoanalyst, a woman, Dr. Benedict, told us a good many interesting things. This, for example: The wife adapts better than the husband to modern society; if she does not have a job, she has things to keep her busy (the housework, the upbringing of the children). On the other hand, the man, if he is not working, if he does not have a *position,* a *function,* has nothing to do in an urban society. In ten years, if the new system of introducing women everywhere is continued, the competition of women thus becoming more and more real—in ten years there will be millions of neurasthenic men and millions of dollars will be spent to take care of them. Because, adds Dr. Benedict, women superior to men (due to their faculty of adaptation), and if this superiority is encouraged, the psychomental instability of men will worsen.

Fascinated by the anthropocosmic structure of the Supreme Goddess, the Universal Mother, among the Kogi, a Colombian tribe of Sierra Nevada. Rarely does one meet so coherent, systematic, and transparent a valorization of maternity as the source of the real. Everything which exists was conceived. Creation is a procreation. All modes of being—even that of death—were conceived by the Universal Mother. And everything man does he does inside the Cosmos, which, although created, remains inside the Mother. For the first time, the differences between the four intrauterine modes of existence are expressed with clarity and precision: the prenatal mode, that of earthly existence, the post-mortem mode, waiting for reincarnation, finally the mode of being of the dead person who decides to remain in the womb of the Mother.

Death is obviously an invention of the Masculine Spirit, adversary of the Mother. But even death does not succeed in wresting anything from the jurisdiction of the Mother—since the dead return to the universal womb. Such a cosmic maternal vision is met only in Indian mystical doctrine. Thus one understands why the idea of supreme divinity is interdependent with the conception that men have of the origin of the real and of the mystery of creation. The "sex" of the divinity is merely the consequence of this primordial intuition.

How "conditioned" were the imagination and fantasy of the conquistadors and explorers of South America! The Amazon River was so named by Carvajal because, he affirmed, women similar to those of whom Homer spoke struggled heroically against the soldiers of Orellana, at the mouth of the Rio Negro. Likewise the fabulous Ewaipanomas were described as having "their eyes on their shoulders and their mouth between their breasts." The image is found in Pliny the Elder, and it was constantly reactualized by all mythical geographies: "Ethiopia," Asia, the Far East. It could certainly not be missing in the tales of those who penetrated more and more deeply into the interior of the new continent in search of the mythical Paititi (El Dorado).

With what sadness I'm reading the chronicles and letters of the first missionaries to the Andean region. The terror of the populations taking refuge in the *selva;* they believed that those who presented themselves as priests were merely the spies of conquistadors seeking gold, silver, and slaves. They would recognize a monk only when he would eat with them the food prepared by their wives.

The religious creativity of the Christian West must not be looked for solely in the theology or the history of the Church, but also in the "occult" underground currents, in the mythology of secret societies, in the alchemy of the Renaissance, in the mythical geographies of the Middle Ages and of the Baroque. Preromanticism and romanticism exalt the function of dreams and of imagination. It was at the same time that the discovery of the "Night" and "the organic" took place, and so many other experiences which, if they were not completely new, were for the first time fully carried out, interpreted, and, especially, transformed into guiding principles.

I am thinking, for example, of Novalis, who rediscovered "the dialectic of the sacred," to wit, that nature, such as it shows itself to us, does not represent absolute reality but is only a cipher. His extraordinary intuition: that it is not necessary to die, to become "spirit," in order to be able to communicate with higher worlds, and that, beginning here below, one can know beatific experience. Some day someone must point out how ancient, even archaic, were the ideas of Novalis: one must also try to explain due to what circumstances these ideas were so long forgotten or voluntarily ignored. . . .

The fascination of travel derives not only from spaces, forms, and colors—the places one goes or through which one travels—but also from the number of personal "times" one reactualizes. The more I advance in life, the more I have the impression that journeys take place, concomitantly, in time and space. A landscape, a street, and an event certainly have their freshness and their charm, but at the same time they release innumerable little memories—some apparently without any interest, but no less moving and ultimately precious; it is thus that one recovers forgotten or neglected fragments of a "personal history." In a certain sense, when I travel through familiar or unknown geographic spaces, I travel at the same time in the past, in my own history. What delights me in this anamnesis brought about and nourished by traveling is first of all its spontaneity; it is impossible to anticipate or specify what fragment of the past will be given back to me at the end of a street in which I walk. When I go into a cathedral

I never know if I will find there the memory of other sanctuaries seen in days gone by—or if I will remember a book or a man of whom I have not thought for years, or if I will catch myself hearing an old melody, a conversation long forgotten.

That means, among other things, that a travel journal, to the degree in which the one who writes it tries to capture at least a part of everything "which has happened to him," must run the risk of being confused with a book of autobiographical notes and fragments. Is it solely a matter of that, of the recovery of the past? It could be that the process is more complicated and more subtle: a journey which takes place across different landscapes, forms, and colors, arouses a series of associations just as precious for the secret history of the soul as are, in a Jungian analysis, the associations brought about by hearing certain words, names, legends, or myths, or as is the contemplation of certain paintings or drawings.

Index